The Essential Middle School

Second Edition

The Essential Middle School

JON WILES
University of South Florida

JOSEPH BONDI
University of South Florida

Macmillan Publishing Company
New York

Maxwell Macmillan Canada
Toronto

Maxwell Macmillan International
New York   Oxford   Singapore   Sydney

Editor: Robert B. Miller
Production Editor: JoEllen Gohr
Art Coordinator: Peter A. Robison
Photo Editor: Anne Vega
Text Designer: Debra A. Fargo
Cover Designer: Robert Vega
Production Buyer: Pamela D. Bennett

This book was set in Caledonia by Carlisle Communications, Ltd., and was printed and bound by Book Press, Inc., a Quebecor America Book Group Company. The cover was printed by Phoenix Color Corp.

Macmillan Publishing Company
866 Third Avenue
New York, New York 10022

Macmillan Publishing Company is part of the
Maxwell Communication Group of Companies.

Maxwell Macmillan Canada, Inc.
1200 Eglinton Avenue East, Suite 200
Don Mills, Ontario M3C 3N1

Library of Congress Cataloging-in-Publication Data
Wiles, Jon.
   The essential middle school / Jon Wiles, Joseph Bondi.
     p.   cm.
   Includes bibliographical references and index.
   ISBN 0-02-427640-5
   1. Middle schools. I. Bondi, Joseph. II. Title.
  LB1623.W48   1992
  373.2'36 — dc20
                                             92-24299
                                               CIP

Printing: 2 3 4 5 6 7 8 9

Photo credits: Robert Finken, pp. 127, 233, and 245; Jean-Claude LeJeune, pp. 1, 23, 53, 64, and 77; Gail Meese/Macmillan, p. 101; David Strickler, p. 205; Courtesy of Donna Windham/ Richland School District, Columbia, South Carolina, p. 181; and Gale Zucker, pp. 84 and 149.

This book is dedicated to special people in our lives:
our children, Amy and Michael Wiles and Pam, Beth, and Brad Bondi,
who provide us daily joy,

Our wives, Margaret Wiles and Patsy Bondi,
who are marvelous companions, mothers, and teachers,

Our mothers, Hilda Wiles and Virginia Bondi,
whom we love and respect as mothers and great schoolteachers,

Our mentors, too numerous to mention,
who taught us how essential the middle school is
for emerging adolescent learners.

Preface

The Essential Middle School is widely used as a resource on education in the middle grades. The authors are appreciative of this usage and credit the distinction to two causes: the format found in the first edition and the fact that the book is written for practitioners attempting to implement the middle school concept, rather than for persons studying the concept. When the book was conceived in 1980 — long before the first edition appeared in 1986 — the intent was to guide intermediate educators toward a new form of schooling; that is, to offer a handbook for establishing or converting a facility so as to meet student needs at this level of education.

Today, it is clear that the middle school has moved into the organizational mainstream and is likely to continue to dominate intermediate education as educators prepare for the twenty-first century. As of the early 1990s, a body of literature, associations, conferences, and legislation all are emerging to promote the middle school concept and philosophy. Consequently, the focus of this new version of *The Essential Middle School* shifts from *what* to *how,* in other words, from understanding the middle school concept to developing and implementing programs. This new focus reflects the maturity of the middle school movement since its inception in the 1960s.

It is important to note that the middle school is no longer simply a U.S. phenomenon; the authors have watched with delight as its philosophy became international in application. Since 1980, we have worked in more than forty states and a dozen foreign nations to help develop meaningful intermediate programs. The numerous illustrations and examples in this new edition reflect those efforts, and we are grateful to the schools and agencies that shared their work with us.

This edition takes readers through the steps that school personnel encounter in planning and developing a middle school—whether a new one or one being converted from a standing facility. Like all good curriculum planning, programs originate with a rationale, a philosophy, or set of dominant beliefs. Using a deductive "if-then" logic, planners next reduce such beliefs to identifiable commitments or priorities, program concepts, organizational patterns, and instructional strategies and practices at the classroom level. The chapter organization in this edition follows this curriculum development pattern:

Chapter 1 outlines the rationale, origins, advantages, functions, and tasks of a middle school, along with the setting of parameters for its unique identity. Chapter 2 identifies the target population, emerging adolescents, and specific characteristics that make their needs the foremost driving force at this educational level. Chapter 3 profiles the ideal middle school teacher and defines the professional preparation, teaching strategies, and classroom management styles recommended for this particular environment. Chapter 4 gets into the specifics of how to design an effective program, using as a prototype the 1990 Duval County (Jacksonville, Florida) middle school conversion. Chapter 5 deals with the specifics of organization—team teaching, interdisciplinary teaming, flexible modular scheduling. Chapter 6 identifies instructional leadership provided by teachers and the patterns of instruction they use. The chapter also discusses the organization of learning and learning designs. Chapter 7 shows how to develop creative instructional activities, materials, and learning environments. Chapter 8 offers pointers on planning (preliminary and ongoing) a middle school and developing a curriculum using the Wiles-Bondi Curriculum Management Plan as a model. Chapter 9 instructs on how to implement service delivery, keeping in mind that implementation of inservice training, building facilities, and special programs is also an ongoing process. Chapter 10 shows how to monitor and evaluate the program continuously. Chapter 11 gives a brief outlook on the future direction of the middle school.

One of the book's key tools, one that reinforces the "how-to" focus of this edition, is the "Selected Learning Activities" component found at the end of each chapter. Furthermore, Chapters 1 through 10 are supplemented by end-of-book appendixes that include numerous examples (forms, questionnaires, models, charts, and so on) that expand on the topics discussed and a glossary of selected terms common to the middle school setting.

Over the past decade, school districts have debated the "means" versus the "end" of middle school education—for example organizational practices like teaming and advisory guidance. Successful middle schools, however, have kept their eye on the ball by being philosophically consistent and building a program around knowledge gained from human development research. We hope this edition will clarify this major stumbling block to implementation.

Finally, we hope that readers will seek greater understanding of preadolescent development and the historic role of intermediate education by following the notes and references into the literature that are listed at the end of each chapter. We believe the reader will find comfort in the consistency of thought in U.S. education over the years about what schools should be doing for older children and young adolescents. The middle school is not only a logical extension of those consistent themes, it is also a source of pride for instructional workers in this nation.

ACKNOWLEDGMENTS

The authors are indebted to the many schools and school districts that allowed us to use many of the materials, schedules, and program descriptions illustrated in this book. Particularly, we would like to acknowledge the support of Larry Zenke, Charles Cline, and Betty White of the Duval County, Florida, School District, and Joseph DeChurch of the Dade County, Florida, School District. Lucretia R. Payton-Stewart, Georgia State University, and Dennis Pataniczek, State University of New York, College of Brockport, reviewed the manuscript and offered many helpful suggestions.

Finally, we are grateful to the in-between-agers we have taught and the dedicated teachers and administrators in middle schools and school districts who have helped us acquire the ideas and insights in middle school education we have presented in this book.

Contents

Chapter 6

Identifying Instructional Leadership   127

Chapter 7

Developing Creative Instructional Activities, Materials, and Learning Environments   149

Chapter 8

Planning Considerations in Establishing a Middle School   181

Chapter 9

Service Delivery and Implementation   205

Chapter 10

Evaluating the Middle School 233

Chapter 11

Outlook for Middle Schools 245

Appendixes

The Essential Middle School

1

Rationale for the Middle School

*A successful middle school depends
more on faculties than facilities,
more on people than on the purse.*

INTRODUCTION

The middle school represents a unique contribution to American education. Most contemporary educational programs in the United States are adaptations of historic forms and ideas. Although it is true that many of the ideas that contribute to today's middle school existed previously, the combination of philosophy, organization, and instructional practices to support a program rationalized by human development research is novel. It is the direction and purpose that distinguishes the middle school from its predecessor, the junior high school, and all other content-centered programs.

This chapter seeks to help the reader understand the concept of the American middle school. The **middle school** is a philosophically directed program of education with clear priorities and objectives. Its organization, strategies, and practices are focused on the preadolescent learner, and its programs seek nothing less than the successful transition of these learners through this difficult and unique period of human development.

Origins of Middle School Education

The foundations of middle school education are old, as are many of the practices found in modern middle schools. Among the key concepts from the past are child-centeredness and learning strategies that actively involve the student. The catalyst for these ideas, within the context of middle school education, is research on human development. Some of the instructional techniques found in the middle school, such as teaming,[1] are also not new. However, as we shall see, bringing these practices together in a pattern so as to implement a new program is unique. In short, the middle school is a novel pattern of education woven from old ideas and practices.

If we study European educational thought from the previous century, we are introduced to many of the intellectual forebears of the middle school. Rousseau, Pestalozzi, and Froebels[2] spoke about the learner and suggested teaching and learning strategies that were both personal and active. Rather than seeing the child as an incomplete adult, or evil, as many adults of their time did, these enlightened scholars accepted a natural quality in childhood and portrayed the child as competent and good. For these early theorists, the role of teaching was not to "correct" students or "fill them up" with knowledge, but rather to guide the student as he or she unfolded.

Another early belief in America was that education should be relevant to the needs of learners. Benjamin Franklin, writing in 1740, spoke of the need for utility:[3]

> As to their studies, it would be well if they could be taught everything that is useful—but their time is short and it is therefore proposed that they learn those things that are most useful.

One of the major events that introduced American educators to a child-centered view of schooling was the centennial celebration held in Philadelphia in 1876. Here, many of their ideas were exhibited and discussed in earnest. There is evidence that as early as 1895 this "second" philosophy of education was firmly in place. In the words of the National Education Association's Committee of Fifteen on Elementary Education:[4]

> Modern education emphasizes the opinion that the child, not the subject of study, is the guide to the teacher's efforts. To know the child is of paramount importance.

By the turn of the twentieth century, a child-centered philosophy of education and a growing body of information about human development often appeared in tandem. Unlike traditionalists, who saw education as a process of information transfer and an educated person as a purveyor of unusual information, America's new educators held that schooling was for the development of the individual learner. Citing studies of human development, they prescribed approaches and strategies for educating students.

In his book titled *Adolescence* (1904), which was based on his quantified studies of youth in New York City, psychologist G. Stanley Hall described the effect of puberty as either a scientific or a philosophical evolution:[5]

> With the advent of puberty, and the beginning of the adolescent period, there is a marked acceleration in the development of the whole psychic life. The mind, which has been expanding throughout childhood, now expands more rapidly. The intellect essays larger fields of conquest in the way of knowledge. The emotional nature becomes endowed with a fever, sensitive to the subtle shades of the beautiful and the sublime. And the will seems to awaken to a new realization of its own power.

Using this growing body of knowledge, educators began to prescribe new methodology and pedagogy. John Dewey, America's most famous educator, stated the case thusly:[6]

> Education . . . must begin with a psychological insight into the child's capacities, interests, and habits. It must be controlled at every point by reference to these same considerations. These powers, interests, and habits must be continually interpreted— we must know what they mean.

Within two decades following the turn of the century, "progressive" education (as opposed to traditional education) had established itself. Questions raised by the new thinking with respect to the purpose and form of education were reflected by the Committee on the Reorganization of Secondary Education. Meeting from 1913 to 1918, this commission recommended a broader, more utilitarian purpose for secondary education with seven cardinal principles (directions) including citizenship training, vocational preparation, and worthy home membership.[7] By the early 1940s, phrases like "life education" were common in the literature.

Differences in the assumptions of traditional education versus those of progressive education cannot be overemphasized in that they help explain why the middle school is not simply a warmed-over junior high school. Hilda Taba puts it this way:[8]

> . . . the variations in the conceptions of the function of education are not idle or theoretical arguments. They have definite concrete implications for the shape of educational programs, especially the curriculum. If one believes that the chief function of education is to transmit the perennial truths, one cannot but strive toward a uniform curriculum and teaching. Education takes on a different shape when the major function is seen as fostering creative thinking or problem solving. As such, differences in

these concepts naturally determine what are considered "essentials" and what are the dispensable "frills" in education.

Observing the influences of these changes over three decades, Leonard Koos, a widely read junior high school advocate, identified eight influences on secondary education:[9]

1. Organization of elementary and secondary education into three tiers
2. Recognition of the need for gradualism in transition
3. Adjustments made in the area of physical education
4. Modification in learning to suit the cognitive power of the student
5. Ability of the school to adjust to the mental maturity of the student
6. Addition of extracurricular offerings to meet new social interests
7. Provision of more opportunity for moral guidance and inspiration
8. Recognition of the need to reduce unnecessary stress on students

The impact of studies of student development had wide-ranging consequences as even noneducators, like philosopher Alfred N. Whitehead, began to see the need for a more modern methodology:[10]

Do not teach too many subjects—let the main ideas which are introduced into a child's education be few and important, and let them be thrown in every combination possible.

The period from 1930 to 1960 saw many new instructional practices that stemmed from the growing awareness of human development research. Under the label of "individualizing," techniques such as team teaching, cooperative learning, outdoor (organic) education, and open-space facilities were created. Most often, however, these techniques, intended to enhance the education of the individual learner, were superimposed on a content curriculum without much effect. In the words of William Alexander, "father" of the American middle school:[11]

A review of the plans made and implemented yesterday leaves no doubt that the dominant assumption of past curriculum planning has been the goal of subject matter mastery through a subject curriculum, almost inextricably tied to a closed school and graded school ladder, to a marking system that rewards successful achievement of fixed content and penalizes unsuccessful achievement, to an instructional organization based on fixed classes in the subjects and a time table for them.

Finally, in the early 1960s the forces of human development research were pushing American education closer to a reformation of both the purpose and structure of schooling. Of particular influence were the translations of Jean Piaget's work,[12] a major study of human development from ages ten to fourteen by the University of California at Berkeley,[13] and the first efforts to integrate this nation's schools.

By 1965, the United States was "primed" for the invention of a number of new educational programs including early childhood education, middle school education, gifted education, and special education. All of these new programs shared the common denominator of being focused on human growth and development, and collectively they ushered in a new era in American education. To fully understand the changes that occurred at the middle level, one must review the history of the junior high school that preceded the middle school.

The Junior High School

For secondary education, the period following the Civil War was one of rebuilding. Most states had experienced a disruption of both secondary and higher education in the 1860s, and it wasn't until 1872 that legal mandate existed to have tax-supported secondary education.[14] By the early 1890s, the overall quality of secondary education was uneven, and a committee of secondary leaders as well as colleges was called to study the problem. The main committee, the Committee of Ten,[15] recommended standardization of courses, credits, and times needed for college entrance, effectively "locking in" the high school curriculum. Another committee recommended reducing the secondary years so as to create a six-year high school. Such a six-six plan was in effect in the United States until around 1910.

Problems inherent with the six-year high school were familiar for anyone working at the intermediate level of education. Secondary schools reported that students seemed too "immature" for the studies required. Discipline was a common problem and "dropping out" was often cited. Part of the problem was that the high school was experiencing tremendous growth during this period (an increase from a mere two hundred thousand pupils in the mid-1890s to nearly five million by the mid-1920s) and a new program for the full six years was not developed. By 1905, the six-year high school was under heavy criticism.

In 1909, the first junior high school, with grades seven through nine, was introduced in Columbus, Ohio; another followed in Berkeley, California, in January of 1910. Reasons given by Superintendent Frank Bunker in the latter case were to reduce the high school dropout rate and relieve overcrowding in the high school.[16] In 1919, the North Central Association of Colleges and Secondary Schools defined the junior high school as one in which grades seven through nine were placed in a building of their own with a special teaching staff and administrators. The junior high school was on the way. By 1920, approximately four hundred junior high schools were in existence, and the number would grow to nearly sixty-five hundred by the mid-1950s.

The early literature of the junior high school movement is virtually indistinguishable from the early literature of the middle school: Both speak of the specialness of an age group going through the onset of puberty; both call for an adaptive curriculum sensitive to the uniqueness of individual learners; and both program descriptions call for an active and practical curriculum that engages the student. The key differences between the junior high school and the middle school that replaced it is that the latter organized to provide such a curriculum whereas the former never did.

Although the majority of junior high schools were composed of grades seven through nine, there were a number of other grade combinations, such as eight and nine, seven through ten, and six through eight. Many six-through-eight configurations were found in the Southeast because for many years high school in that region only went through the eleventh grade. Prior to the turn of the century, even some public schools were called middle schools (see Figure 1.1) and had grade combinations of five through eight. Figure 1.2 shows the evolution of intermediate schools.

FIGURE 1.1   A middle school certificate from 1898

FIGURE 1.2   Evolution of American schools

Elementary	Early 1800s–1890	Grades 1–6, 1–8
Elementary Secondary	1890–1910	Grades 1–6, 7–12 1–8, 9–12
Elementary Junior high Senior high	1910–1960	Grades 1–6 7–9 10–12
Elementary Middle school High school	1960–Present	Grades K–5 6–8 9–12

There are many reasons why the junior high school failed to create a program to match the rhetoric. Already mentioned was the tremendous growth of the high school during this period, with the result that most resources went to new facilities and materials. Alas, most junior high schools during the fifty-year period of its existence were located in old high school buildings. Also cited was the inability to train teachers for this new level, a problem that still exists in the 1990s. But most important was the inability of the junior high school to shake off the traditional content-focused curriculum that defined school success by courses mastered and carried out through a "high school–like" departmentalization of teachers and schedule. In fact, in its final years junior high schools, having activities such as marching bands, full-blown interscholastic events, proms, and cap-and-gown graduations, were often indistinguishable from high schools.

The Carnegie unit assigned to grades nine and above for the purpose of achieving a uniform preparation for high school (Committee of Ten) exerted a powerful influence on the junior high school. Often, all courses were organized in a fifty-minute, six-period-day format, for the sake of standardization. Later, the movement of the ninth grade to the high school while creating grades six-through-eight middle schools freed the newer form of this Carnegie unit burden.

The junior high school was not without its critics, and attempts were made to reform the program and organization of the junior high through the addition of exploratory programs and core teaching. William Gruhn and Harl Douglass conducted a study of the junior high school in the 1940s and identified six basic functions of the junior high school:[17]

1. *Integration,* designed to help students use the skills, attitudes, and understandings previously acquired and integrate them into effective and wholesome behavior.
2. *Exploration,* to allow students the opportunity to explore particular interests so that they can have access to better choices and actions, both vocational and academic. Students will develop a wide range of cultural, civic, social, recreational, and avocational interests.
3. *Guidance,* to help students make satisfactory social, emotional, and social adjustments toward becoming mature personalities.
4. *Differentiation,* to provide diverse educational opportunities and facilities in accord with varying student backgrounds, personalities, and other individual differences so that each pupil can achieve most economically and completely the ultimate aims of education.
5. *Socialization,* to furnish learning experiences intended to prepare students for effective and satisfying participation in a complex social order as well as future changes in the social order.
6. *Articulation,* to provide for a gradual transition from preadolescent education to an educational program suited to the needs of adolescent girls and boys.

Finally, in the 1950s serious calls for reform of the junior high school could be heard, first from the traditionalists following Russia's launch of *Sputnik*[18] in 1957, and later by reformers with the onset of racial integration. The highly standardized junior high school had failed to achieve the student-focused school envisioned by early theorists like Thomas Briggs, Leonard Koos, Vernon Bennett, and Calvin Davis.

However, a second generation of "junior high" educators, led by curriculum devel-opers like William Alexander, John Lounsbury, and Gordon Vars, stood ready to try again. Following Alexander's coining of the term *middle school* to describe innovative junior highs in 1967,[19] the middle school movement was under way.

WHY A MIDDLE SCHOOL?

Four factors led to the emergence of the middle school. First, the late 1950s and early 1960s were filled with criticisms of American schools, classroom and teacher short-ages, double and triple sessions, and soaring tax rates; books like *Why Johnny Can't Read* triggered new concerns about the quality of U.S. schooling. The successful launching of *Sputnik* created an obsession for academic achievement especially in science, foreign languages, and mathematics.

At this time a renewed interest in college preparation led to a call for a four-year high school where specialized courses like computer sciences and microbiology could remain under the direction of the college preparatory school—the high school. Like-wise, the inclusion of grades five and six in an intermediate school promised to strengthen instruction by allowing subject specialists to work with younger students. Many of the first middle schools were organized with grades five through eight.

A second factor was the effort to eliminate racial segregation. *The Schoolhouse in the City* stated that the real force behind the middle school movement in the larger cities (New York City, for example) was the elimination of *de facto* segregation.[20]

A third factor was the increased enrollment of school-aged children in the 1950s and 1960s. The shortage of buildings resulted in double, even triple, school sessions in school districts. Because older students in high schools were able to cope with overcrowding better than younger students, the ninth grade was moved to the high school to relieve the overcrowded junior high school. The same rationale was used to relieve the elementary school by moving the fifth and/or sixth grade to the junior high school.

A fourth factor that favored emergence of the middle school was the "band-wagon effect." This resulted when one middle school received favorable exposure in books and periodicals, and some administrators determined that the middle school was "the thing to do."

All of the four factors above may not have been the most valid reasons why middle schools were organized; but even if for the "wrong reasons," educators seized the right opportunities to develop programs designed for the preadolescent and early adolescent learner.

It is ironic that in the early 1990s the same four factors influencing middle school development exist except for two changes, i.e., the criticism of schools is not directed toward language, science, and mathematics excellence, but toward basic skills in reading and mathematics, and the increased enrollment of the 1950s and 1960s has become a declining enrollment in the 1990s.

Today, junior high schools are being reorganized into middle schools to elim-inate segregation, to alleviate population and building problems brought on by declining enrollment, to improve basic skills programs in the middle grades, and because "other districts have middle schools and we should too."

Although these are *de facto* reasons for reorganizing junior high schools into middle schools, we believe the following rationale, which provides a more relevant and appropriate program and learning environment for "transescent"[21] learners, is easier to justify:

1. To provide a program especially designed for the ten- to fourteen-year-old going through the unique "transescent" period of growth and development. There is recognition that students in this age range constitute a distinct grouping— physically, socially, and intellectually.
2. To build on the changed elementary school. Historically, the post-*Sputnik* clamor to upgrade schools prepared the way for elementary school personnel to accept the middle school concept. The introduction of the "new" science, the "new" social studies, the "new" mathematics, and the "new" linguistics in elementary schools eroded the sanctity of the self-contained classroom. As part of the reorganization of curriculum that followed *Sputnik*, elementary teachers tended to cultivate a specific content area in the curriculum. This led to a departure from the self-contained classroom toward more sharing of students among teachers.
3. Dissatisfaction with the existing junior high school. In most cases, the junior high school did not become a transitional school between the elementary and senior high school. Unfortunately, it became a miniature high school with all the sophisticated activities of the high school. Instruction was often formal and discipline-centered, with insufficient attention given to the student as a unique individual.
4. To facilitate educational change. A more rapid and comprehensive change is frequently effected by creating a new institution rather than attempting to remodel an old one. Teachers and administrators in a new school, free from the constraints and traditions of an existing school, are more receptive to innovations and new ideas.[22]

Of all the reasons advanced for the existence of the middle school, numbers 1 and 4 cited above stand out. A special program is needed for the ten- to fourteen-year-old. The wide range of physical, social, and intellectual growth calls for an individualized program that is lacking in most junior high schools. The middle school provides for individual differences, with the program tailored to fit each student. The middle school, through a new program and organization, provides for much-needed innovations in curriculum and instruction. Thus, educators have provided an innovative atmosphere for implementing those practices long talked about but seldom effected.[23]

Advantages

Early in the middle school movement, a comprehensive list of sixteen advantages it offers was compiled. These advantages still exist today:[24]

1. It gives this unit a status of its own, rather than a "junior" classification.
2. It facilitates the introduction in grades five and six of some specialization and team teaching in staff patterns.

3. It facilitates the reorganization of teacher education, which is sorely needed to provide teachers competent to teach in the middle school. Because existing patterns of the elementary or the secondary teacher training program suffice, a new pattern must be developed.
4. Developmentally, children in grades six through eight are probably more alike than children in grades seven through nine.
5. Because they are undergoing the common experience of adolescence, sixth through eighth graders should have special attention, special teachers, and special programs, which the middle school permits.
6. It provides an opportunity for gradual change from the self-contained classroom to complete departmentalization.
7. Additional facilities and specialists can be made available to all children one year earlier.
8. It permits the organization of a program that emphasizes a continuation and enrichment of basic education in the fundamentals.
9. It facilitates extension of guidance services into the elementary grades.
10. It helps to slow down the "growing-up" process from kindergarten through eighth grade because the oldest group is removed from each level.
11. It puts children from the entire district together one year earlier, thus aiding their social development.
12. Physical unification of grades nine through twelve permits better coordination of courses for the senior high school.
13. It eliminates the possibility of some students and parents not being aware of the importance of the ninth grade as part of the senior high school record, particularly in terms of college admission.
14. It eliminates the need for special programs and facilities for one grade and eliminates the problems created by the fact that the ninth grade is functionally a part of the senior high school.
15. It reduces duplication of expensive equipment and facilities for the one grade so that funds can be spent on facilities that benefit all grades.
16. It provides both present and future flexibility in building planning, particularly when it comes to accommodating a changing school population.

Functions

Middle schools, both in recognition and in numbers, have become a separate intermediate institution in America. Cumulative experience, research, and proof that "the middle school works" have resulted in its widespread acceptance by students, teachers, administrators, and parents. We have defined the middle school as a transitional school concerned with providing the most appropriate program to cope with the personal and educational needs of emerging adolescent learners. The Association for Supervision and Curriculum Development has identified the middle school as an institution that has the following features:[25]

□ A unique program adapted to the needs of the preadolescent and early adolescent student.
□ The widest possible range of intellectual, social, and physical experiences.

☐ Opportunities for exploration and development of fundamental skills, while making allowances for individual learning patterns. It should maintain an atmosphere of basic respect for individual differences.

☐ A climate that enables students to develop abilities, find facts, weigh evidence, draw conclusions, determine values, and keep their minds open to new facts.

☐ Staff members who recognize and understand the student's needs, interests, backgrounds, motivations, goals, stresses, strains, frustrations, and fears.

☐ A smooth education transition between the elementary school and the high school, while allowing for the physical and emotional changes taking place due to transescence.

☐ An environment where the child—not the program—is most important and where the opportunity to succeed is ensured for all students.

☐ Guidance in the development of mental processes and attitudes needed for constructive citizenship and the development of lifelong competencies and appreciations needed for effective use of leisure.

☐ Competent instructional personnel who will strive to understand the students whom they serve and develop professional competencies that are both unique and applicable to the transescent student.

☐ Facilities and time that allow students and teachers an opportunity to achieve the goals of the program to their fullest capabilities.

Table 1.1 illustrates the unique and transitional nature of the middle school.

The middle school, then, represents a renewed effort to design and implement a program of education that can accommodate the needs of the preadolescent population.

TABLE 1.1 The Middle School: Unique and Transitional

	Elementary	Middle	High
Teacher-student relationship	Parental	Adviser	Instructor
Teacher organization	Self-contained	Interdisciplinary team	Department
Curricular emphasis	Skills	Exploration	Depth
Schedule	Self-contained	Block	Periods
Instruction	Student-directed	Balance	Teacher-directed
Student grouping	Chronological	Multi-age developmental	Subject
Building plan	Classroom areas	Team areas	Department areas
Psychomotor development	Skills and games	Skills and intramurals	Skills and interscholastics
Utilization of media	Classroom groups	Balance	Individual study
Guidance	Diagnostic/ developmental	Teacher helper	Career-vocational
Teacher preparation	Child-oriented generalist	Flexible resource	Discipline specialist

It is a broadly focused program, drawing its philosophy and rationale from the evolving body of knowledge concerned with human growth and development. The middle school represents a systematic effort to organize the schooling experience in such a way as to facilitate the maximum growth and development of all learners.

The middle school program consists of arrangements and activities that attempt to tie formal learning directly to the developmental needs of the student. To date, identified "developmental tasks" represent the most promising criteria for curriculum development, which intersects school activity with learner growth and development.

Developmental Tasks

The school does not represent our society's only mechanism for preservation and adaptation. The family, the religious institution, and the media, all contribute to society's educative processes. The public school, however, still remains the only formally sanctioned institution created and supported to preserve and promote that society.

A problem that has plagued educational planners throughout this century is how to determine the scope of the school's responsibility in educating children. As social, economic, and political forces have acted on our nation, the dimension of school operation and the role of the school has fluctuated. Today the scope of schools' responsibilities is immense. The educative process has expanded to serve forty-five million pupils each day, or fifteen times as many individuals as were in the armed services at the height of the Vietnam War. With such size has come increasing diversity of responsibility and concern.

Obviously, public schools cannot continue to expand their concerns and commitments indefinitely. They must, through program planning, identify those areas that can be dealt with within the boundaries of available resources. Schools must develop a focus and set standards for the determination of the curriculum.

One way in which schools might work responsibly with young people of all backgrounds and capacities has been called the *developmental tasks* of growth. As formulated by sociologist Robert Havighurst in the early 1950s, developmental tasks of human growth represent universal steps in a culture toward achieving adulthood. An assumption made in considering developmental tasks as possible criteria for school planning (an assumption that is essential to the acceptance of the middle school rationale) is that the comprehensive development and expansion of human potential is an important concern of the school.

During the past twenty years, developmental psychologists, educators, sociologists, and others have identified many "tasks" regularly encountered by all individuals in our society as they progress from childhood to adolescence. Examples of such tasks are shown in Table 1.2.

Whereas these developmental tasks are only suggestive of the kinds of concerns and needs experienced by young persons between early childhood and adolescence, they do indicate some areas where school programs can intervene meaningfully in the developmental process.

At the early childhood level, representing the corresponding school years from nursery school through the third grade, there might be a focus on the following categories of needs:

□ *Social adjustment,* an introduction to institutional living, a building of relationships with other children and adults, the encouragement of socially acceptable behaviors.
□ *Initial physical development,* the encouragement of gross motor skills and specialized tasks associated with the schooling process. Also, the detection and correction of progress-retarding deficiencies, such as visual and learning problems.
□ *An awareness of self,* the establishment and awareness of self-identity as an individual. The development of autonomy, an exploration of roles, the discovery of interests and talents.

TABLE 1.2   Examples of Developmental Tasks

Adolescence
Establishing emancipation from parent dependency
Exploring occupational projection selection
Completing value structure
Mastering self-acceptance

Preadolescence
Handling major body changes
Asserting independence from family
Establishing sex-role identity
Dealing with peer-group relationships
Controlling emotions
Constructing a values foundation
Pursuing interest expression
Utilizing new reasoning capacities
Developing acceptable self-concept

Late Childhood
Mastering communication skills
Building meaningful peer relations
Thinking independently
Exploring self-acceptance
Finding constructive outlets for expression
Using role projection

Middle Childhood
Structuring the physical world
Refining language and thought patterns
Establishing relationships with others
Understanding sex roles

Early Childhood
Developing motor control
Emerging self-awareness
Mapping out surroundings
Assigning meaning to events
Exploring relationships with others
Developing language and thought patterns

□ *Academic readiness,* consisting of learning basal knowledge, developing learning skills, establishing symbols literacy, promoting positive attitudes toward schooling.

□ *Sensory development,* encouraging expansion of the five senses including aesthetic appreciation and an awareness of environmental beauty. (No priority for importance is intended by the order of these categories.)

In the intermediate years, corresponding to grades four through eight, the focus of programs might be:

□ *Social development and refinement,* to facilitate the acceptance of new roles and responsibilities, to teach the interdependence of individuals in society, to explore social values, to teach basic communications and human relations skills.

□ *Promotion of physical and mental health,* an intensive program of exercise designed to develop conditioning and coordination. An accompanying component used to promote positive physical and mental health practices. Basic sex education.

□ *Development of self-concept and self-acceptance,* to promote feelings of worth in all individuals, to accentuate strengths, to aid in the development of realistic perceptions and expectations of self, to foster increased independence, to assist in values exploration, to explore and expand interests.

□ *Academic adequacy,* to ensure literacy, to aid in the organization needed for academic achievement, to teach skills for continued learning, to introduce knowledge areas, to explore career potentials as they relate to interests, to develop independence and autonomy in learning, to foster critical thinking.

□ *Aesthetic stimulation,* to develop latent talents in art, music, writing; to promote an understanding of human aesthetic achievement; to develop a capacity for the satisfying use of leisure time. (No priority for importance is intended by the order of these categories.)

In the secondary school, corresponding to the first years of the high school and perhaps into the postsecondary years (nine through thirteen), the following program focus might be utilized:

□ *Social maturation,* promoting increased independence and autonomy in decision making, exploring the rights and responsibilities of adulthood and citizenship, studying marriage and family life, exploring socially acceptable means of communication.

□ *Refinement of health,* defining and analyzing the meaning of good health for individuals and society—including personalizing positive health plans, emphasizing programs of individual health development and maintenance, and studying causes of poor health (drugs, alcoholism, smoking, obesity).

□ *Supporting self-actualization,* assisting in values, clarification, exploration of careers and education as extensions of individual needs and interests, the correction of minor psychological and emotional problems, the identification and emphasis of personal strengths.

□ *Academic specialization,* the development of specialization in knowledge and learning skills, an exploration of academic opportunities, the refinement of critical and analytical thinking, and an emphasis on the utility of knowledge in everyday living.

□ *Aesthetic refinement*, the pursuit of quality living, an emphasis of social existence, the refinement of aesthetic talents, the development of satisfying hobbies, an understanding of human capacities for further achievements. (No priority of importance is intended by the order of these categories.)

Utilizing developmental tasks as criteria for planning school programs suggests some global areas of focus for activity development. Following are some continuums of concern:

Early Childhood	**Intermediate**	**Secondary**
Social adjustment	Social development	Social maturation
Initial physical development	Promotion of physical development	Refinement of physical health
Self-awareness	Self-acceptance	Self-actualization
Academic readiness	Academic adequacy	Academic specialization
Sensory development	Aesthetic stimulation	Aesthetic refinement

>———— Continuums of Growth in School ————→

Even though educators must analyze student needs at each level of education, it is interesting to view in isolation the tasks and possible roles of schooling at the intermediate level of education:

Tasks

Late Childhood
Mastery of communication
Building of peer relationships
Thinking as an individual
Acceptance of self
Finding means of expression
Role projection

Preadolescence
Handling physical change
Asserting independence
Establishing sex-role identity
Refining peer relationships
Controlling emotions
Constructing a values foundation
Pursuing interests
Use of reasoning capacity
Developing self-concept

School Roles

1. *Social development and refinement*
   Acceptance of responsibility
   Interdependence of individuals
   Exploration of social values
   Human relations
   Communication skills

2. *Promotion of physical and mental health*
   Conditioning and coordination
   Understanding hygiene
   Sex education
   Understanding nutrition

3. *Development of self-concept and self-acceptance*
   Accentuate strengths
   Self-analysis
   Increased responsibility
   Values exploration
   Interest expansion

4. *Academic adequacy*
   Basic literacy
   Organize for academic achievement
   Skills for continued learning
   Introduce knowledge areas
   Explore career potential
   Develop learning autonomy
   Critical thinking

5. *Aesthetic stimulation*
   Develop latent talents
   Promote aesthetic appreciation
   Develop leisure-time activities

Table 1.3 examines the program of each level of schooling.

Matching some of the developmental tasks of late childhood and preadolescence with some of the possible roles of the school during the corresponding grade levels highlights interesting conditions that exist in intermediate education. Few programs in the middle grades justify their experiences in terms of student needs. The narrowness of the curriculum in most intermediate schools is a historical hybrid derived from other levels of schooling.

If educational planners choose to use the developmental needs of the students being served as criteria for curriculum development, the school must broaden its definition of an *education*. There must be a greater concern for social and emotional dimensions of preadolescent development because academic preparation and physical development represent only part of the needs of emerging adolescents.

Our growing awareness of the affective dimensions of learning—feelings, attitudes, emotions, and the like—suggests that we must deal with preadolescents in a more sophisticated and comprehensive manner. We can no longer afford to ignore the environmental conditions that surround the schooling process. Further, we must acknowledge that our objectives in formal schooling require altered teaching behaviors as well as intellectual growth.

It seems obvious that the kinds of administrative and curricular arrangements made by the school at both the building and classroom levels will need to be

TABLE 1.3 Program by Level of Schooling

Elementary School	Middle School	High School

Introduction to School
Socialization
Beginning Skills
Beginning Learnings
Introduction to Disciplines
    Social studies
    Science
	Personal Development
	Refinement of Skills
	
	Continued Learnings
	Education for Social
	Competence
	
	Interdisciplinary Learnings
		Comprehensive
		    Vocational training
		    College preparatory
		In-depth Learnings
		    Chemistry
		    Algebra
		    World history
		    American literature
		Career Planning

	Organization and *Developmental Skills*	
K–5	6, 7–8	9–12
K–3 4–5	6–8	
Early Late childhood childhood	Transescence	Adolescence

rethought and redesigned. Greater program flexibility and diversity will have to be introduced in all facets of school life. Activity will have to be broadened and enriched.

ESTABLISHING AN IDENTITY FOR THE MIDDLE SCHOOL

Education for emerging adolescents has received an intensive reexamination over the past decade. One result has been the verification of a need for a school with a differentiated function for the ten- to fourteen-year-old age group. That need for a distinct school—unlike the elementary, high school, or even the junior high school—is more defensible than ever in light of recent information about growth and development of emerging adolescents. Changing social conditions have also helped establish the need for a school in the middle with an identity of its own. As middle schools have grown in number and quality, a number of common elements have helped establish an identity for the middle school, including:

☐ Absence of the "little high school" approach.
☐ Absence of the "star system," where a few special students dominate everything, in favor of an attempt to provide success experiences for greater numbers of students.
☐ An attempt to use instructional methods more appropriate to this age group: individualized instruction, variable group sizes, multimedia approaches, beginning independent study programs, inquiry-oriented instruction.
☐ Increased opportunity for teacher-student guidance (may include a home base or advisory group program).

□ Increased flexibility in scheduling and in student grouping.

□ At least some cooperative planning and team teaching.

□ At least some interdisciplinary studies, where teachers from a variety of academic pursuits provide opportunities for students to see how the areas of knowledge fit together.

□ A wide range of exploratory opportunities, academic and otherwise.

□ Increased opportunity for physical activity and movement, and more frequent physical education.

□ Earlier introduction to the areas of organized academic knowledge.

□ Attention to the skills of continued learning, those skills that will permit students to learn better on their own or at higher levels.

□ Accent on increasing the student's ability to be independent, responsible, and self-disciplined.

□ Flexible physical plant facilities.

□ Attention to the personal development of the student: values clarification, group process skills, health and family life education when appropriate, career education.

□ Teachers trained especially for, and committed to, the education of emerging adolescents.

Neil Atkins, a pioneer in the middle school movement, early identified the features of the middle school that distinguish it as uniquely appropriate for the children it serves.[26] Three of these features include:

Attitudinal stance: The uniqueness of the middle school comes not so much in grade organization, courses, grouping, or schedules as it does in matters of attitude, perception, and sensitivity. The mission of the school is viewed as neither remedial nor preparatory. The transitional nature of students age ten to fourteen is not only recognized but also valued. Therefore, the middle school can be characterized as having the capacity to accommodate children whose chronological age is dominated with problems of coping with change—changing interests, changing personal relationships, and changing bodies.

Operational flexibility and innovative practice: Translated into operational terms, this means the middle school should be characterized organizationally by flexibility, instructionally by individualization, and environmentally by sensitivity to changing needs of the age group it serves. Middle school students are viewed as individuals and not groups for whom instructional decisions are made.

The experimental attitude brought on by increased sensitivity and awareness about child development has led to innovative practices and programs in the middle school.

Supportive instructional strategies: Another distinguishing feature of the middle school is the shift in emphasis from mastery of knowledge to utilization of knowledge. Prominent features of the program include diagnostic teaching, individualized instruction, self-directed learning, and learner-centered evaluation. These closely interrelated strategies lead to a central goal of the middle school—namely, to support the student's effort to move as a learner from dependence to independence. The organizational manifestation of instructional strategies is to remove gradually any institutional restraints on movement and use of materials and equipment. Self-concept is strengthened through the power of competence, and a sense of inquiry and commitment to learning is fostered through the choices of alternative courses of action.

SUMMARY

The middle school model for intermediate education evolved from the earlier programs of the junior high school. Although the expressed goals of the junior high school and the middle school are similar, the middle school represents a new and different way of working with emerging adolescents.

Historically, the junior high school has tended to imitate the curriculum of the senior high school. By contrast, the middle school was established as a school with its own special identity and organization. The social changes of the 1960s and 1970s, such as fluctuating enrollments, desegregation, and other factors, provided the right opportunities for educators to launch this new school form. Because of its unique structure, the middle school may be able to achieve the goals only articulated by the early junior high.

The emergence of the middle school has resulted in a renewed interest in the developmental characteristics of pupils between early childhood and adolescence. These common developmental tasks of growth represent one planning base on which conceptualizing the intermediate school program can build.

We believe that the purposeful design of the middle school program will result in an educational experience that proves highly effective for students in their intermediate years.

SUGGESTED LEARNING ACTIVITIES

1. Tracing the history of the junior high school, try to identify those factors that led to the eventual establishment of the middle school.
2. List five differences between the junior high school and the middle school. If the goals of the junior high school and those of the middle school are basically the same, how is the middle school unique?
3. Write a philosophical statement defending the emerging middle school design. Try to determine what parts of the middle school concept are essential.

NOTES

1. Teaming was formally recognized by the National Association of Secondary School Principals in the early 1950s. The teacher as adviser program was in existence at Eagle Lake High School in Los Angeles in 1940. Even teacher empowerment existed as early as 1936 in Shaker Heights, Ohio.
2. For an overview of these contributions, see "A New Look at Progressive Education," *ASCD Yearbook*, 1972.
3. Cited in Leonard V. Koos, *The American Secondary School* (New York: Ginn and Company, 1927), 20.
4. As cited in *The Curriculum: Retrospect and Prospect*, NSSE Yearbook, 1971, p. 5.
5. Koos, op. cit., p. 71.
6. "A New Look at Progressive Education," p. 21.
7. Commission on the Reorganization of Education, *Cardinal Principles of Secondary Education*, Bureau of Education, 1918.

8. Hilda Taba, *Curriculum Development: Theory into Practice* (New York: Harcourt Brace, 1962), 30.
9. Koos, op. cit., p. 94.
10. A. N. Whitehead, *Aims of Education* (New York: Macmillan, 1929), 18.
11. William Alexander, "Curriculum Planning as It Should Be," an address to the ASCD Annual Conference, Chicago, 1971.
12. See J. Flavell, *The Developmental Psychology of Jean Piaget* (New York: Van Nostrand, 1963) for a comprehensive treatment of this topic.
13. In 1962 the University of California study documented that 95 percent of all American children enter puberty between ages ten and fourteen, leading to an early prescription for a grades five-through-eight middle school.
14. The *Kalamazoo* decision, Michigan State Supreme Court, 1872.
15. Committee of Ten, NEA, chaired by Charles Eliot, president of Harvard.
16. Frank Bunker, *The Junior High School Movement: Its Beginnings* (Washington, DC: Roberts Publishing, 1935).
17. William Gruhn and Harl Douglass, *The Modern Junior High School*, (New York: Ronald, 1956), 31–32.
18. When the Russians launched *Sputnik* (their first satellite), traditionalists attacked the junior high curriculum as being "watered down" and nonacademic. When integration of schools began in earnest in 1959, junior highs were criticized for being too academic and unresponsive to individual differences.
19. Alexander used a grant from the W. K. Kellogg Foundation to identify schools having a fifth-through eighth-grade or sixth- through eighth-grade organization and possessing some innovations like team teaching. Three hundred were found in the United States in 1967.
20. Educational Facilities Laboratories, *The Schoolhouse in the City* (New York: EFL, 1966), 10.
21. *Transescence* is the stage of development which begins prior to the onset of puberty and extends through the early stages of adolescence. Since puberty does not occur precisely at the same chronological age in human development, the transescent designation is based on the many physical, social, and emotional changes in the body chemistry that appear prior to the time when the body gains a practical degree of stabilization over those complex pubescent changes. Donald Eichhorn, *The Middle School*, Center for Applied Research in Education, 1966, p. 3.
22. A report to the State Commission on Middle School, Middle Schools in Florida, Tallahassee: State Department of Education, 1972, pp. 2–4.
23. Joseph Bondi, *Developing Middle Schools: A Guidebook,* (Wheeling, IL: Whitehall Publishing Company, 1972), 12.
24. Pearl Brod, "The Middle School—Trends toward Its Adoption," *Clearinghouse* 40 (February 1966), 331–33.
25. ASCD Working Group. In *The Middle School We Need* (Washington, DC: Association for Supervision and Curriculum Development, 1975), 2–3, Used with permission.
26. Neil Atkins, "Rethinking Education in the Middle," *Theory into Practice* 7 (June 1968), 118–19.

SELECTED REFERENCES

Alexander, W. et al, *The Emergent Middle School* (New York: Holt, Rinehart, Winston, 1968).

Association for Supervision and Curriculum Development, *The Middle School We Need* (Washington, DC: ASCD, 1975).

Blair, A. and Burton, W., *Growth and Development of the Preadolescent* (New York: Appleton-Century-Crofts), 1951.

Briggs, T., *The Junior High School* (Boston: Houghton-Mifflin) 1920.

Commission on the Reorganization of Secondary Education, *Cardinal Principles of Secondary Education*, Bulletin 1918 (Washington, DC: U.S. Department of the Interior, Bureau of Education, 1918).

Conant, J., *Recommendations for Education in the Junior High School Years: A Memorandum* to School Boards (Princeton, NJ: Educational Testing Service, 1960).

Douglas, A., *The Junior High School,* Fifteenth Yearbook, National Society for the Study of Education, Public School Publishing Company, 1916.

Eichhorn, D., *The Middle School* (New York: Center for Applied Research in Education, 1966).

Flavell, J., *The Developmental Psychology of Jean Piaget* (Princeton, NJ: Van Nostrand, 1963).

Lounsbury, J. and Marani, J., *The Junior High School We Saw: One Day in the Eighth Grade* (Washington, DC: ASCD, 1964).

2

The Middle School Student

Nothing is so unequal as the
equal treatment of unequals.

An early adolescent is. . .

a canvas to be filled.
a field to be tilled.
clay to be molded.
a bulb to develop.
a diamond to be cut.
a challenge to be met.
a poem to be written.
a song to be sung.
a fragrance to be released.
a life to be saved.
a friend to be made.
a gift to the future.
a bridge to the stars.
a pain in the heart.
a tear in the eye.
energy to be channeled.
a riddle to be solved.
a birdsong in December.
a candle to be lit.
a rain for the sod.
the right hand of God.
—Georgia Ensminger, Oldham
Middle School, LaGrange Kentucky.
Used with permission.

INTRODUCTION

The most important pupils in today's schools is that diverse group caught in the middle years—the years between childhood and adolescence. A growing body of knowledge shows that what happens to students between the ages of ten and fourteen determines not only their future success in school, but success in life as well.

Writings on the subject are filled with short, sometimes clever, descriptions of young adolescents—"awkward and clumsy," "filled with turbulent emotions," "displays emerging independence," "trying." Yet, who *are* these young adolescents in our schools' middle grades?

This chapter is designed to give the reader a better understanding of the characteristics of emerging adolescent learners and resultant implications for school programs. It also provides a study of the problems that affect a modern society, problems that exert a profound influence on an impressionable age group.

The poem in Figure 2.1 reflects the uncertainty of the emerging adolescent who is neither boy nor man, neither girl nor woman. Because we often do not understand the behavior of others, we are likely to attribute the worst possible motives to them. This especially holds true for young adolescents. When confronted with normal behaviors of young adolescents, such as loud talking or wearing out-

FIGURE 2.1   Understanding the emerging adolescent learner

How high is the sky?
Who invented the tie?
Why was I born?
Who am I?
What is the reason?
When is a season?
Where am I going—
This I really have to know.

Source: Fred Buckman, Fitzgerald Middle School, Largo, Florida. Used with permission.

landish clothes, we believe they are done purposely to frustrate or infuriate us. David Elkind,[1] a child psychologist, has, through the interpretation of his studies and those of Piaget (see Figure 2.2), provided us with insights into the troubling behaviors of emerging adolescents.[2]

A common problem of young adolescents is their tendency to interpret situations more complexly than is warranted. For instance, simple decisions about what slacks or dress to wear are overcomplicated by bringing in extraneous concerns about how and why the clothes were bought in the first place. In school, young adolescents often approach their subjects at a much too complex level and thereby fail in them—not because the studies are too hard, but because they are too simple.

Elkind attributes such behaviors to newly attained thinking capacities made possible through what Piaget calls *formal operations*. Formal operations allow a pupil to hold many variables in mind at the same time, to conceive ideals and contrary-to-fact propositions. But in the young adolescent, these newly attained formal operations often are not under full control. The capacity to think of many alternatives is not immediately coupled with the ability to assign priorities and to decide which choice is best. That is why young adolescents sometimes appear backward, when in fact they are too bright.

Formal operations also allow young adolescents to think about other people's thinking. This ability is not always coupled with the ability to distinguish between what is of interest to others and what is of interest to self. Because the emerging adolescent is concerned with all the physical and social changes that are going on, he believes everyone else is equally preoccupied with his appearance or behavior. Young adolescents, then, surround themselves with an imaginary audience.

The imaginary audience makes this age group extremely self-conscious; they believe they are the center of everyone's attention. Fantasies of making a touchdown or singing before a large audience are common imaginary audience fantasies in which the youth is the center of everyone's attention.

FIGURE 2.2   Stages of intellectual development as described by Piaget

Stages of Development—Middle Years	7–15 Age Range
Concrete Operations	7–11 years
Ability to think out problems previously "worked" out. Logical thought, e.g., genuine classification, learning to organize objects into a series; reversing operations (as in arithmetic).	
a. learns to master logical operations using material with a concrete content	
b. unable to think abstractly about a problem	
c. understands the principle of conservation leads directly to an awareness of reversibility	
d. can use various approaches to the solution of a problem	
e. concerned with the relationship of the parts to the whole	
f. can perform the operation of serializing	
g. language becomes primarily sociocentric while egocentric speech decreases	
h. can comprehend the following four concrete operational groupings: combinativity, reversability, associativity, and identity or nullifiability	
Formal Operations Comprehension of abstract concepts, e.g., ability to form "ideas" and reason about the future, ability to handle contrary-to-fact propositions, and ability to develop and test hypotheses.	11–15 years
Substage A	11–12 to 14–15 years
Appears to be a preparatory stage in which adolescents may make correct discoveries and handle certain formal operations, but the approach is cumbersome and they are not yet able to provide systematic and rigorous proof.	
Substage B	14–15 years onward
Adolescents are capable of formulating more elegant generalizations and advancing more inclusive laws. Most of all they are able to provide spontaneously more systematic proof, since they can use methods of control.	
A higher degree of mastery of the formal operations; they have the ability to make logical combinations in the following four ways: by conjunction, by disjunction, by implication, by incompatibility.	

Source: Table form adapted from Ernest R. Hilgard and Richard C. Atkinson, *Introduction to Psychology,* 4th ed. (New York: Harcourt, Brace and World, 1968). The information presented here represents a synthesis of descriptions of Piaget's theory of intellectual development cited in Robert F. Biehler, *Psychology Applied to Teaching* (Boston: Houghton Mifflin, 1971), p. 81; and Herbert Ginsburg and Sylvia Opper, Piaget's *Theory of Intellectual Development* (Englewood Cliffs, NJ: Prentice-Hall, 1969), pp. 26–206.

Groups of young people sometimes contrive to create an audience by their loud and provocative behavior. What is of immediate interest to them often annoys adults within listening range. The pervasive imaginary audience of young adolescents accounts for both their self-consciousness and their distasteful public behavior.

Vandalism in schools, which seems so irrational, becomes less so when one understands that it is often done with audience reaction in mind. While committing the act, the young vandal speculates about how outraged the audience will be.

The center-stage, I-me world of emerging adolescents leads them to believe they are special and not subject to the natural laws that pertain to others. The young girl who becomes pregnant, or the young boy who experiments with drugs, believes *others* will get caught, "not me."

The *self* is an all-important preoccupation of young people, and they assume that what is common to everyone is unique to them. One example is the son who says, "Dad, you just don't know how it feels to be in love," or the daughter who says, "Mom, you just don't know how much I need extra allowance."

The reverse preoccupation also occurs, that is, young adolescents may feel that everyone is concerned with the freckles on their nose. Any argument to the contrary carries little impact because it is arguing with another person's reality.

As young people grow and mature, they begin to share their concerns with others and develop friendships in which intimacies are shared. The tragic, self-destructive behavior of many young adolescents often occurs because they have a sense of loneliness brought on by the belief that their problems are uniquely theirs.

The emerging adolescent often displays hypocritical behavior. For instance, he will refuse to allow a brother or sister in his room to borrow things, but will go into his father's or mother's study, borrow a typewriter, calculator, or cassette player, and not return it. Hypocrisy is but another by-product of formal operations that have not been fully elaborated. The young adolescent is able to conceptualize fairly abstract rules of behavior but lacks the experience to see their relevance to concrete behavior. The youth who believes roles are for everyone else but him or her upsets adults who regard such behavior as self-serving. Again, it must be remembered that this behavior results from intellectual immaturity, not from lack of moral character.

Adolescent idealism often results in the ability to conceive and express high moral principles, but not the ability to find concrete ways to attain them. As adolescents mature and begin to engage in meaningful activities, they learn the need to work toward ideas. The middle school can be a place where young people can become pragmatic without having to become cynical about ideals and moral principles.

Piaget and Elkind have helped middle school educators shift a whole set of behaviors attributed to emerging adolescents from the realm of "bad" to the realm of "behavior typical for the age." By recognizing that behaviors of middle school students reflect intellectual immaturity, middle school educators can themselves become more rational in their reactions to those students.

CHARACTERISTICS OF EMERGING ADOLESCENTS AND IMPLICATIONS FOR THE MIDDLE SCHOOL

Preadolescents and early adolescents experience dramatic physical, social, emotional, and intellectual changes that result from maturational changes. More biological changes occur in the bodies of ten- to fourteen-year-olds than any other age group, with the exception of children in their first three years of life. The middle school has benefited from recent research relating to children going through the major transition from late childhood to adolescence. Those research data have provided additional validated facts about the physiological and psychological dynamics acting in and on emerging adolescent learners.

When junior high schools were first developed more than eighty years ago, only generalized data regarding growth and development of students were available. Although important longitudinal studies featuring the growth and development of boys and girls were conducted between 1930 and 1960, the results of those studies had little impact on the educational program of young adolescents.

The middle school has attempted to use data pertinent to growth and development of ten- to fourteen-year-olds to justify certain organizational patterns. Unfortunately, some of the data are incorrect. An example is data relating to the earlier maturation of girls. Middle school literature is filled with statements purporting to show that American girls are reaching sexual maturity at a younger and younger age. Such statements were often used to justify moving sixth-grade and, in some cases, fifth-grade students into the middle school. In reality, there are no comparative studies indicating that the average age at which girls first menstruate has changed. The most conclusive study was conducted in 1976 by the National Institutes of Health, where it was reported that no significant age difference existed in the first menstrual period (menarche) between girls in the study and their mothers. Seven hundred eighty-one girls participated in this study conducted at the Massachusetts Institute of Technology and Massachusetts General Hospital. (Girls in the study were of similar background and about the same height and weight of girls about the same age studied in 1943, 1954, and 1973.) These results also did not support the belief that each generation is taller and healthier than the last.

Because the transitional years between childhood and adolescence are marked by distinct changes in the bodies and minds of boys and girls, the success of the middle school depends on teachers and administrators understanding each learner and her unique developmental pattern. Table 2.1 details characteristics of emerging adolescent learners, together with implications for the middle school.

The extreme differences in the rate and scale of growth and development among preadolescents is dramatized in Figure 2.3. Most of these conditions might be found in a typical eighth-grade middle school classroom. Figure 2.4 examines the shaky bridge linking childhood to adolescence.

Needs Suggested by Growth and Development Characteristics

The foregoing discussion of physical, emotional, social, and intellectual characteristics of students and the implications for the middle school suggest two terms: *transition* and *difference*. We must develop a school to encompass the transitional nature of the group as a whole and to consider the vast differences within the group.

Middle graders need security on one hand and freedom to experience and explore on the other. They need an environment that protects them from themselves without smothering the "self."

Although variations among individuals are marked, certain basic needs appear to be common among this age group:

□ To be safe and free of threat   □ To be recognized
□ To be loved   □ To be independent
□ To be part of a group with identification and acceptance

TABLE 2.1 Development of Emerging Adolescents and Its Implications for the Middle School

Characteristics of Emerging Adolescents	Implications for the Middle School
Physical Development	
Accelerated physical development begins in transescence, marked by increase in weight, height, heart size, lung capacity, and muscular strength. Boys and girls are growing at varying rates. Girls tend to be taller for the first two years and tend to be more physically advanced. Bone growth is faster than muscle development, and the uneven muscle/bone development results in lack of coordination and awkwardness. Bones may lack protection of covering muscles and supporting tendons.	Provide a health and science curriculum that emphasizes self-understanding about body changes. Guidance counselors and community resource persons (e.g., pediatricians) can help students understand what is happening to their bodies. Schedule adaptive physical education classes to build physical coordination. Equipment design should help students develop small and large muscles.
In pubescent girls, secondary sex characteristics continue to develop, with breasts enlarging and menstruation beginning.	Intense sports competition; avoid contact sports. Schedule sex education classes; health and hygiene seminars.
A wide range of individual differences among students begins to appear. Although the sequential order of development is relatively consistent in each sex, boys tend to lag a year or two behind girls. There are marked individual differences in physical development for boys and girls. The age of greatest variability in physiological development and physical size is about age 13.	Provide opportunities for interaction among students of different ages, but avoid situations where physical development can be compared (e.g., communal showers.) Emphasize intramural programs rather than interscholastic athletics so that each student may participate regardless of physical development. Where interscholastic sports programs exist, number of games should be limited, with games played in afternoon rather than evening.
Glandular imbalances occur, resulting in acne, allergies, dental and eye defects—some health disturbances are real and some are imaginary.	Provide regular physical examinations for all middle school students.
Boys and girls display changes in body contour—large nose, protruding ears, long arms—have posture problems, and are self-conscious about their bodies.	Health classes should emphasize exercises for good posture. Students should understand through self-analysis that growth is an individual process and occurs unevenly.

TABLE 2.1 *continued*

Characteristics of Emerging Adolescents	Implications for the Middle School
Physical Development	
A girdle of fat often appears around the hips and thighs of boys in early puberty. Slight development of tissue under the skin around the nipples occurs briefly, causing anxiety in boys who fear they are developing "the wrong way."	Films and talks by doctors and counselors can help students understand the changes the body goes through during this period. A carefully planned program of sex education developed in collaboration with parents, medical doctors, and community agencies should be developed.
Students are likely to be disturbed by body changes. Girls especially are likely to be disturbed about the physical changes that accompany sexual maturation.	
Receding chins, cowlicks, dimples, and changes in voice result in possible embarrassment to boys.	Teacher and parental reassurance and understanding are necessary to help students understand that many body changes are temporary in nature.
Boys and girls tend to tire easily but won't admit it.	Advise parents to insist that students get proper rest: overexertion should be discouraged.
Fluctuations in basal metabolism may cause students to be extremely restless at times and listless at others.	Provide an opportunity for daily exercise and a place where students can be children by playing and being noisy for short periods.
	Encourage activities such as special-interest classes and "hands-on" exercises. Students should be allowed to physically move around in classes and avoid long periods of passive work.
Boys and girls show ravenous appetites and peculiar tastes; may overtax digestive system with large quantities of improper foods.	Provide snacks to satisfy between-meal hunger as well as nutritional guidance specific to this age group.
Social Development	
Affiliation base broadens from family to peer group. Conflict sometimes results due to splitting of allegiance between peer group and family.	Teachers should work closely with the family to help adults realize that peer pressure is a normal part of the maturation process. Parents should be encouraged to continue to provide love and comfort even though they may feel rejected.

TABLE 2.1 *continued*

Characteristics of Emerging Adolescents	Implications for the Middle School
Social Development	
	Teachers should be counselors. Home-base, teacher-adviser house plan arrangements should be encouraged.
Peers become sources for standards and models of behavior. Child's occasional rebellion does not diminish importance of parents for development of values. Emerging adolescents want to make their own choices, but authority still remains primarily with family.	Sponsor school activities that permit students to interact socially with many school personnel. Family studies can help ease parental conflicts. Parental involvement at school should be encouraged, but parents should not be too conspicuous by their presence.
	Encourage cocurricular activities. For example, an active student government will help students develop guidelines for interpersonal relations and standards of behavior.
Society's mobility has broken ties to peer groups and created anxieties in emerging adolescents.	Promote "family" grouping of students and teachers to provide stability for new students. Interdisciplinary units can be structured to provide interaction among various groups of students. Clubs and special-interest classes should be an integral part of the school day.
Students are confused and frightened by new school settings.	Orientation programs and "buddy systems" can reduce the trauma of moving from an elementary school to a middle school. Family teams can encourage a sense of belonging.
Students show unusual or drastic behavior at times—aggressive, daring, boisterous, argumentative.	Schedule debates, plays, playdays, and other activities to allow students to "show off" in a productive way.
"Puppy love" years emerge, with a show of extreme devotion to a particular boy or girl. However, allegiance may be transferred to a new friend overnight.	Role-playing and guidance exercises can provide the opportunity to act out feelings. Provide opportunities for social interaction between the sexes—parties and games, but not dances in the early grades of the middle school.

TABLE 2.1 *continued*

Characteristics of Emerging Adolescents	Implications for the Middle School
Social Development	
Youth feel that the will of the group must prevail and sometimes can be almost cruel to those not in their group. They copy and display fads of extremes in clothes, speech, mannerisms, and handwriting; very susceptible to media advertising.	Set up an active student government so students can develop their own guidelines for dress and behavior. Adults should be encouraged not to react with outrage when extreme dress or mannerisms are displayed.
Boys and girls show strong concern for what is "right" and for social justice; also show concern for less-fortunate others.	Foster plans that allow students to engage in service activities, for example, peer teaching, which allows students to help other students. Community projects (e.g., assisting in a senior citizens club or helping in a child care center) can be planned by students and teachers.
They are influenced by adults—attempt to identify with adults other than their parents.	Flexible teaching patterns should prevail so students can interact with a variety of adults with whom they can identify.
Despite a trend toward heterosexual interests, same-sex affiliation tends to dominate.	Plan large group activities rather than boy-girl events. Intramurals can be scheduled so students can interact with friends of the same or opposite sex.
Students desire direction and regulation but reserve the right to question or reject suggestions of adults.	Provide opportunities for students to accept more responsibility in setting standards for behavior. Students should be helped to establish realistic goals and be assisted in helping realize those goals.
Emotional Development	
Erratic and inconsistent behavior is prevalent. Anxiety and fear contrast with reassuring bravado. Feelings tend to shift between superiority and inferiority. Coping with physical changes, striving for independence from family, becoming a person in his own right, and learning a new mode of intellectual functioning are all emotion-laden problems for emerging adolescents. Students have many fears, real and imagined. At no other time in development is he or she likely to encounter such a diverse number of problems simultaneously.	Encourage self-evaluation among students. Design activities that help students play out their emotions. Activity programs should provide opportunities for shy students to be drawn out and loud students to engage in calming activities. Counseling must operate as a part of, rather than an adjunct to, the learning program. Students should be helped to interpret superiority and inferiority feelings. Mature value systems should be encouraged by allowing students to examine options of behavior and to study consequences of various actions.

TABLE 2.1 *continued*

Characteristics of Emerging Adolescents	Implications for the Middle School
Emotional Development	
	Encourage students to assume leadership in group discussions and experience frequent success and recognition for personal efforts and achievements. A general atmosphere of friendliness, relaxation, concern, and group cohesiveness should guide the program.
Chemical and hormone imbalances often trigger emotions that are little understood by the transescent. Students sometimes regress to childlike behavior.	Adults in the middle school should not pressure students to explain their emotions (e.g., crying for no apparent reason). Occasional childlike behavior should not be ridiculed.
	Provide numerous possibilities for releasing emotional stress.
Too-rapid or too-slow physical development is often a source of irritation and concern. Development of secondary sex characteristics may create additional tensions about rate of development.	Provide appropriate sex education and encourage participation of parents and community agencies. Pediatricians, psychologists, and counselors should be called on to assist students in understanding developmental changes.
This age group is easily offended and sensitive to criticism of personal shortcomings.	Sarcasm by adults should be avoided. Students should be helped to develop values when solving their problems.
Students tend to exaggerate simple occurrences and believe their problems are unique.	Use sociodrama to enable students to see themselves as others see them. Readings dealing with problems similar to their own can help them see that many problems are not unique.
Intellectual Development	
Students display a wide range of skills and abilities unique to their developmental patterns.	Use a variety of approaches and materials in the teaching-learning process.
Students will range in development from the concrete-manipulatory stage to the ability to deal with abstract concepts. The transescent is intensely curious and growing in mental ability.	Treat students at their own intellectual levels, providing immediate rather than remote goals. All subjects should be individualized. Skill grouping should be flexible.

TABLE 2.1 *continued*

Characteristics of Emerging Adolescents	Implications for the Middle School
Intellectual Development	
Middle school learners prefer active over passive learning activities and prefer interaction with peers during learning activities.	Encourage physical movement, with small group discussions, learning centers, and creative dramatics suggested as good activity projects. Provide a program of learning that is exciting and meaningful.
Students are usually very curious and exhibit a strong willingness to learn things they consider useful. They enjoy using skills to solve "real-life" problems.	Organize curricula around real-life concepts (e.g., conflict, competition, peer group influence). Provide activities in formal and informal situations to improve reasoning powers. Studies of the community and the environment are particularly relevant to the age group.
Students often display heightened egocentrism and will argue to convince others or to clarify their own thinking. Independent, critical thinking emerges.	Organized discussions of ideas and feelings in peer groups can facilitate self-understanding. Provide experiences for individuals to express themselves by writing and participating in dramatic productions.
Studies show that brain growth in transescents slows between the ages of twelve and fourteen.	Learners' cognitive skills should be refined; continued cognitive growth during ages twelve to fourteen may not be expected.
	Provide opportunities for enjoyable studies in the arts. Encourage self-expression in all subjects.

FIGURE 2.3 Portrait of a thirteen-year-old

6 feet 2 inches tall	*or*	4 feet 7 inches tall
Trips going up the stairs	*or*	An Olympic gold medal winner with a perfect 10.0 in parallel bar competition
An alcoholic or a drug addict	*or*	A Sunday school leader and Little Leaguer
Wears dental braces	*or*	Competes in Miss Teenage America
Looking forward to quitting school	*or*	Curious and enthusiastic about learning
Unable to read the comic page	*or*	Reads the *Wall Street Journal*
Has trouble with whole numbers	*or*	Solves geometry problems easily
A "regular" in juvenile court	*or*	An Eagle Scout
Already a mother of two	*or*	Still plays with dolls

Source: Beth J. Bondi

FIGURE 2.4   The shaky transition from childhood to adolescence

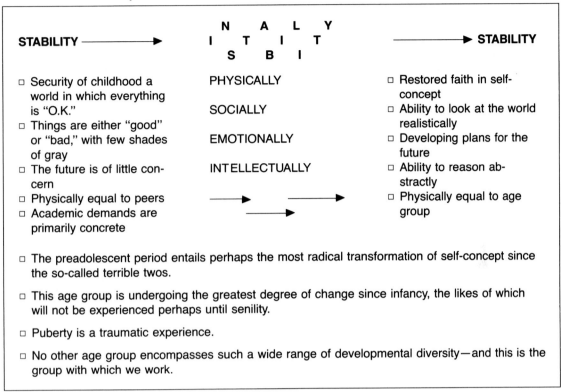

□ The preadolescent period entails perhaps the most radical transformation of self-concept since the so-called terrible twos.

□ This age group is undergoing the greatest degree of change since infancy, the likes of which will not be experienced perhaps until senility.

□ Puberty is a traumatic experience.

□ No other age group encompasses such a wide range of developmental diversity—and this is the group with which we work.

Preadolescence is a restless age for girls and boys. The torture of trying to sit still in school is obvious, and some pupils learn to perform remarkable feats of contortion without falling out of their chairs. Therefore, a school atmosphere in which physical movement is integral to the educative process is of high priority for the preadolescent. Activity-related learning (for example drawing, designing, constructing, and making displays), as well as moving from classroom to library or from classroom to play center, is vital to the preadolescent. In other words, a steady grind at the school desk is undesirable at this restless age.

Personal development is beginning to undergo significant and perplexing alterations and frequently children commence a self-searching quest on which they seek to "locate" themselves in a shifting social complex—a journey some adults never complete satisfactorily. Despite a commitment to fair play, these youth nonetheless must struggle to establish a relationship between their own sense of values and the value inconsistencies of others, especially adults.

Transescents are curious, explorative, and interested in many things. They are in the early stages of the conflict between their desire to be independent and the necessity to depend on others. They live in a world of shifting sands—unsure of themselves, unsure of their environment, and puzzled by the relationship between the two.

Pupils need guidance in the middle years to help them grow and develop into fully functioning individuals. The middle school has been suggested as a school for producing such individuals. Perhaps the message found in the following letter from a junior high school student will help illustrate the needs of young adults at this critical turning point.

Who Am I?

I have many things I want
to say but—
No one will listen.
I have many things I want
to do but—
No one will let me.
There are so many places
I want to go but—
No one will take me.
And the things I write
are corrected but—
No one reads them.
Who am I?
—*A sixth grader*

EMERGING ADOLESCENTS: VICTIMS OF A CHANGING SOCIETY

Normal developmental or maturational changes that occur in ten- to fourteen-year-olds create a set of problems unlike those experienced by any other age group. Middle school students of the 1990s are also faced with another set of problems, not of their own making: They have become victims of a changing society that no longer has time or inclination to provide the nurturing environment that emerging adolescents need to grow and to develop into fully functioning adults. Even though a considerable body of knowledge proves that success in school, and indeed success in life, depends on what happens to preadolescent and early adolescent students, this group is the least understood, the least cared for, and the most fragile in our society.

Misunderstood and Neglected

Today's social institutions operate on the premise that all students between the ages of ten and fourteen are difficult, disruptive, obstreperous, and almost impossible to deal with. Parents and educators alike know that early adolescent bodies begin to mature sometime in the middle school years, but they do not understand why some students "grow up" early while others are slow to reach physical maturity. Even though physical growth is often traumatic and unpredictable, some parents and educators are unaware to what extent transescents can be affected by the changes occurring in their bodies. Although the onset of menstruation, acne, and development of secondary sex characteristics, for example, may create tensions that affect their school performance, girls still are expected to display the same behavioral patterns every day. Consider how emerging adolescent girls begin to compete with their mothers in ways mothers do not understand and which may create conflicts at home.

Boys are also affected by a society that leads them to believe men should be tall, broad-shouldered, and narrow-hipped—the so-called all-American look. Long before puberty, boys believe that being tall is equated with being masculine. Tall, early-maturing boys get picked as team captains, date the prettiest girls, and are chosen class leaders whether they exhibit leadership qualities or not. Often, early maturers are thrust into situations where they are expected to behave like adults socially when they are still mere children.

On the other hand, life is often difficult for the late maturer, but when he does catch up he may have gained in the long run from his painful experiences. Because they have had to live with and overcome a delicate problem of their own, late maturers are often more sensitive, more thoughtful, and more understanding in dealing with other people than are early maturers.

Adults often treat emerging adolescents as small children. Because students are grouped by chronological age, a thirteen-year-old, sexually active girl is expected to possess the same basic interests as a thirteen-year-old boy who may still be two years away from puberty. Too many schools maintain age segregation and grade structures based on chronological age rather than on maturation.

In addition to physical growth, social changes occur in the middle school years. As indicated earlier in the chapter, emerging adolescents begin to pull away from adults and gravitate toward peers, as evidenced by dress, habits, and language. Without understanding the dynamic of this transformation from dependent, obedient, sweet child to independent, disobedient, ill-tempered young adolescent, adults misread signals and become impatient and short-tempered. Worst of all, they may abdicate their responsibility as adults and parents by no longer going to PTA meetings when their sons or daughters reach grade seven, ceasing to visit the school, and hesitating to show approval or disapproval of their children's behavior. Consider parents who have called the middle school teacher or principal and said, "I don't know what to do with my daughter; *you* do something."

Society has created a myth about boys and girls in transescence, the myth that they will somehow grow up by themselves and that adults should "leave them alone" until they are mature adolescents.

The survey in Figure 2.5 has been administered to over twenty-five thousand middle school students from all socioeconomic levels. Students were asked to rank the eleven values (all important values to emerging adolescents), from most important to least important. Their teachers were also asked to rank the values and indicate how they thought students would rank the values. Results of the survey are listed in Figure 2.6.

FIGURE 2.5   Values survey: parent–student

Rank 1 (*most* important) to 11 (*least* important).   I am a: _____ Student
                                                                                 _____ Parent

Self   **Other**
_____ A comfortable life (nice house, plenty of money)   _____
_____ Equality (brotherhood; equal chance for all, rich or poor, black or white, man or   _____
          woman)
_____ Family security (family getting along together, all living together, all caring for   _____
          each other)
_____ Self-respect (liking yourself, feeling good about what you do)   _____
_____ Sense of accomplishment (doing something worthwhile for society; making a   _____
          lasting contribution)
_____ Freedom (being independent, having free choice)   _____
_____ Happiness (personal contentment)   _____
_____ True friendship (having friends who are close and loyal)   _____
_____ Exciting life (fun-filled, active, enjoyable)   _____
_____ World at peace (no wars, riots, less crime and violence)   _____
_____ Good education (opportunity to finish high school—go on to college or further   _____
          training)

FIGURE 2.6   Results of values survey

Ranked by Students	**Ranked by Teachers**	**As Teachers Believed Students Would Rank**
Family	Family	World at peace
Freedom	Self-respect	True friendship
Happiness	Equality	Family
Self-respect	Freedom	Exciting life
Comfortable life	World at peace	Happiness
True friendship	Sense of accomplishment	Comfortable life
Good education	Happiness	Self-respect
World at peace	True friendship	Freedom
Exciting life	Good education	Sense of accomplishment
Equality	Comfortable life	Equality
Sense of accomplishment	Exciting life	Good education

Overwhelmingly, students and teachers chose family security as their most important value. The results clearly indicate that middle school students do not want their parents to abdicate their parental responsibility.

The middle school years for ten- to fourteen-year-olds are characterized by emotional instability. It is difficult for some adults to understand why students are happy one moment and sad the next, why chemical changes in the body trigger certain emotions, or how chemical and hormonal imbalances affect their personalities.

As mentioned in Table 2.1, middle school years are "puppy love" years. It has been said that only a middle schooler can meet a person of the opposite sex, go steady, and break up—all through a third person.

A final area in which understanding is lacking lies in achievement. The widest range of achievement occurs in the middle grades. Students falling a half-year behind grade level in elementary school reading find themselves two to three years behind by the time they reach middle school. Parents do not understand why middle school educators do not eliminate affective programs (those that help pupils understand themselves) and simply concentrate on basic skills. Parents need help in understanding that there should be a balance in the curriculum among personal development activities, basic skills programs, and content studies.

As for our society's negligence in caring for emerging adolescents, it is possible to quantify some of that neglect. Middle schools cannot fulfill all the needs of emerging adolescents; yet some would hold the schools solely responsible for the health and well-being of this age group. Only 5 percent of the generalists who practice pediatrics or family medicine have received training in adolescent health care. Although millions of dollars are spent on juvenile delinquency in the United States, less than 1 percent of grants and research funded by the National Institute for Child Health and Human Development places a primary emphasis on preadolescents and early adolescents.

Most national voluntary organizations and clubs have experienced declining memberships among young adolescents. Furthermore, too little national research has been conducted on middle school learners. As a result, there seems to be little relationship between what many schools do and what is actually known about young adolescents. The major tasks of adolescence include separation, individualization, and commitment; yet, few aspects of schooling have accommodated those tasks. The middle school must do so in the midst of a society that is often too busy to care. Middle school leadership must help parents and the community understand that only through their combined efforts will middle graders receive the care and nurture they need to make a successful transition from childhood to adolescence.

MIDDLE GRADERS: A MOST FRAGILE SOCIAL GROUP

As casualties of a changing society that is fraught with social problems, emerging adolescents are faced with a number of adverse conditions, as described briefly in the following subsections.

Deteriorating Family Structure

The status of the U.S. family, a key social institution, is changing, according to HEW findings.[3] For example, the divorce rate exceeds 50 percent—the highest in the world; consequently, 1 in every 4 children in public schools comes from a nontraditional home, with one-half of them spending all or part of their childhood with one parent (more than twelve million youth beyond age eleven live in a single-parent home). Seventy million live with stepparents.

FIGURE 2.7 A changing America

> Of 100 children born today:
> □ 12 are born out of wedlock
> □ 41 are born to parents who divorce before the child reaches 18
> □ 5 are born to parents who separate
> □ 2 will experience the death of a parent before reaching 18
> □ 40 will reach 18 without experiencing any of the above

More than 50 percent of all mothers with children under age one work outside the home. Only 8 percent of families have both parents at home with the father as the sole provider, which leaves more than 40 percent of divorced, separated, or single mothers with no financial assistance from the fathers of their children.

Given the declining birthrate, there are fewer children in the family unit. In addition, child mortality rates have risen since 1960, with children between the ages of ten and twenty-five affected most.

Another side effect of the changing society, according to HEW, is increased mobility—about 1 in 4 Americans relocates each year (job migration, reassignment, family breakup, and so forth).

Psychologists regard the lack of a stable home environment as the primary contributor to delinquency, an opinion backed by attitude polls (in particular, recent Gallup polls) revealing that parents blame themselves for their children getting into trouble and failing to achieve in school.

Figure 2.7 summarizes this bleak family outlook.

Juvenile Delinquency, Crime, and Violence

Unfortunately, the values foundation (mentioned in Chapter 1) among early adolescents is sorely jeopardized, as reflected in growing delinquency, crime, and violence among this age group.[4]

Of all persons arrested for serious crimes (e.g., rape, murder, robbery) in the United States, 43 percent are juveniles—despite the fact that juveniles age seven to eighteen account for only 20 percent of the population. The peak age for committing violent crime among this group is fourteen.

Youth crime rose 293 percent from 1975 to 1990 and is increasing by more than 10 percent annually; in 1992, 15,000 murders were committed by teenage boys. More than 100,000 gang members are in Los Angeles alone; and in 1991, they committed more murders than were recorded in all of Western Europe in a single year.

According to the National Center for Health Statistics (1992), every day 135,000 children take a gun to school, and every fourteen hours a child age five or younger is murdered. One million Americans are behind bars, with another 2.6 million on probation or parole; 1 in every 4 black males, age twenty to twenty-nine, are in jail. One in eight children now entering kindergarten will end up in the juvenile justice system.

A more subtle contributor to delinquency, crime, and violence is television and its effect on preadolescent and adolescent life-style choices.[5] It is estimated that this age group spends one-third of their waking hours watching TV—which means that the developmental environment of the average child includes eighteen thousand hours of TV viewing. The implication? Because television violence has increased, teenagers charged with violent crimes often blame the influence of this medium.

Sex and Teen Pregnancy

More youth are sexually active at earlier ages, according to HEW.[6] By age nineteen, 69 percent of all teenagers have had intercourse, but only 1 in 5 regularly use effective contraception, despite having multiple partners. AIDS will attack more than 120,000 persons each year—many of them teenagers. Each year, 2.5 million teens are infected with a sexually transmitted disease.

Of an estimated fourteen million sexually active teens, only one million are enrolled in family planning clinics, despite the fact that more than 50 percent of fifteen-to nineteen-year-olds are sexually active. Among sexually active boys in the middle school, the average age at which they lost virginity is 11.1 (11.7 for middle school girls for whom the age of menarche (onset of menstruation) ranges from 9.1 to 17.7 years). Typical middle grade males think about sex every five minutes.

Each year, one million girls between ages ten and eighteen give birth out of wedlock—again, the highest rate in the Western world. Two-thirds of teen pregnancies are not among minorities, not among the poor, and not among residents of the inner cities. Each day, forty teenage girls give birth to their third child, and 60 percent of girls who have a baby before age sixteen will have another within two years. From a legal standpoint, most states consider age nine the beginning of childbearing years.

Fifteen percent of babies born to girls age ten to eighteen were to those age ten through thirteen. Twenty-five percent of babies born with birth defects are born to adolescent mothers. Two-thirds of teen marriages end in divorce within five years, and 60 percent of those who remarry will divorce a second time.

Although teens comprise only 18 percent of all sexually fertile women, they account for 46 percent of out-of-wedlock births and 31 percent of all abortions.

In Figure 2.8, how it feels to be a teenager and pregnant is poignantly described by a thirteen-year-old unwed mother.

Alcohol and Drugs

Alcohol and drug abuse among teenagers is increasing at an alarming rate.[7] One in three adolescents is a problem drinker, and one in fifteen has tried cocaine. Twenty-five to 30 percent of all fourth graders feel some pressure to use alcohol and other dangerous drugs.

Children of alcoholics have a 25 to 50 percent chance of developing this disease, which means that seven to fourteen million children may develop alcoholism if the common estimate of ten million adult alcoholics is used.

FIGURE 2.8   Lonely death

I remember the fun we once had.
We got our kicks out of being bad.

And remember the time we both skipped school?
Everyone thought that we were cool.

Remember last summer we let nothing take our joy away?
We made out in the barn on top of the hay.

Remember the time you gave me your ring?
I was so happy that I could sing.

And do you remember the kisses we once shared?
And the day you said you'd always care?

Remember the day we went all the way?
You know for that move we must pay.

I'm in a home for unwed mothers.
But what do you care, you've got so many others.

While writing this I'm fighting the pain—
I'm bearing a child who has no name.

The doctor came in a few minutes ago,
He said there was trouble—
"Oh God, please, no!"

I found out soon he wasn't lying.
The nurse just said that I was dying.

The baby they say will be all right.
But I'll be somewhere else tonight.

—*A seventh grader*

By the end of the ninth grade, 20 percent of adolescents will suffer a drinking problem.

Education, Literacy, and Employment

Nationwide, 3,800 teenagers drop out of school each day. National Assessment of Educational Progress tests for 1992 reveal that only 39.3 percent of seventeen-year-old students could understand and explain complicated reading materials.

Estimates among business leaders are that, by the year 2000, 75 percent of all entrants into the job market will have insufficient verbal and math skills to compete in a changing arena. Business spends at least $35 billion a year for remedial training of its employees.[8]

At the turn of the century, 80 percent of new workers will be minorities, including women. In 1991, 5.1 million adults moonlighted—the largest number in U.S. history.

Health Care

The physical health status of America's children is still inferior to that in other countries.[9] Despite massive government investments in health care services, about 20 percent of children in the United States, age seven to eleven, have serious health problems; many do not receive proper health care. So-called full-service schools now include on-site health services for students and their parents, along with other social services that are located on-site.

Between 1980 and 1990, the average age of beginning smokers dropped from fourteen to ten. The number of girls age thirteen through seventeen who began smoking rose 5 percent during the same decade.

The mental health status of youth is a major concern in the United States as well as in other countries.[10] This nation's mental health sources (as reported by HEW) show the second-leading cause of death among teenagers—after accidents—to be suicide, which doubled between 1980 and 1990.

Whereas in Germany and Japan the reason most often cited for teen suicide is stress, in the United States apathy and rejection are singled out as the major contributing factors among adolescents and postadolescents. More specifically, insecurity in family life is cited.

Note Figure 2.9, a checklist for identifying potential teen suicide.

SOCIAL CHANGES: IMPLICATIONS FOR MIDDLE SCHOOL YOUTH

Early adolescence is characterized by numerous developmental changes, among them cognitive and social changes that produce dramatic results. All of the changes are normal and occur at differing rates; however, coping with these changes is a major task for transescents and for the adults who serve them. Nowhere are those changes more evident than during the middle school years. (Table 2.2 illustrates some of the benchmarks for physical maturation.)

Other changes, such as altered family structures and different working patterns of adults, have left a substantial number of American youth vulnerable to reaching adulthood unable to adequately handle requirements of the workplace, commitments to relationships with families and friends, and responsibilities of participating in a democratic society.

Compounding normal changes in preadolescents and early adolescents—as dramatic as they are—have been changes in the surrounding society that nurtures those youth. In addition to the changes in family structure described earlier, U.S. demographics have undergone startling variations. For example, by the year 2010, 38 percent of all Americans under age 18 will be black, Hispanic, Asian, or other minority. (Hispanics will be the largest minority group in the United States by 2009.) In the biggest states—California, New York, Texas, and Florida—minority children will be a majority by 2010.[11] For many youth, the first real assimilation with children from other cultures will come in the middle school years (it is not unusual in middle schools in Los Angeles, New York, and Miami to hear fifty different languages spoken).

FIGURE 2.9 Adolescent suicide checklist

Indicators	Yes	No
1. A social isolate, a loner	____	____
2. Has deformity or chronic disease	____	____
3. Home life unstable over long period	____	____
4. Has history of regular student-parent conflict	____	____
5. Recently lost parent or other significant person	____	____
6. Family experiencing financial troubles	____	____
7. Lives in unstable, transitional neighborhood	____	____
8. Married at early age (15–20 years)	____	____
9. Evidences sexual identity crisis	____	____
10. Displays sexual promiscuity unchecked by actions of parents	____	____
11. Voices feelings of pessimism, worthlessness	____	____
12. Appears fatigued, reports insomnia	____	____
13. Acts despondent or is unusually quiet	____	____
14. Shows accelerating neglect of appearance	____	____
15. Reports pressure from parents concerning ability to meet school or social expectations	____	____
16. Develops pattern of varied sicknesses during school hours	____	____
17. Displays irregular emotional outbursts, anger	____	____
18. Displays unusual social anxiety in school	____	____
19. Suddenly becomes promiscuous or flirtatious	____	____
20. Writes or speaks of suicidal thoughts	____	____
21. Becomes unusually aggressive, boastful	____	____
22. Begins heavy use of drugs	____	____
23. Evidences neglect of schoolwork	____	____
24. Unable to concentrate on schoolwork	____	____
25. Develops record of excessive absenteeism or unexpectedly drops out of school	____	____

As parents wrestle with divorce, dual careers, and an uncertain economy, they often look to their children to carry part of the load, thrusting them into the hard world of adulthood before they are ready. Child psychologists point to evidence of a growing problem: declining academic achievement; crime in the schools; growing number of cases of depression, suicide, runaways, drug and alcohol abuse, and psychosomatic illnesses (see statistics in previous subsections).

As the number of mothers in the workforce increases, millions of children are being cared for by outsiders—sitters, centers, neighbors, and before-school and after-school programs. High-quality day care is scarce, and many children are shuffled to three or four settings within a day. More than five million children under age thirteen spend a large amount of time unsupervised. Many youth are charged with adult responsibilities—caring for younger siblings and cooking dinner, for example.

Single parents often turn to their children as confidants, discussing with them personal problems and family finances. At the time, young children may not resent the hurried pace, but in early adolescence they pay parents back for all the real and

TABLE 2.2   Benchmark Ages in Adolescent Maturation

	Physical Development	
	Girls	*Boys*
Early	11–13	12–14
Middle	13–16	14–17
Late	16–19	17–24

	Puberty Benchmarks	
	Boys	
	Begin	*End*
Height spurt	10½	24
Testicles	10	17
Penis	11	17
	Girls	
	As Early as	*As Late as*
Height spurt	9½	14½
Breast	8	13½
First period	8½	16½

imagined slights committed against them during childhood. Only one child in five is able to maintain a good relationship with both divorced parents. Thus, divorce is perhaps the greatest factor affecting early adolescents in the past twenty years.

As for the declining health status of the nation's children, a two-year study, "Profile of Child Health in the United States" (1990), conducted by the National Association of Children's Hospitals and Related Institutions, found an estimated twelve million children to be without health insurance. Between 1980 and 1990, the number of child abuse cases rose 55 percent.

Mobility has affected middle school youth more than any other school-age group. For example, parents tend to move, split, find other jobs "after the kids are out of elementary school." The move to the Sunbelt brought on by job opportunities, grandparents living nearby, and the desire to "start a new life in paradise," also is a part of the mobility scenario.

The fragile nature of the middle schooler is reflected in many ways: The search for acceptance leads to alcohol and drug use, pregnancy, and gang affiliation. Students "wear their feelings on their sleeves"; that is, they worry about fairness. That sense of fairness is often seen on the playground where middle school students spend half their time making up rules to games they play.

Teachers need to be especially sensitive to the physical and social needs of these students. Many of the programs (advisory, guidance, family teams) discussed later in the text are responses to these needs. The impressions on students made by a middle school teacher are lasting. Interviews with high school students demonstrate that the

FIGURE 2.10   Hierarchy of student needs

Self-fulfillment	Individual growth
	Increased responsibility
	Achievement
Self-esteem	Recognition
	Status
Sense of belonging	Interpersonal relationships
External expectations	Work performance
	Rules, regulations
Security	Classroom conditions
	School conditions
	Home conditions

Adapted from A. H. Maslow, *Personality and Motivation.*

personal needs met by high school teachers are much more important than cognitive knowledge attained.

Students, like all persons, have needs. Those needs are not equal but rather are ordered. A hierarchy of needs can be identified, allowing teachers to view student motivation in an analytic fashion. Needs of middle school students are ordered into a hierarchy, as demonstrated in Figure 2.10.

RESPONDING TO STUDENT NEEDS

In 1986, the Carnegie Corporation of New York established the Carnegie Council on Adolescent Development, which in 1989 published *Turning Points: Preparing Youth for the 21st Century.* That document focused national attention on middle grades education. Pointing out the dramatic social changes affecting young adolescents, and the many needs of the age group, the document stated that "middle grades schools—jr. high schools, intermediate schools, and middle schools—are potentially society's most powerful force to recapture millions of youth adrift, and help every young person thrive during adolescence."[12]

The Carnegie task force called for middle schools that:

Create small communities for learning where stable, close, mutually respectful relationships with adults and peers are considered fundamental for intellectual development and personal growth. The key elements of these communities are schools-within-schools (or house plan), in which students and teachers grouped together as teams, with small group advisories that ensure that every student is known well by at least one adult.

Teach a core academic program that results in students who are literate, including in the sciences, and who know how to think critically, lead a healthy life, behave ethically, and assume the responsibilities of citizenship in a pluralistic society. Youth service to promote values for citizenship is an essential part of the core academic program.

Ensure success for all students through elimination of tracking by achievement level and promotion of cooperative learning, flexibility in scheduling, and adequate resources (time, space, equipment, and materials) for teachers.

Empower teachers and administrators to make decisions about the experiences of middle graders through creative control by teachers over the instructional program linked to greater responsibilities for students' performance, governance committees that assist the principal in designing and coordinating school-wide programs, and autonomy and leadership within subschools (or houses) to create environments tailored to enhance the intellectual and emotional development of all youth.

Staff middle grades with teachers who are expert at teaching young adolescents and who have been specifically prepared for assignment to the middle grades.

Improve academic performance through fostering the health and fitness of young adolescents by providing a health coordinator in every middle grade school, access to health care and counseling services, and a health-promoting school environment.

Re-engage families in the education of young adolescents by giving families meaningful roles in school governance, communicating with families about the school program and students' progress, and offering families opportunities to support the learning process at home and at the school.

Connect school with communities, which together share responsibility for each middle grade student's success, through identifying service opportunities in the community, establishing partnerships and collaborations to ensure students' access to health and social services, and using community resources to enrich the instructional program and opportunities for constructive after-school activities.

Responding to student needs in planning a middle school program involves each community in examining the needs and interests of their own students. Surveys, questionnaires, and existing data on student mobility, achievement, school failures, parent backgrounds, can guide middle school planners in preparing programs to meet student needs. Examples of survey instruments developed by the authors and used extensively in school planning can be found in Appendices 1 and 2. The authors do not suggest that these efforts are applicable to all communities, rather that the approaches used may be of some practical value to communities developing middle schools.

ESSENTIAL GOALS FOR STUDENTS

If lasting attitudes toward self, others, school, and life itself are formed during the middle school years, we must identify those goals that are essential to adult success. Figure 2.11 outlines goals and indicators the authors suggest. They are by no means all inclusive, but reflect the attitudes and skills employers often cite as critical to job success.

Figure 2.12, written by Pam Bondi (now an attorney) sums up her version of what a middle schooler is all about.

FIGURE 2.11 Wiles-Bondi essential goals for middle school students

Thirst for Knowledge

- Reading key books
- Joining academic clubs
- Corridor curriculum
- Significant adult-tutor interaction
- Has own library
- Reads newspapers, watches news

Positive Attitude

- Enthused about learning
- Participates in activities—Total involvement
- Completes tasks
- Volunteers
- Joins service organizations
- Does community service

Courteous

- Dresses properly
- Practices etiquette
- Introduces self-eye contact
- Less aggressive, less aggressive language
- Carries on family conversations
- Can serve as host or hostess at gatherings

Achievement

- Maintaining and improving test scores
- Reduced failures, less failure notices
- Less retention
- Better average grades
- More students on the honor roll
- Less of a high school dropout
- Meet needs of high achievers as well as low
- Honors—For spelling, mathematics, music, science, and such

Organization

- Brings materials to school and class
- Homework is done more frequently
- Keeps a calendar
- Brings gym clothes
- Uses time wisely
- Asks questions to determine clarity

Problem Solving

- Uses subject matter information
- Solves word problems
- Applies knowledge to "real world"
- Engages in hands-on activities
- Use analysis skills and critical thinking skills
- Can think creatively

Responsibility

- Cares about self, others, environment
- On time, prompt
- Less vandalism
- Cares about wrong-doing
- Lowered discipline problems
- Ability to change behavior
- Serves as peer tutor
- Helps keep school clean

Respect for Others

- Sensitivity to others, sensitivity for disabled
- Uses proper language. Sarcasm lessened
- Helps others, engages in peer learning
- Respects different races and cultures

Health

- Exercises
- Proper diet
- Deals with stress
- Eliminates smoking, drinking, drugs
- Practices safe health habits with opposite sex
- Can identify and avoid activities that lead to AIDS
- Participates in life-long sports

FIGURE 2.12 What is a middle schooler?

What is a middle schooler?
I was asked one day.
I knew what he was,
But what should I say?

He is noise and confusion.
He is silence that is deep.
He is sunshine and laughter,
Or a cloud that will weep.

He is swift as an arrow.
He is a waster of time.
He wants to be rich,
But can not save a dime.

He is rude and nasty.
He is polite as can be.
He wants parental guidance,
But fights to be free.

He is aggressive and bossy.
He is timid and shy.
He knows all the answers,
But still will ask "why."

He is awkward and clumsy.
He is graceful and poised.
He is ever changing,
But do not be annoyed.

What is a middle schooler?
I was asked one day.
He is the future unfolding,
So do not stand in his way.
— *Pamela Jo Bondi,*
a former eighth grader

The authors encourage middle school teachers and administrators to utilize the guidlines suggested in Chapter 1 and this chapter to conduct a thorough study of the students they will serve. A focus on individualization should follow.

SUMMARY

Emergent adolescent learners are characterized by their diversity and unique patterns of development. They are curious, physical creatures who are full of energy and imagination and interested in many things.

The physical, social, intellectual, and emotional changes that take hold during these transitional years between childhood and adolescence necessitates a school atmosphere in which middle graders age ten to fourteen can grow and develop into fully functioning mature adolescents.

Along with normal (but sometimes traumatic) maturational changes, this age group must also contend with social problems that typify the 1990s. These problems, due primarily to the breakdown of the U.S. family structure, include increased rates of teen suicide, teen pregnancy, alcoholism, drug abuse, higher crime among youth, job and family mobility, among others. Although these social ills do not affect this age group exclusively, they do affect them at their most impressionable stage of development.

The more knowledgeable middle school staff and administrators are about this age group, the better equipped they are to plan and design a facility tailored to meet their unique learning needs. This chapter provided a detailed profile of today's middle schoolers. The following chapter will focus on the kind of teacher best suited to instruct them.

SUGGESTED LEARNING ACTIVITIES

1. Conduct a values survey like the one found in Figure 2.5. How do your results compare with those found in Figure 2.6?
2. Develop procedures for studying the students in your middle school. What processes and instruments would you use to gather information about students?
3. Prepare a list of characteristics of emerging adolescents with implications for your middle school program.
4. Develop a position paper on the need for sex education in the middle school.
5. Prepare a slide-tape presentation illustrating various physical, social, intellectual, and emotional characteristics of transescent youth.
6. Prepare an oral presentation for parents that would make them more aware of the social problems affecting middle school students.

NOTES

1. David Elkind, *A Sympathic Understanding of the Child: Birth to Sixteen* (Boston: Allyn and Bacon, 1974). Elkind continues his theme of "behavior typical for the age" in numerous other publications. The authors are grateful to Dr. Elkind for furnishing background information for this section from talks delivered to professional groups and other notes he has generously shared with us.
2. Leona Zacharias, William Rand, and Richard Wurtman, "A Prospective Study of Sexual Development and Growth in American Girls: The Statistics of Menarche," *Obstetrical and Gynecological Survey* 31 (April 1976): 325–27.
3. U.S. Department of HEW, "Annual Summary for the United States: Births, Marriages, Divorces, and Deaths," National Center for Health Statistics, 1992.
4. U.S. Department of HEW, National Institute for Child Health and Development, Annual Report, 1992.
5. U.S. Department of HEW, National Clearing House for Mental Health Information, Annual Report, 1992.
6. U.S. Department of HEW, National Institute of Child Health and Development, Annual Report, 1992.

7. U.S. Department of HEW, National Institute on Alcohol and Drug Abuse, Annual Report, 1992.
8. Carnegie Council on Adolescent Development, *Turning Points: Preparing American Youth for the 21st Century* (New York: Carnegie Corporation, 1989).
9. Periodic Reports from the American Association for Physical Education and Recreation, Washington, D.C.
10. U.S. Department of HEW, National Institute of Mental Health, Annual Report, 1992.
11. *American Demographics*, U.S. Bureau of the Census, 1992.
12. Carnegie Council, op. cit.

SELECTED REFERENCES

Association for Supervision and Curriculum Development, Working Group on the Emerging Adolescent Learner, Joseph Bondi, chairman, *The Middle School We Need* (Washington, DC: ASCD, 1975).

Carnegie Council on Adolescent Development, *Turning Points: Preparing American Youth for the 21st Century* (New York: Carnegie Corporation, 1989).

Elkind, David. *A Sympathic Understanding of the Child: Birth to Sixteen* (Boston: Allyn and Bacon, 1974).

Foundation for Teaching Economics, ERIC Clearing House on Social Studies, et al, *Citizenship for the 21st Century* (Bloomington: Indiana University, 1991).

Wiles, Jon, and Bondi, Joseph. *Working with At-Risk Middle School Students* (Tampa: Wiles, Bondi and Associates, 1991).

3

The Middle School Teacher

*The teacher we are looking for in the
middle school is less the sage on the
stage and more the guide on the side.*

INTRODUCTION

The middle school teacher is the key to fulfilling the philosophy that guides the middle school movement. This is because, in addition to having those characteristics needed for all teachers, the middle school educator must have a potent "chemistry" that is sympathetic to, and compatible with, a student population whose most striking feature is their diversity.

To help identify this special individual, this chapter will examine five critical areas: personal characteristics, teacher competencies, professional preparation, appropriate teaching strategies (interaction analysis, verbal patterns, classroom questions, independent study), and procedures for classroom management and discipline.

Appendix 3 supplements the information in the chapter with models for inservice training and inservice program designs.

PERSONAL CHARACTERISTICS

Although the following characteristics are important for all teachers, they are particularly relevant in the middle school because of the special needs of students at this level of development.

□ The teacher likes children. It is difficult to identify such a person; therefore, subjective answers must be relied on: Does she enjoy students who are active, energetic, and loud? Is he flexible, adaptable, and sensitive to quick changes in pupils' moods and needs? Does she establish rapport easily with students?
□ The teacher believes in and practices the middle school concept and philosophy.
□ The teacher displays enthusiasm for, and commitment to, working with older children and younger adolescents.
□ The teacher possesses a wide variety of skills, abilities, and talents.
□ The teacher sees as his main goal the development of the creative potential of each child.
□ The teacher is knowledgeable in subject areas and brings them to the level of the learner.
□ The teacher can work effectively in close collaboration with fellow teachers in cooperative planning and team teaching.
□ The teacher has an open mind toward innovation and change.
□ The teacher is alive intellectually, physically, and socially.
□ The teacher is compassionate, tolerant, and flexible.

Perhaps the most important attributes of the middle school teacher are an honest desire to work with this age group, flexibility and adaptability, enthusiasm, a good sense of humor, compassion, and tolerance.

Flexibility and adaptability are essential because middle school teachers must be prepared to make use of intense periods of interest that are characteristic of the "middlescent."

A child tends to emulate the enthusiasm displayed by the teacher, so to function most effectively a middle school should be staffed with teachers who demonstrate enthusiasm about trying new methods and ideas.

Children in the transitional period between childhood and adolescence are subjected to pressures from parents, peers, and teachers. A teacher's sense of humor in the school environment provides a safety valve for mounting pressures. Teachers of "in-between-agers" must be patient. The great disparity in ability to understand directions and in attention spans calls for a patient approach.

Each child needs at least one person within the framework of the school with whom he or she can relate. Thus, the teacher also becomes a counselor.

In an effort to identify teacher competencies that are essential to a middle school's success, a number of states have moved to a competency-based approach in teacher preparation. Gordon Lawrence, an early leader in the middle school movement, has identified twenty key competencies needed by middle school teachers (see Figure 3.1).

Through the work of various doctoral students and researchers, a number of middle school competencies have been validated by those knowledgeable about the middle school. We have listed forty-one of those competencies at the end of this section. Because competencies are complex and multidimensional, behavior patterns are not easily measured. Lawrence identified six types of measurement for middle school competencies:

1. *Measurement of abstract information,* a memory operation. Whether textbook knowledge or firsthand experience, the teacher can describe physical or intellectual developmental traits of emerging adolescents.

2. *Conceptual measurement,* the ability to conceptualize abstract information in operational terms. For example, a teacher's ability to use abstract information in writing a lesson plan.

3. *Dispositional measurement,* the disposition to act in a way that uses appropriate abstract information. Measurement of this dimension involves a substantial affective component. An example is evaluating a videotape class activity and measuring the reaction of the viewer to the restless body movement of students.

4. *Structured performance,* the ability to perform a defined task when requested. Such a task might be to plan and conduct a fifteen-minute lesson during which student talk, as measured by a Flanders System of Interaction Analysis,[1] might be maximized. (The Flanders System is discussed later in this chapter.)

5. *Performance unconstrained by the measurer,* the ability to employ certain skills when the situation calls for them. For instance, can a skill be demonstrated on the request of an observer?

6. *Measurement of long-term consequences ensuing from performance,* defining and measuring a competency by the long-term outcomes it affects in persons or events. Long-term pupil growth is hard to measure because a number of factors (in addition to the teacher) influence pupil growth over a long span of time.

Presented below is a selected list of teacher competencies compiled from other scholars. This list, when compared with the twenty selected by Lawrence, indicates the primary skills needed for successful middle school teaching.

1. Possesses knowledge of preadolescent and early adolescent physical development, including knowledge of physical activity needs and the diversity and variety of physical growth rates.

FIGURE 3.1   Key competency areas for middle school teaching

1. Shows awareness of his own behavior patterns and how they are influenced by situations and by his beliefs; awareness of personality characteristics; acceptance of a variety of behavior in others that differs from own.
2. Interacts constructively with other adults and with transescents; shows regard for persons; is approachable, responsive, and supportive.
3. Understands the physical development process of the transescent student and organizes his teaching according to that process.
4. Understands the intellectual developmental process of the transescent student and organizes his teaching according to that process.
5. Understands the socioemotional development process of the transescent student learner and organizes his teaching according to that process.
6. Understands the career developmental process of the transescent student and organizes his teaching according to that process.
7. Understands and applies various theories of the teaching-learning process; analyzes the learning patterns of individual students, prescribes for these, and evaluates results.
8. Incorporates a knowledge of group dynamics in his teaching and helps students understand group process: group decision making, leadership skills, and peer influence.
9. Promotes positive relationships between the school and the community, between the teacher and parents, and between various subcultures in the school.
10. Organizes curriculum plans and opportunities appropriate to the middle school (those that facilitate the developmental tasks of transescence and are responsive to community problems).
11. Uses appropriate procedures of managing an instructional program—designing, conducting, evaluating and revising curriculum and instruction.
12. Makes effective presentations using appropriate media.
13. Deals effectively with unusual classroom problems.
14. Counsels individual students, promoting self-direction through indirect guidance.
15. Helps students to consider alternative values and to develop personal workable valuing systems.
16. Teaches students techniques of problem solving.
17. Provides opportunities and guidance to help students become independent learners (define own goals and problems, identify resources, and evaluate outcomes).
18. Designs and conducts group activities according to the kinds of learnings facilitated by the different groupings.
19. Has skills of working in cooperative teaching situations with other teachers, paraprofessionals, and resource persons.
20. Accepts responsibility of multidisciplinary instruction: plans thematic and coordinated studies with other teachers and assists them in teaching subjects outside his own area of specialization.

Source: From Gordon Lawrence, University of Florida—Middle School Project. Used with permission.

2. Commands knowledge of preadolescent and early adolescent intellectual development, with emphasis on the transition from concrete to formal levels of mental development.
3. Has a knowledge of recognized developmental theory and personality theory, which can be utilized in identifying appropriate learning strategies for this age group.

4. Understands the socioemotional development, including the need to adjust to a changing body.

5. Possesses the necessary skills to allow interaction between individual students as well as the opportunity to work in groups of varying sizes.

6. Understands the cultural forces and community relationships that affect the total school curriculum.

7. Can organize the curriculum to facilitate the developmental tasks of preadolescence and early adolescence.

8. Understands the transitional nature of grades five through eight as they bridge the gap between the children of the lower elementary grades and late adolescents and early adults of the upper grades.

9. Possesses the skills needed to work with other teachers and school professionals in team teaching.

10. Can plan multidisciplinary lessons and/or units and teach them personally or with other professionals.

11. Commands a broad academic background, with specialization in at least two allied areas of the curriculum.

12. Possesses the skill to integrate appropriate media and concrete demonstrations into presentations.

13. Can develop and conduct learning situations that promote independent learning and maximize student choice and responsibility for follow-through.

14. Possesses the knowledge and skills that allow students to sort information, set priorities, and budget time and energy.

15. Can teach problem-solving skills and develop lessons that are inquiry-oriented.

16. Has ability to teach students how to discover knowledge and use both inductive and deductive methods in the discovery of knowledge.

17. Possesses the knowledge and skills necessary to use role-playing, simulation, instructional games, and creative dramatics in teaching the content as well as the affective domain in a middle grade classroom.

18. Commands the knowledge and skill needed to organize and manage a classroom, which allows individuals to learn at a rate commensurate with their ability.

19. Possesses verbal behaviors that promote student input in a variety of group settings.

20. Has the knowledge and skills needed to diagnose strengths and weaknesses, to determine learning levels of individuals, to prescribe courses of action, and to evaluate the outcomes.

21. Has experience in innovation and possesses the skill to experiment with teaching techniques to find ones that are most effective in given situations.

22. Can teach the communication skills of reading, writing, and speaking in all subject areas.

23. Commands knowledge of reading techniques that enable students to progress and improve their reading in the subject areas.

24. Has a knowledge of the techniques necessary to promote positive self-concepts and self-reliance.

25. Possesses a knowledge of group dynamics and the ability to organize groups that will make decisions and provide their own leadership.

26. Has a knowledge of careers and the ability to help students explore career options.
27. Possesses skills necessary to effectively manage groups of students in activity settings.
28. Possesses the ability to recognize difficulties which may be emotional and/or physically based.
29. Works with extracurricular activities in the school.
30. Gathers appropriate personal information on students using questionnaires, interviews, and observation.
31. Provides frequent feedback to students on learning progress.
32. Functions calmly in a high-activity environment.
33. Handles disruptive behavior positively and consistently.
34. Builds learning experiences for students based on learning skills (reading, math) obtained in elementary grades.
35. Works cooperatively with peers, consultants, resource persons, and paraprofessionals.
36. Exhibits concern for students by listening and/or empathizing with them.
37. Selects evaluation techniques appropriate to curricular objectives in the affective domain.
38. Utilizes values clarification and other affective teaching techniques to help students develop personal value systems.
39. Provides an informal, flexible classroom environment.
40. Cooperates in curricular planning and revision.
41. Evaluates the teaching situation and selects the grouping techniques most appropriate for the situation: large group instruction (100+ students), small group instruction (15–25 students), or independent study.

PROFESSIONAL PREPARATION

Although most states have adopted (or plan to adopt) middle school certification requirements, teacher education institutions have been slow in developing preservice programs to prepare middle school teachers. The 1980s saw most middle school teachers "re-tooled" to teach in the middle school. Middle school teachers, already certified in either elementary or secondary education, were allowed to add a special middle school certification through completion of required inservice training. However, the 1980s failed to produce substantial numbers of preservice teachers specializing in middle school education. The thrust of teacher preparation for middle school teachers in the 1990s will continue to be in the area of inservice education.

Because many state departments of education and teacher-training institutions could not divest themselves from the elementary-secondary syndrome, middle school certifications have typically been housed in either elementary or secondary departments. In eighty years of education in the middle grades—in either the junior high school or middle school—educators have still not been convinced that this stage of education is an entity and deserves equal recognition with the elementary and senior high schools.

Middle school leaders in the 1990s must continue the fight to establish adequate preservice and inservice training programs for middle school teachers. Later chapters will stress the need for strong training programs for administrators and other resource persons in the middle school (some examples of which appear in Appendix 3).

Staff Development

Because most training of middle school teachers follows preservice, staff development (or inservice) is a critical dimension of middle school operations and an ongoing activity. Programs implemented without adequate preparation will prove to be disappointing to students and staff alike. In fact, programs installed without a *comprehensive* and *sustaining* inservice component are destined for failure.

The 1980s were characterized by a surge in middle school development; unfortunately, much of the staff education that accompanied program changes was inadequate and, worse, a wasted effort. Hucksters masquerading as middle school "experts" roamed the country entertaining teachers with stories (mostly made up) about adolescent students. Despite their limited backgrounds, these opportunists provided guidance in middle school education or passed off the work of others as their own.

The samples of inservice models found in Appendix 3 counter that haphazard approach with an effective plan that is both comprehensive and sustaining. The best staff development is planned locally, delivered locally, and continues beyond initial implementation (more on this in Chapter 9).

Inservice Training Content

An effective program for inservice training will cover at least eight areas:

1. Dealing with motivation and disciplinary problems in the classroom
2. Applying effective teaching strategies
3. Understanding characteristics and dynamics of middle school students
4. Dealing with low achievers
5. Mastering grouping (and regrouping) techniques
6. Enhancing learner self-concept
7. Understanding techniques for guiding and advising students
8. Using paraprofessionals and volunteers to enhance the middle school experience

The Training Process

Delivery of inservice training will be guided by five general directives:

1. Be systematic and ongoing.
2. Conduct training at the building level whenever possible.
3. Focus on identified needs as indicated by teacher surveys and other needs assessment strategies.
4. Use a combination of staff development activities—temporary duty, inservice workshops, staff meetings, summer institutes for example.
5. Engage in continuous monitoring and evaluation of training program components.

Training activities should accommodate the varied needs and interests of participants in terms of time, content, and delivery system. For example, staff development should occur during the contract day; therefore, options such as teacher release time, faculty and departmental meetings, paid workshops, and summer institutes should be provided.

Content options should address cognitive and affective areas related to the following: affective practices and processes for middle school instruction, specific needs of the middle school student, and individual needs of staff members.

Personnel who conduct training should consider these five delivery options:

1. Primary responsibility for developing and coordinating inservice activities and materials to lie with staff development and research department personnel
2. District teachers and administrators having middle school–related expertise to be identified and called on to serve as resources to individual schools
3. Staff development specialists, curriculum specialists, and personnel from other support services to provide training and follow-up services as needed
4. Consultants to be contracted as budget allows
5. The Teachers Training Teachers (TTT) Model to be used (a peer teachers training program—see Appendix 3)

Staff learning opportunities will be designed to accommodate different learning styles and learner needs—for example hands-on workshops, demonstrations, reading and audiovisual materials, lectures, curriculum-building activities, small group problem-solving discussions, and large group presentations.

Funding

The middle school renewal program must be provided for by adequate funding so as to guarantee high-quality staff development. (The importance of funding and other resource appropriations is addressed in Chapter 8.)

Administrator Training

As perhaps the most immediate source of teacher support, administrative team members must be effective leaders if the renewal program is to survive. Therefore, administrators need to attain competency in three areas:

1. Comprehension of the essential middle school philosophy
2. Training that will enable them to supervise new strategies added to middle school programs (e.g., teaming, adviser/advisee program, enrichment program)
3. Proficiency in monitoring and evaluating the middle school program at the building level

APPROPRIATE TEACHING STRATEGIES

The essential middle school requires teaching skills that differ from those needed in the elementary and high school settings. Unlike the solitary craftsperson found in the departmentalized high school or the self-contained elementary school, the middle school teacher usually works with a team of teachers, as prescribed by the Carnegie ("familial") directives listed in Chapter 2. Therefore, middle school teachers must be capable of working not only with emerging adolescent learners but with other adults. This latter skill—working with other adults—often is more difficult to master, especially for veterans who have spent most of their careers working independently.

Also, other skills must be learned—for example working with small groups of students in advisement, parent conferencing, and records maintenance (student profile folders and team minutes). (Examine Appendix 3 for descriptions of those skills; see especially the workshop outlines.) Instructional approaches (cooperative learning, large and small group interaction, peer teaching and tutoring by students, minicourses, and interdisciplinary units) are all part of the teacher's repertoire and will be dealt with at length in Chapter 7.

Implementing a new program and organizational pattern will not guarantee success. Teachers also must examine classroom methodology and select appropriate teaching strategies. Understanding the dynamics of transescents provides the background for choosing the most effective strategy or strategies. For instance, this age group cannot sit still for long periods of time; if teachers devise learning situations that involve movement, manipulation of objects, and other forms of active participation, then more learning will occur.

As middle school programs have emerged in the past twenty years, methods and instruments have been developed to help teachers apply innovations more systematically. These innovations ultimately improve the quality of teachers coming out of preservice and inservice training programs. The following sections identify four of these systems that are particularly relevant to the middle school: interaction analysis, verbal patterns of teachers, classroom questions, and independent study.

Interaction Analysis

Observation systems that measure classroom interaction probably show the most promise as learning devices for preservice and inservice teachers. *Systematic observation* is defined here as a technique that identifies, examines, classifies, and/or qualifies specific teaching activities. Of the observation systems available, the thirteen-category modification of the Flanders System of Interaction Analysis of verbal behavior is probably best applied to middle school settings.

The thirteen-category system, which takes into account the verbal interaction between teachers and pupils in the classroom, enables one to determine whether the teacher controls students in such a way as to increase or decrease freedom or action. Through the use of observers or by using audiotape or videotape equipment, a teacher can review the results of a teaching lesson. Every three seconds an observer writes down the category number of the interaction she has just observed. The numbers are recorded in sequence in a column. Whether the observer is using a live classroom or tape recording for her observations, it is best for the observer to spend ten to fifteen minutes getting oriented to the situation before categorizing. The observer stops classifying whenever the classroom activity is inappropriate, for instance, when there is silent reading, or when various groups are working in the classroom, or when children are working in their workbooks. In the thirteen-category system, teacher statements are classified as either indirect or direct. This classification gives central attention to the degree of freedom a teacher gives to the student.

In a given situation, the teacher can choose to be indirect, that is, maximize freedom of a student to respond, or be direct, that is, minimize freedom of a student to respond. Teacher response is classified under the first nine categories.

Student talk is classified under three categories, and a fourth category provides for silence or confusion where neither a student nor the teacher can be heard. All categories are mutually exclusive, yet totally inclusive of all verbal interaction that occurs in the classroom. Figure 3.2 describes the categories in the thirteen-category modification of the Flanders System of Interaction Analysis.

The social forces at work in the classroom are so complex that it appears on the surface to be difficult to analyze them. The teacher's interaction with middle school students, which is a portion of the total social process, seems almost as difficult to identify. Nevertheless, teacher-pupil contacts have been classified into specifically defined behavioral acts by various researchers who have studied teacher behavior. The Flanders System and other such systems are excellent means of sensitizing middle school teachers to their own verbal behavior in the classroom and helping them monitor their interaction with students.

Nonverbal communication in the classroom is another dimension of teaching that has drawn the attention of researchers. Middle school students are especially cognizant of body messages, both real and imaginary, that their teachers send out. Nonverbal communication is often referred to as a silent language, and individuals send messages through a variety of conventional and nonconventional means. Thus, a teacher's facial expressions, bodily movements, and vocal tones all convey feelings to students. For example, although a student may hear a teacher verbally praise her work, the teacher's facial expression may communicate disapproval of that work. A teacher who fails to understand the nonverbal message conveyed to pupils may not be able to comprehend their responses to him. In analyzing a classroom, then, it is just as important to examine *how* the teacher says what he has to say and how he behaves and expresses feelings as *what* the teacher says, does, and feels. How teachers communicate their perceptions, feelings, and motivations can be identified with facial expressions, gestures, and vocal tones. Such expressions determine in large measure how pupils perceive those teachers.

In examining the significance of nonverbal communication in the middle school, it is important to understand that teaching is a highly personal matter, and prospective and inservice teachers need to face themselves as well as to acquire pedagogical skills. Middle school teachers need to become more aware of the connection between the messages they communicate and the consequences that follow. They also need to capitalize on the nonverbal cues expressed by students as keys to their clarity and understanding. Whereas nonverbal interaction in the classroom is less amenable to systematic objective inquiry than verbal interaction, the meanings pupils give to a teacher's nonverbal message have significance for learning and teaching.

Through continued study of nonverbal behavior, middle school teachers can sharpen, alter, and modify nonverbal messages they transmit to students. The advantages of adding nonverbal analysis in a study of teaching is that middle school teachers can look at their behavior in two ways—what their behavior means to pupils, and how their behavior is interpreted by their pupils.

FIGURE 3.2   Description of categories for a thirteen-category modification of the Flanders System of Interaction Analysis

	Category Number	Description of Verbal Behavior
T E A C H E R / **INDIRECT**	1	*Accepts feelings:* Accepts and clarifies the feeling tone of students in a friendly manner. Student feelings may be of a positive or negative nature. Predicting and recalling student feelings are also included.
	2	*Praises or encourages:* Praises or encourages student action, behavior, recitation, comments, ideas, and so forth. Jokes that release tension and are not at the expense of another individual. Teacher nodding head or saying "uh-huh" or "go on" are included.
	3	*Accepts or uses student's ideas:* Clarifying, building on, developing, and accepting the action, behavior, and ideas of the student.
	4	*Asks questions:* Asking a question about the content (subject matter) or procedure with the intent that the student should answer.
	5	*Answers student questions (student-initiated teacher talk):* Giving direct answers to student questions regarding content or procedures.
TALK / **DIRECT**	6	*Lecture (teacher-initiated teacher talk):* Giving facts, information, or opinions about content or procedure. Teacher expressing his or her own ideas. Asking rhetorical questions (not intended to be answered).
	7	*Gives directions:* Directions, commands, or orders to which the student is expected to comply.
	8	*Corrective feedback:* Telling a student that his answer is wrong when the correctness of his answer can be established by means other than opinion (i.e., empirical validation, definition, or custom).
	9	*Criticizes student(s) or justifies authority:* Statements intended to change student behavior from a nonacceptable to an acceptable pattern; scolding someone; stating why the teacher is doing what he is doing so as to gain or maintain control; rejecting or criticizing a student's opinion or judgment.
S T U D E N T / **TALK**	10	*Teacher-initiated student talk:* Talk by students in response to requests or narrow teacher questions. Teacher initiates the contact or solicits student's statements.
	11	*Student questions:* Student questions concerning content or procedure that are directed to the teacher.
	12	*Student-initiated student talk:* Talk by students in response to broad teacher questions that require judgment or opinion. Voluntary declarative statements offered by the student, but not called for by the teacher.
	13	*Silence or confusion:* Pauses (short periods of silence) and periods of confusion in which communication cannot be understood by an observer.

$$\text{Indirect-Direct Ratio} = \frac{\text{categories 1, 2, 3, 4, 5}}{\text{categories 6, 7, 8, 9}}$$

$$\text{Revised Indirect-Direct Ratio} = \frac{\text{categories 1, 2, 3}}{\text{categories 7, 8, 9}}$$

$$\text{Student-Teacher Ratio} = \frac{\text{categories 10, 11, 12}}{\text{categories 1, 2, 3, 4, 5, 6, 7, 8, 9}}$$

Source: Originally developed by Ned Flanders, modified by John Hough and Joseph Bondi.

Teacher Verbal Patterns

Research has provided more and better information about teaching performance. The use of systematic observational instruments now identifies those teaching behaviors that exert great control on pupil learning in middle school classrooms.

The first pattern, identified through the use of the Flanders System (or modification thereof), is called simply the *excessive teacher-talk* pattern. This occurs when teachers talk two-thirds or more of the time in the classroom. If this is the case, there is very little time left for students to participate. Middle schools that emphasize extensive student participation in their own learning should encourage the use of feedback from interaction analysis so that teachers can become aware of and able to control the amount of time they talk in the classroom. Just this one use alone renders interaction analysis an effective teaching and supervisory tool.

The second verbal pattern demonstrated by teachers is *recitation*. Arno Bellack, a pioneer in describing verbal behaviors of teachers and pupils, has observed that no matter what teachers' differences are in ability levels or backgrounds, their actions and responses are much alike.[2] In addition to monopolizing the talking, teachers' major activity is asking and reacting to students' questions that call for factual answers. As a pedagogical process, the question-answer sequence was recognized fifty years ago when teacher education consisted of considerable training in the skill of asking questions. Unfortunately, this process is still employed, despite the fact that each successive generation of educational leaders, no matter what their differences, has condemned the rapid-fire, question-answer pattern of instruction. Training

Middle school teachers must like children and share their enthusiasm for new learning.

programs for middle school teachers should develop new processes that keep teachers from following a similar pattern.

A classroom in which recitation is the major activity suggests a high-pressure atmosphere; it also suggests that the teacher is doing most of the work. Asking a lot of questions also means that little attention is given to individual student needs. The most that can be gained from rote recitation are verbal memory and superficial judgment.

By combining the Flanders System with the Gallagher-Aschner System (which identifies types of questions asked in the classroom), and Bloom's Taxonomy of Education Objectives (a kind of multidimensional approach), middle school teachers can break the recitation pattern. Again, teachers must be provided with effective feedback, which allows them to "read" and modify their own verbal behavior.

The third verbal pattern is called *classroom management*. This pattern consists of teacher responses to unacceptable behavior and teacher communications indicating transitions in learning activities. As will be studied in the next section, Kounin has developed a system for analyzing the classroom management aspect of teaching. Such things as how a teacher notifies pupils of a change in activity and how and when a teacher reacts to improper student behavior, are aspects of teacher skill in working with pupils that relate to pupil growth. This includes pupil growth in a number of areas, not just in subject matter.

The fourth verbal pattern is *teacher acceptance*. This includes teacher acceptance of student ideas and feelings. A number of observational systems have been used to categorize teacher acceptance of ideas and feelings. There is ample evidence that teachers who accept students' ideas and feelings enhance learning in the classroom. Much work is yet to be done in identifying how teachers react to students of a different race or socioeconomic level.

The last teacher behavior is called the *flexibility pattern*. Most teachers like to think they are flexible individuals who can adjust to any circumstances. Unfortunately, teachers who are products of outdated training methods are quite often the opposite. Their behavior is so stereotyped that students can often predict a particular teacher's reaction to different student behaviors. For instance, some students soon learn that it does not pay to ask questions in a certain classroom or that in another the teacher will talk 90 percent of the time. Nowhere is flexibility of teacher behavior more important than in the middle school.

Teachers can learn to be more flexible in their verbal behavior. Through interaction analysis teachers can get feedback from systematic observation of their verbal behavior. The middle school can provide the setting for teachers to use observational systems to identify and control those verbal behaviors that affect pupils learning.

Classroom Questions

In the Flanders (or modified Flanders) Systems of Interaction Analysis, one category of behavior deals with questions. That category concerns a teacher asking questions about content or procedure in order to elicit a student response. For the middle school teacher to obtain a greater understanding of her questions, other types of feedback instruments must be used.

The Gallagher-Aschner System of analyzing and controlling classroom questioning behavior has been widely used in preservice and inservice programs (see Table 3.1). In their work with the system, Gallagher and Aschner have found that most teacher behavior falls in the first level, cognitive-memory, but that even a slight increase in divergent questions leads to a major increase in divergent ideas produced by students.

The Gallagher-Aschner and other systems of analyzing and controlling classroom questions should be used to help train teachers to stimulate productive thought processes in middle school classrooms.

Independent Study and the Teacher's Role

Independent study demands a look at the role of the teacher and the kind of teacher needed for middle schools. The teacher plays a crucial role in stimulating and supporting independent study in the following ways and situations:

TABLE 3.1 The Gallagher-Aschner System: A Technique for Analyzing and Controlling Classroom Questioning Behavior

1. *Cognitive-Memory:* Calls for a specific memorized answer or response; anything that can be retrieved from the memory bank.

   1a. What is 2 × 3?
   1b. When did Florida become a state?
   1c. What is a noun?
   1d. At what temperature Centigrade does water boil?

2. *Convergent:* Calls for a specific (single) correct answer, which may be obtained by the application of a rule or procedure; normally requires the consideration of more than a single quantity of information and/or knowledge.

   2a. What is 30.5 × 62.7?
   2b. How long did the prohibition law remain in effect?
   2c. Diagram this sentence.
   2d. How many calories are required to melt 160 grams of ice at 0° C?

3. *Divergent:* Allows students a choice of more than one alternative or a chance to create ideas of his own; more than a single answer is appropriate and acceptable.

   3a. What is 10 to three other bases?
   3b. What might have been the effects on the growth of the United States had there not been a Civil War?
   3c. Write a short story about Halloween.
   3d. Design an apparatus that will demonstrate the law of conservation of matter.

4. *Evaluative:* Calls for development and/or establishment of relevant standard of criteria of acceptability involving considerations such as usefulness, desirability, social and cultural appropriateness, and moral and ethical propriety, then comparing the issue at hand to these; involves the making of value judgments.

   4a. Is 10 the best base for a number system?
   4b. Was the Civil War defensible?
   4c. Is English the best choice for a universal language?
   4d. Should we continue our space program now that we have landed on the moon?

Source: J. J. Gallagher and Mary Jane Aschner, "A Preliminary Report: Analyses of Classroom Interaction," *Merrill-Palmer Quarterly of Behavior and Development* 9 (1963): pp. 183–94.

The Teacher as a Supporter of Independent Study. If independent study is to be effective, the student must develop self-discipline and self-direction—which cannot be done if the teacher assumes the role of police officer or spy. Instead, the teacher must ask this basic question: Is the student's behavior appropriate for the situation, the learning activity, and the setting?

What is appropriate student behavior?

- It is *not* distracting or disturbing to others.
- It is *not* endangering the student or others.
- It *is* helping the student satisfy a worthwhile need. For example, the need to relax and let off steam is worthwhile—given the appropriate setting and means.

What can be done if the student's behavior is unsatisfactory and inappropriate?

Sometimes the simplest and best answer is to change the environment, not the behavior. ("Your talking in the library is bothering others. Why not go down to the lounge where you can talk without bothering anyone?")

The basic rule, however, is to use the least amount of direction that will enable the student's behavior to become satisfactory. Sometimes a stern look or a quiet word will suffice; overreaction should be guarded against.

What is the teacher's role in stimulating independent study? In answering this question, several points should be remembered:

- Know the student's interests and appeal to them, but also make a distinct attempt to broaden those interests.
- Stress the importance of independent study; the student will be subconsciously influenced by your own attitude toward it.
- Suggest areas for independent study that relate to and emanate from curricular concerns. The best independent study is not extraneous to, but is an intrinsic part of, the curriculum.
- Do not stress what is known about the subject but what is unknown; not what has been discovered but what remains undiscovered.
- Pique interest by dropping hints about projects the student might undertake. Resist the temptation to give answers; instead, raise questions.
- Teach the student how to raise the right kinds of questions. Not to denigrate serendipity, asking the right questions is crucial.
- Set a good example by telling the student the results of your own independent study.

CLASSROOM MANAGEMENT AND DISCIPLINE

The changing family structure and increased conflict found in all elements of our society have led to concern about a general breakdown in school discipline and the need for better classroom management. There are a number of ways in which better management can be achieved in the classroom. Inexperienced middle school teachers enter the classroom filled with pedagogical terms—*social control, group dynamics, behavior patterns,* and *democratic procedures.* These terms mean little to the worried teacher who must get Johnny or Mary to sit down and keep quiet—at least long enough for the teacher to get the day started. Therefore, classroom management becomes an important aspect of teaching in the middle school.

Management of Transitions

Jacob Kounin has found a surprising number of aspects of teacher behavior that relate directly with a student's involvement in class. An interesting aspect of Kounin's work is that much of it is concerned with the management of transitions from one unit to another, rather than from the teaching within a unit. The following are examples:[3]

> *Group alerting* occurs when the teacher notifies pupils of an imminent change in activity, watches to see that pupils finish the current activity, and initiates the new one only when all class members are ready. In contrast, *thrusting*, occurs when the teacher "bursts" in on pupil activity with no warning and no sensitivity to anything but the teacher's own needs.
>
> *Stimulus boundedness* describes behavior that suggests the teacher is trapped by a stimulus, like a moth by a flame. For example, a piece of paper on the floor leads to interruption of activities while the teacher complains to the class about it or tries to find out how it got there.
>
> *Overlap* refers to the teacher's ability to carry on two operations at once. For example, while the teacher is working with a reading group, another pupil asks a question about arithmetic. The teacher reacts by helping with the arithmetic while keeping the reading group going.
>
> A *dangle* occurs when the teacher calls for the end of one activity, initiates another one, then returns to the previous activity. For example, "Now, pupils, put away your arithmetic books and papers and get out your spelling books; we're going to have spelling." After the pupils have put away their arithmetic materials and gotten out their spelling materials the teacher asks, "Oh, by the way, did everybody get problem four right?"
>
> A *truncation* occurs if the teacher never gets back to the new activity initiated (for example, if in the previous example he never returns to the spelling).
>
> *With-it-ness* is how the teacher demonstrates his awareness of deviant behavior, a management technique that is assessed both for timing and for target accuracy. Timing involves stopping the deviant behavior before it spreads, and target accuracy involves identifying the responsible pupil. If, for example, whispering in the back of the room spread to several other children and at this point the teacher criticizes one of the class members who joined in, this behavior would be scored negatively both for timing and for target accuracy.

The Kounin examples illustrate the ways teachers can maintain the group without hindering classroom learning. In analyzing classrooms, we must not ignore the techniques of group management that teachers must utilize daily. Teachers must be provided feedback of their own behavior if they are to improve instruction.

Issues Unique to Emerging Adolescents

What is good discipline? Certainly not a classroom in which no one except the teacher speaks. A classroom in which students respond willingly and quickly to the teacher's routine requests is a well-controlled class. A middle school teacher who can maintain good working conditions and control noise without losing composure promotes a good learning environment.

The 1991 Gallup poll of attitudes toward public schools indicated, as it had in the past ten years, that discipline was the major problem facing the nation's public schools. Furthermore, parents still blame themselves for the problems of discipline, motivation, and drug and alcohol addiction that frequently begin in the home.

Despite the breakdown of the family and parental guilt, however, middle school teachers still must cope daily with disciplinary problems in the classroom. Statistics reveal that the prime cause of teacher dropout after a few years is inability to develop effective disciplinary procedures.

Teaching in the middle school can be a rewarding and creative experience. It can also be highly frustrating because at no other grade level are students so capable of being uncooperative or disruptive to the teaching-learning process. Teachers who are successful in working with emerging adolescents often appear to have accomplished a "magic hold" over their students. Closer analysis, however, reveals that such teachers simply have a greater understanding of their students' development and have structured disciplinary procedures to fit the students whom they instruct.

The authors hold to three key premises about discipline as it pertains to emerging adolescents. First, most disciplinary problems experienced in the classroom are natural rather than unnatural acts and as such will take care of themselves. Second, the majority of problems can be averted by revising the students' instructional program. Third, establishing a clear set of teachers' expectations can make existing disciplinary procedures more effective over a period of time.

A Period of Stress and Uncertainty

Middle school teachers would do well to resurrect their own experiences at this age. Fond memories come more easily than painful ones, and sometimes it is difficult for teachers to recall the many problems, uncertainties, pressures, and fears of their own early adolescence. Yet today, relationships with parents, peer-group pressures, problems of identity, self-image, opposite-sex relationships, and needs for status still form the nucleus of concerns for most young adolescents. The point is that the stress experienced by early adolescents is genuine. Teachers who can "get inside their students" will have a greater chance of reacting effectively to their behavior.

When confronted with stressful situations, adults call on previous experience to act in ways that minimize social and personal pressures. Emerging adolescents generally do not have such a perspective; their childhood experiences are inappropriate for the adult world. Thus, they react to stressful conditions in unpredictable and inconsistent ways, ways that often are unacceptable to adults.

Teachers hold certain expectations for student behavior, and when those expectations are not met, they react in adult fashion. Unfortunately, not all teachers hold the same expectations for student behavior or react in the same manner to unacceptable behavior.

Disruptive behavior in the middle school is more common than most teachers acknowledge. National statistics [4] on extreme forms of student disruption are shocking, and such statistics often show the young adolescent to be a principal offender. In school districts where student misconduct is considered to be a minor problem, a tremendous amount of disruptive behavior and delinquent activity is ignored.

Part of the difficulty in confronting disruption and building effective disciplinary procedures stems from the lack of a clear definition of the problem itself. "Discipline problems" in schools can range from gum chewing to outright physical aggression. Until the problem is clearly defined, establishing effective procedures to redress it will remain a hit-or-miss proposition.

Some middle grade students not only are unruly but also hostile toward the learning process. They seem to lack self-control and revert to a childlike dependence on physical aggression when confronted by authority. Others, usually habitual offenders of school codes, seem unable to distinguish between right and wrong. Emerging deviant behaviors seem to achieve full bloom in the late intermediate years. For many teachers, a major problem is the *range* of disciplinary difficulties they confront.

Tasks of Development

Aside from undergoing a period of transformation, middle schoolers are developing physically at their own rates. This fact is manifested in the difference in size and weight among ten- to fourteen-year-olds. The teacher, however, acknowledges that students differ in ways other than physical appearance—social maturity, for instance. Emotional stability is variable, as is the ability to conceptualize and rationalize. Given a roomful of young adolescents, the overriding common denominator *is their difference*.

Borrowing from sociologist Robert Havighurst's conceptualization, the young adolescent might be perceived as engaged in a set of developmental tasks that must be accomplished as the student passes into adulthood.[5] One task, for instance, is to accept a changing body and the accompanying self-image. Another might be to learn to get along with others in a social setting or to control emotions and express oneself in socially acceptable ways. These tasks must be confronted by the student in his or her unique pattern of mastery in dealing with each task.

The concept that is difficult for many teachers to understand, however, is that few young adolescents are mature in all realms of development. A seventh-grade girl may look twenty years old physically and still act like a child. A small, bookish-looking sixth grader may be fully mature only in intellectual capacity. All students in the intermediate grades are in transition, passing through a certain period and mastering basic social tasks as they go. If teachers could understand this basic fact of individuation, they would have a much clearer idea of how to establish more effective disciplinary procedures. Probably no single set of regulations can be applied uniformly at all times in one intermediate classroom—not even by the best teacher.

Most teachers possess a multitude of effective responses to classroom problems, "weapons" that include praise, voice control, facial expressions, gestures, finger snapping, physical proximity, touch, isolation, and expulsion from the classroom. Students also possess a repertoire of counteracting behaviors. The result is that sometimes teachers and students engage in escalation games, the most popular of which is for students to test or bait the teacher without receiving the maximum punishment. The underlying cause of such a deteriorating situation is that some teachers attempt to enforce a uniform code of behavior, which, as already noted, is virtually impossible for this age group. Only if the "tightest lid" is applied can a class full of young adolescents be controlled in this manner. Such a classroom is usually characterized by a lot of discipline but very little real learning. For all of these reasons, then, effective *and consistent* procedures must be institutionalized throughout the school.

Establishing Disciplinary Procedures: Specific Guidelines

Four guidelines are useful for establishing and enforcing disciplinary procedures. They must be (1) known by all involved, (2) flexible enough to accommodate student differences, (3) appropriate to the behavior, and (4) involve others who are important to the student being disciplined.

Like students, even the best teachers have some bad days, but one thing critical to emerging adolescents is consistency in their daily lives and in their search for patterns to which they can adjust. Teachers who take time to think through the concept of discipline *together with students* will eliminate unpredictability in their intervention measures when a problem arises.

Although spelling out rules of discipline is important, it is equally important to acknowledge student differences when applying punishment. Students are keenly aware of their own uniqueness, and their tolerance for "situational application" of discipline (e.g., as it fits the situation) will surprise most teachers. If procedures can be thought of as a continuum rather than a cause-and-effect relationship, each student can be helped to become more responsible in the classroom. In some cases, behavior can be modified by continually extending trust and responsibility.

Disciplinary procedures must be appropriate to the behavior exhibited. One leading cause of infractions in the middle grades is a teacher who responds in the same way regardless of the conditions. That is, if the same punishment is meted out for daydreaming as for physical aggression, students will sense the injustice, and eventually they and the guilty teacher will become adversaries.

Finally, whatever procedure is used, other persons who are significant to the child—another teacher, parents, or peers—must be involved so that the punishment will be reinforced.

Schoolwide Response Patterns

Although it is beneficial for every teacher to think about disciplinary procedures in a systematic way, it is even more important that a faculty address this concern as a unit. Through discussion, the entire staff may coordinate a collective response to major disruptions. For example, does the whole faculty consider certain behaviors to be completely reprehensible or merely mischievous? What would be the appropriate collective response to the student? Can the school manage some episodes by using diversionary tactics? Are certain problems considered "natural" because they arise routinely, whereas others are so basic as to demand a change in school structure?

The authors believe that in many cases, suppression responses are inappropriate, due to the ever-changing nature of this particular population; and that to use such measures should be a tactic of last resort. Such heavy-handedness appears to run counter to the growth tasks of gaining independence, status, and self-control. A restructured school environment and a responsive system for classroom management can contribute to such growth and development. Figure 3.3 outlines a middle school disciplinary plan that deals with all except major infractions. (A sample disciplinary notice appears in Appendix 7.)

How Can Institutions Help?

During the past decade, intermediate education has experienced a major renewal, with educational programs designed to accommodate student differences and facilitate passage through the early adolescent years. These institutional changes have had a positive effect in reducing disciplinary problems among students. The overall effect of these changes has been to *personalize* or *humanize* education in the intermediate grades.

The changes that have been incorporated into programs for emerging adolescents can be divided into two major categories: (1) changes that make the instructional program more humane and (2) changes that make the instructional program more adaptable to student needs. Under ideal conditions an entire school would adapt changes like the activities mentioned in the following paragraphs; however, they can be implemented in one classroom setting.

One method for personalizing a program is for teachers to conduct an assessment of student needs. To the degree that interests can be determined and a composite of student development outlined, instruction can be designed to serve learners. Common sense and experience suggest that all persons are receptive to learning that meets their needs.

Another way to improve programs is to break down large group administrative units into smaller, more intimate groups. In many schools the "school-within-a-school" concept has been used to guarantee that individual students enjoy continuity of social contact during the school day. A dominant theme of the young adolescent period is a feeling of loneliness, and within classrooms, small tasks groups can overcome this problem.

Keeping records presents another way to make the school program more humane and personal. To the degree that teachers can monitor growth through effective record keeping, student needs and problems can be pinpointed and confronted. Such record keeping should go beyond simply maintaining files on academic progress and would be most effective if written like entries in a diary.

Schools and their teachers can seek to provide a wider range of student guidance services. To overcome the uneven ratio of guidance counselors to students (1:450+ in most intermediate schools), peer counseling can be used in a number of activities of varying emotional intensity. In classroom settings, teachers can use a variation on adviser/advisee activity and provide in-the-hall "walking advisement." This way, each student will be assured access to an adult with whom she can converse.

FIGURE 3.3 Middle school disciplinary plan

CATCH THEM DOING GOOD

Dear Parents:

We would like to introduce you to our middle school disciplinary plan. All classes, excluding exceptional education, will use this plan.

I. In general, we have a high expectation for our students and their behavior. This plan, based on providing *positive* and *negative* consequences for classroom behavior, is highly structured and is based on a demerit and reward system. It will be implemented with fairness and consistency in all classes.

II. Students will be issued demerits in class when school rules are broken or class instruction is disrupted, specifically if the student breaks the following rules:

□ Students must be on time for class.
□ Students must be prepared with materials and supplies.
□ Students must not use unacceptable language.
□ Students must help maintain a positive and undisrupted learning environment by:
—not talking unless requested by teacher.
—not being out of seat unless requested by instructor.
—not throwing paper, pencil, or other objects.
—not chewing gum or eating snacks.

The students have been told about these rules and know the importance of enforcing them in class.

III. The accumulation of demerits and the resultant disciplinary action will follow this plan:

□ 3 demerits: Phone call or note to parents
□ 4 demerits: After-school detention (team)
□ 5 demerits: Team conference (with student and team teachers) and parent notification
□ 6 demerits: Guidance referral (counseling)
□ 7 demerits: Parent conference
□ 8 demerits: House leader—in-school or out-of-school suspension

At the beginning of each nine-week period, all demerits will be erased and every student will start with a "clean slate."

IV. Good behavior will result in positive consequences. Some examples are as follows:

□ We will schedule parties and activities.
□ Students will receive awards/certificates for improving their behavior.
□ Students with good academic record and no demerits will be rewarded.

We welcome your suggestions/comments about the disciplinary plan and look forward to working with parents to provide each child with the best education possible.

Thank you.

TEAM _____ DATE _____
STUDENT SIGNATURE _____
PARENT SIGNATURE _____
SUGGESTIONS/COMMENTS _____
_____
_____

Teachers can seek more parental involvement in the school experience. To assume that lessons given in a six-hour school day can encompass the many lessons outside the school is shortsighted. Teachers need the support and help of parents that is obtainable only to the degree that parents are given a meaningful role. Their presence in a classroom setting means additional adult figures and, correspondingly, more adults who can work in small groups with young adolescents. School-business partnerships also can provide caring adults (e.g., employee volunteers, mentors, tutors) and will be examined further in Chapter 9.

Another major change that schools and teachers can make is to adjust intermediate school programs so that they are more adaptable to student needs. One way is to place the curriculum on a continuous progress basis, a benefit of which is that older students or students who repeatedly have failed can become involved without suffering humiliation.

Another way of adapting the program is to make the class schedule more flexible within major time periods. In this way, neither the teacher nor student is a slave to the clock, and discussions and activities that strike a responsive chord can be maintained. Such flexibility also teaches time management and allows students to have greater control over their school day.

Yet another way to enhance adaptability is to "program" constructive and creative outlets into the school day. This can be done by allowing students to earn "free time" in class, or by scheduling exploratory activities that "stretch" the student's experience. Such creative outlets can do much to de-emphasize unfair competition among students and at the same time provide opportunities for all students to find areas of strength.

A fourth way of making the school or class program more adaptable is to integrate school and social experiences. Young adolescents have a great need to master social experiences like communicating with others, overcoming shyness, learning etiquette, and projecting sex roles. The classroom that integrates these strong needs with learning has fewer motivational problems.

Finally, the school can be more adaptive if it will provide more than one way of learning. Each teacher has a favorite learning style and preferred delivery system for learning. Rather than excluding those students who do not learn well by traditional methods, teachers can find alternative learning paths for different students.

SUMMARY

More than any other single factor, teachers hold the key to success of the essential middle school. Along with personal characteristics generally desired in a teacher (likes children, is enthusiastic, is committed to the middle school philosophy, and so on), researchers have identified specific teacher competencies needed. Among these are awareness of physical, intellectual, and socioemotional needs of transescents; knowledge of personality and developmental theory; ability to merge media (demonstration, lecture, audiovisual, and so forth) into appropriate presentations; and ability to work cooperatively with peers.

In addition to discussing the teacher's role, this chapter presented suggestions for the professional preparation of middle school teachers. Central to this preparation is the commitment of certifying agencies and teacher training institutions to revise training programs so as to create a middle school that is neither elementary nor secondary but has an identity of its own.

Implementation will be successful only if teachers can select appropriate teaching strategies. Several instruments and innovations were described—the Flanders System and the Gallagher-Aschner System, analysis of teacher verbal patterns, and independent study, among others.

Classroom management and issues surrounding discipline among this age group were discussed and guidelines provided for coping with behavior problems in the classroom.

SUGGESTED LEARNING ACTIVITIES

1. Ask students to develop a list of personal characteristics of middle school teachers whom they most admire.
2. Identify the ten most important teacher competencies of the middle school teacher competencies identified in this chapter. Give reasons why you selected the ones on your list.
3. Design an outline of a preservice or inservice training program for middle school teachers.

What courses and/or experiences would you include?
4. Use the modified Flanders System or the Gallagher-Aschner System in your classroom to analyze a given teaching-learning situation.
5. Develop a list of disciplinary procedures for working with emerging adolescents.

NOTES

1. Ned Flanders, *Teacher Influence-Pupil Attitudes and Achievement* (Washington, DC: Research Monograph 12, HEW, 1965).
2. Arno A. Bellack, et al., *The Language of the Classroom* (New York: Teachers College Press, 1966).
3. Jacob S. Kounin, *Discipline and Group Management in Classrooms* (New York: Holt, Rinehart and Winston, 1970).

4. U.S. Department of HEW, National Institute of Mental Health, Annual Report, 1992.
5. Robert J. Havighurst, *Developmental Tasks and Education* (New York: Longmans, Green, 1952).

SELECTED REFERENCES

Association for Supervision and Curriculum Development, Working Group on the Emerging Adolescent Learner, Joseph Bondi, chairman, *The Middle School We Need* (Washington, DC: ASCD, 1975).

Wiles, Jon, and Bondi, Joseph, *A Guide and Plan for Conducting Ten Workshops with the NEA Middle School Training Program* (Washington, DC: National Education Association, 1985).

_____, *Discipline and Safety in Middle Schools* (Tampa: Wiles, Bondi and Associates, Inc., 1991).

_____, *Training Programs for Middle School Teachers* (Tampa: Wiles, Bondi and Associates, Inc., 1992).

4

Designing an Effective Program

*The great range of differences
found in middle school students demands
a broad and relevant program.*

INTRODUCTION

A middle school program should reflect the philosophy of the school itself. For this reason it may be difficult to find an identical program in any two schools, even within the same school district. But because of the common goal that drives middle school philosophy—to provide education for ten- to fourteen-year-olds who are in transition physically, socially, emotionally, and intellectually—certain elements form a unifying thread that runs throughout the successful middle school curriculum.

This chapter will examine each of those elements that give this level of education its identity and vitality. The heart of the chapter is a model on which a balanced program can be designed.

THE BALANCED CURRICULUM

The Association for Supervision and Curriculum Development (ASCD) has described a number of criteria that make for a balanced middle school program. These criteria are summarized below.

Learning experiences should be provided for transescents at their own intellectual levels and relate to immediate rather than remote academic goals. So as to account for the full range of students who are at many different levels of concrete and formal operations, a wide variety of cognitive learning experiences should be made available. In addition, learning objectives should be sequenced to allow for the transition from concrete to formal operations. Toward this end, a diversified curriculum of exploratory and/or fundamental activities should result in daily experiences that will stimulate and nurture intellectual development. For example, opportunities should be provided for development of problem-solving skills, reflective-thinking processes, and awareness for the order of the student's environment. Cognitive experiences should be so structured that students can progress in an individualized manner. That is, as much consideration should be given to *who* the student is and becomes (his self-concept, sense of self-responsibility, and attitudes toward school and personal happiness) as is given to *how much* and *what* he knows. However, within the structure of an individualized learning program, students can interact with one another—social interaction is not an enemy of individualized learning.

Furthermore, notes the ASCD, a curriculum must be flexible enough that all areas taught reveal opportunities for further study, help students learn how to study, and help them appraise their own interests and talents. In addition, the middle school should continue the developmental program of basic skills instruction started in the elementary school, with emphasis on both developmental and remedial reading. A planned sequence of concepts in the general education areas must be promoted, with major emphasis on the interests and skills for continued learning, a balanced program of exploratory experiences and other activities and services for personal development, and appropriate attention to the development of values.

A balanced program must combine and integrate areas of learning to break down artificial and irrelevant divisions of curriculum content. Some previously departmentalized areas of the curriculum should be combined and taught around integrative themes, topics, and experiences. (Interdisciplinary/thematic units will be discussed in Chapter 5.) Other areas of the curriculum, particularly those concerned with basic skills that are logical, sequential, and analytical, might best be taught in ungraded or continuous progress programs (discussed in Chapter 6). Inflexible student scheduling, with its emphasis on departmentalization, should be restructured in the direction of greater flexibility.

Methods of instruction should involve open and individually directed learning experiences. For example, students' personal curiosity should be nurtured, with one learning experience inspiring subsequent activities. The role of the teacher should be more that of a personal guide and facilitator of learning than of a purveyor of knowledge. Thus, traditional lecture-recitation methods should be minimized. Also, curriculum and teaching methods must reflect cultural, ethnic, and socioeconomic subgroups within the middle school student population.

Grouping of students should involve not only cognitive, but also physical, social, and emotional criteria.

Finally, experiences in the arts must be made accessible so that all transescents can enhance their aesthetic appreciation and creative expression.[1]

Despite much progress over the past ten years in developing new and exciting programs for emergent adolescent learners, much remains to be done. Whether middle school programs are housed in structures called middle schools or found in upper elementary grades, junior highs, or secondary schools, their focus must be attuned to the developmental characteristics of this unique group of learners.[2]

It becomes clear, then, that the purpose of a middle school is to offer a balanced, comprehensive, success-oriented curriculum that is designed to bridge the gap between the self-contained environment of the elementary school and the departmentalized structure of the high school. It is also intended to provide experiences that will assist students in making the transition from late childhood to adolescence.

Through the introduction of formal academic discipline and a variety of enrichment and special-interest experiences (detailed in Chapter 7), the middle school curriculum is more exploratory in nature than is that of the elementary school and is less specialized than the high school program. Thus, because skill development balanced with subject-area content is a primary goal, three major components emerge in the middle school curriculum: subject content, personal development, and essential learning skills.

Students experience learning through a program that emphasizes integration of the four core subject content areas—language arts, mathematics, science, and social studies—and the adviser/advisee program. The specifics of what students should learn and how to help them learn are important aspects of *subject content*.

Personal development is designed to foster social, emotional, and moral growth through student-centered curricular and extracurricular activities. This is a school-wide responsibility that involves the entire staff. To help initiate and implement personal development topics, an adviser/advisee program is recommended.

As an outgrowth of its responsibility to refine *essential learning skills* (e.g., reading, speaking, writing, and such) introduced in the elementary school, a middle school program should assist students in becoming more self-directed learners.

TABLE 4.1   A Balanced Curriculum

Subject Content	Personal Development	Essential Learning Skills
3 years math	Adviser/advisee program	School awareness
3 years science	Developmental PE	Community awareness
3 years communication/language arts	Health and nutrition	Reading
3 years social studies	Individual growth	Listening
3 years reading	Social growth	Speaking
3 years developmental PE	Citizenship	Writing
3 years exploratory courses	Creativity	Vocabulary
	Minicourses	Thinking
	Special interests	Problem solving
	Career education	Decision making
	Exceptional education	Study
		Media
		Map
		Reference
		Test taking
		Computer literacy
		Computation and/or calculator

Specifically this means that proficiency in certain basic skills emphasized in all subject areas is key to each student's ability to function effectively in further schooling and in society.

Table 4.1 illustrates an "ideal" curriculum, that is, one that synthesizes the three essential components in a balanced middle school curriculum.

JUNIOR HIGH VERSUS THE MIDDLE SCHOOL: SOME DIFFERENCES

The middle school program differs in a number of ways from its predecessor, the traditional junior high. Table 4.2 highlights some of the key differences.

The personal development component of middle school programs focuses on the developmental differences of emerging adolescent learners rather than on their sameness, as is the case with traditional programs.

The subject content element takes into account existing cognitive and psychomotor skills of preadolescent and early adolescent middle graders.

An effective middle school program also emphasizes those essential learning skills that will be needed throughout school life and adult life.

To educate today's emerging adolescent learners, the middle school will be based on a comprehensive curriculum/program design that in turn is based on an in-depth needs assessment. The balance of this chapter presents a middle school program design that can serve as a prototype for the 1990s and beyond. This design is based on the Duval County (Jacksonville, Florida) school district. Report excerpts for a companion design are found in Appendix 4.

TABLE 4.2 Traditional Junior High versus Middle School: A Study in Contrast

Traditional Junior High	Middle School
Based on high school model	Common, academically oriented core curriculum
Mastery of subject matter	Interdisciplinary academic program
Departmentalized academic program	Team concept
Emphasis on the disciplines	Exploratory elective program
Conference periods scattered throughout the day; seven-period day	Teacher planning time; flexible scheduling; extended blocks of uninterrupted time
Full-semester elective	Collaborative and independent self-contained teaching modes
Homogeneous grouping (tracking)	Equal access to all programs by all students
Full athletic program	Student advisory programs

A DESIGN PROTOTYPE: DUVAL COUNTY MIDDLE SCHOOL

Philosophy: The Nature and Needs of Early Adolescents

Middle school students are in transition between childhood and adulthood. Therefore, children between ages ten and fourteen have very distinctive needs that set them apart from elementary and high school students. Physically, they exhibit wide daily variations in growth and development and energy levels, especially with the onset of puberty. Intellectually, they have a heightened curiosity about the world around them but are easily distracted and have short attention spans. Socially, they are strongly influenced by peers and challenge authority. Emotionally, middle school students are constantly searching for self-identity. Thus, they need a stable yet flexible environment that will meet their changing needs and promote their academic success.

The Nature of the Responsive School

Middle schools must be flexible, student-centered structures responsive to the growth and educational needs of children in transition. By providing for maximum interaction between teachers and students, middle schools encourage the development of independent thinking skills to ensure that students achieve academic success and develop personal responsibility. Teachers, administrators, and support staff must adopt a nurturing approach that emphasizes and attends to each student as a person. Such a school will have the following characteristics:

☐ A student-centered focus that enhances academic progress
☐ An environment that ensures smooth transitions from elementary to middle school and from middle school to high school
☐ A curriculum focused on students' personal development and on skills for continued learning

□ Opportunities to develop constructive, meaningful relationships with peers and adults

□ A focus on students' increasing levels of independence, responsibility, self-discipline, and citizenship through effective decision making

□ Teachers and administrators who are committed to the education of the emerging adolescent

□ A variety of evaluation criteria to assess student progress while maintaining academic excellence

□ An emphasis on developing a safe and caring environment that fosters a genuine interest in learning

□ Meaningful articulation with parents that encourages their involvement in their children's education

In addition, the effective middle school will provide the following:

□ Teachers who are organized into interdisciplinary teams with common planning times and responsibility for the same student population

□ Teacher-based adviser/advisee programs facilitated by guidance counselors

□ Flexible scheduling based on time blocks rather than on fixed-length periods

□ Opportunities for individualized learning that lead to the refinement of existing cognitive and psychomotor skills

□ A structured exploratory program that includes enrichment, independent study, art, music, career education, foreign language, intramural activities, team activities, and peer-group activities

□ Emphasis on basic skills in reading, writing, mathematics, and critical thinking through an integrated curriculum

The Curriculum: An Overview

The middle school will provide a stable yet flexible curriculum to meet each student's academic, affective, and developmental needs while providing an opportunity to participate in an exploratory program. The *goals* of the curriculum are threefold:

1. To foster academic success in all students
2. To implement an affective program such as the adviser/advisee program
3. To provide an exploratory program

Each student will take the following *core curriculum:*

□ 3 years of communications including reading, writing, and speaking
□ 3 years of mathematics
□ 3 years of science
□ 3 years of social studies
□ 3 years of physical education and health
□ 3 years of exploratory electives in art, music, foreign language, and career education courses
□ 3 years of the adviser/advisee program

Exploratory elective programs will be defined by the following parameters:

□ Offerings will vary from school to school based on the school facility, size, and staff.
□ Sixth-grade students will be in a different area each nine-week period. They will be required to choose four different exploratory programs for the year.
□ Seventh-grade students will choose from elective courses of one semester or one year in duration.
□ Eighth-grade students will choose from elective courses of one semester or one year in duration.
□ Possible exploratory elective areas:
  —Career education: Wood/graphics/metal/power/electricity
  —Home economics: Food/clothing/child care
  —Business: Typing/business skills/accounting
  —Fine arts: Drama/journalism/art
  —Foreign language: Spanish/French/Latin
  —Music: Band/chorus/general music
  —Computer: Programming/applications/problem solving

Following is a list of *continual (essential) learning skills* that need to be an integral part of all subjects and courses:

□ Critical thinking
□ Reading
□ Writing
□ Listening
□ Speaking
□ Study skills
□ Vocabulary
□ Problem solving
□ Decision making
□ Social interaction
□ Test taking skills
□ Computer literacy
□ Reference usage
□ Career awareness
□ School awareness
□ Community awareness
□ Citizenship
□ Media usage

Curricular Design: A Model for Setting Standards

1.0 Career Education: A "hands-on" approach allows for personal assessment, technological literacy, and career development. Students will learn the role of technology in the world of work, explore various career fields, and have the chance to set career goals from which they will develop a personal career and educational plan.

1.01   Experiences that demonstrate the relationship of educational achievement to career opportunities
1.02   Orientation to standard career clusters
1.03   Activities that apply basic skills in English, mathematics, science, and social studies to the world of work
1.04   Participation during each of the 3 middle school years in exploratory career programs including business, home economics, and technology/education
1.05   Experiences that develop an understanding and appreciation for the dignity and worth of work

A special-interest class studies ocean life.

1.06 Assessment of the student's personal aptitudes/interests and direction toward relating those aptitudes/interests to career fields

1.07 Individual student development of a 4-year educational plan for grades 9–12 with input from student, parents, and school advisers

1.08 Participation in manipulative activities with tools, materials, and processes to solve practical problems

1.09 Access to an occupational specialist for all students

1.10 The use of computer technology to enhance instruction

1.11 Mastery of the career education curriculum through frequent use of reading, writing, speaking, and listening skills

2.0 Computers and Technology: As society advances technologically, it is imperative that students in grades six through eight be exposed to technology so as to apply it beneficially in their environment.

2.01 Computer studies offered to 6th-grade students through the exploratory wheel

2.02 A computer/technology course for 7th-grade students based on the current 8th-grade Computer Literacy Program modified to include in-depth study in the area of computer applications

2.03 Semester courses in computer logic and problem solving, computer applications, and computer programming offered as elective courses in the 7th and 8th grades, should student demand and available facilities warrant such course offerings

2.04 The incorporation of computers and related technology into all areas of the curriculum, in that research indicates that technology is a viable tool for instruction when that technology is used to supplement, not replace, the curriculum

3.0 Exceptional Education: Every student has the opportunity to become an active participant in, and contributing member of, society through a program designed to meet his or her specific physical, emotional, intellectual, communicative, social, and vocational needs. No student is separated from the educational mainstream without documented evidence that separation or a more restricted environment is for the student's benefit or is necessary to serve his or her best interest.

3.01 Ongoing process for review and revision of the Individual Education Program (IEP) to ensure that individual needs are met

3.02 Provision of the least restrictive environment that provides successful educational and social opportunities

3.03 Full access to all school programs and activities

3.04 Provision of appropriate therapies, adaptive programs (and devices), and transportation

3.05 Curriculum that focuses on students' functional levels and meets the state and local requirements for promotion

3.06 Provision for various scheduling, mainstreaming, and regular education alternatives to meet individual student needs

3.07 The use of computer technology to enhance instruction

3.08 Vocational evaluation and appropriate opportunities for training and career awareness activities

3.09 Affective curriculum that includes problem-solving and coping skills and encourages appropriate behaviors and self-concept

3.10 Provision for challenging activities that promote reasoned, logical, and critical thought

3.11 Mastery of the appropriate academic curriculum areas through frequent use of reading, writing, speaking, and listening skills

4.0 Fine Arts: Art experiences are valuable as a means of teaching creative problem solving and critical thinking through direct performance as well as indirect study. The middle school student should be exposed to two- and three-dimensional art on the exploratory wheel in order to make choices for further courses of study in the arts. Classroom activities should be integrated with the four primary content areas for arts instruction, which includes creating art forms (production), aesthetics, history, and criticism. Every effort should be made to combine aspects of each major area in every unit of study with appropriate assignments and projects.

4.01   Perceptual skills—identifying potential for subject matter by responding to works of art
4.02   Technical skills—producing works of art that relate to media and technique
4.03   Expressive skills—producing art through meaning, composition, and choice of appropriate tools and techniques
4.04   Critical skills—classroom critique sessions on student work as well as master-work providing experiences in making and justifying judgments about the aesthetic quality and merit of works of art
4.05   Art knowledge—offering experiences to learn about historical masterworks through becoming aware of contemporary and local artists and events
4.06   The use of computer technology to enhance instruction
4.07   Mastery of the fine arts curriculum through frequent use of reading, writing, speaking, and listening skills
4.08   Nine-week exploratory art experience for 6th grade

5.0 Foreign Languages: The general philosophy of the program is to promote the educational benefits gained through the study of foreign languages and cultures. Foreign language will be offered as a part of the exploratory wheel for sixth graders, emphasizing the comparison and exploration of a variety of languages and corresponding cultures. For seventh graders, foreign language will be offered as an exploratory semester course, emphasizing basic conversation and cultural awareness of a single foreign language. Eighth graders may take either a semester of foreign language or a yearlong course, emphasizing preparation for high school foreign language study. As with any elective course, foreign language offerings in any school depend on the facilities available, the student demand for the course, and the presence of appropriate instructional staff.

5.01   Skills in listening and speaking in a foreign language
5.02   Skills in reading and writing in a foreign language
5.03   An appreciation and understanding of the historical and cultural values of people who speak foreign languages
5.04   A better understanding of the student's own language
5.05   An awareness of the value of foreign language as an employable communication skill
5.06   A foundation for continuing the study of foreign languages in high school
5.07   The use of computer technology to enhance instruction
5.08   Mastery of the foreign language curriculum through frequent use of reading, writing, speaking, and listening skills

6.0 Health: In addition to the tremendous emotional, social, biological, and intellectual changes that routinely confront the middle school child, today's students also face a number of potentially fatal threats: substance abuse, AIDS and other sexually transmitted disease, increased incidence of suicide, and an increased rate of teenage pregnancy. Therefore, it is essential that students be provided a strong comprehensive health program throughout the middle school years. That program will be best achieved through the integration of health instruction into the physical education and life science classrooms and into the adviser/advisee program. All teachers responsible for health instruction must receive either adequate health inservices or health certification so as to ensure competent instruction in this essential subject area.

6.01   Substance abuse prevention
6.02   Disease prevention
6.03   Personal health and hygiene
6.04   Human growth and development
6.05   Nutrition education
6.06   Safety/first aid (including CPR)
6.07   Health resources in the community
6.08   Consumer education
6.09   Family living
6.10   Mental and emotional health
6.11   Interpersonal relationships
6.12   Structure and function of the human body
6.13   Mastery of the health curriculum through frequent use of reading, writing, speaking, and listening skills
6.14   A yearly minimum of 45 days instruction in comprehensive health education in physical education

7.0 Language Arts: The study of English language arts develops written and oral communication skills and provides opportunities to practice critical reading skills and writing techniques in order to successfully use these essential skills in other subject areas. Provisions for defined skill development in the area of reading are necessary to enable students to make the transition from "learning to read" through the elementary school basal reading program to middle school "reading to learn" in each of the content areas. Such provisions may best be enhanced through the use of at least one reading resource teacher to service each middle school in terms of providing integrated reading assistance to content area teachers for course-specific reading strategies and to individual students in terms of developmental reading instruction, as necessary. The program should consist of integrated instruction in reading, writing, listening, and speaking skills.

7.01   Instruction in reading comprehension at the literal, inferential, and evaluative levels
7.02   Remediation, enrichment, and developmental reading programs
7.03   A sustained silent reading program involving students and faculty members
7.04   Weekly writing practice and instruction
7.05   A diagnostic approach to writing instruction, including immediate feedback to students and use of students' essays as teaching tools
7.06   Practice in listening and speaking skills, including class discussion, group discussion, teacher-student dialogue, following oral directions, and peer feedback
7.07   Integration of reading, writing, speaking, and listening instruction in the language arts classroom rather than emphasis on isolated skills

7.08   The use of computer technology to enhance instruction, particularly in the area of writing

8.0 Mathematics: Today's adolescents and preadolescents (mostly in grades six through eight) need more academic challenge, particularly a strengthened curriculum in mathematics and science. Higher-order analytical and problem-solving skills should provide the thrust for the mathematics curriculum.

8.01   Applying mathematics to problem-solving situations
8.02   Demonstrating estimation and approximation procedures
8.03   Performing mathematical computations
8.04   Recognizing and applying geometric concepts
8.05   Recognizing and applying measurement concepts
8.06   Recognizing and applying the concepts of probability and statistics
8.07   Demonstrating number sense and operation sense
8.08   Demonstrating knowledge of algebraic concepts, the emphasis on which will be undertaken in advanced 7th-grade classes and in 8th-grade pre-algebra, algebra, and general math courses where a sufficient number of students and adequate facilities justify offering those courses
8.09   Hands-on activities that incorporate the use of manipulatives
8.10   Application of mathematics in other content areas
8.11   Additional challenges and activities for those students who demonstrate the desire and talent to expand their study of mathematics to a technologically related field
8.12   The use of computer technology to enhance instruction
8.13   Mastery of the mathematics curriculum through frequent use of reading, writing, speaking, and listening skills

9.0 Music: Because music is a primary expression of every culture, the middle school music education program is designed to develop student sensitivity, cultural values, and the skills necessary to respond to and enjoy music from an aesthetic standpoint. The sixth-grade music program will consist of general music and music appreciation in the exploratory wheel. Sixth-grade students will be restricted from taking band and/or chorus during the school day, but there will be opportunities for interested students through afterschool activities.* The music course of study will include band, orchestra, and chorus for seventh and eighth graders.

9.01   Providing experiences that will develop a basic understanding of the elements of music and the ability to use the skills and knowledge in music
9.02   Developing basic skills in production, performance techniques, music literacy, and music appreciation
9.03   Identifying similarities and differences in the music of various styles and cultures
9.04   Demonstrating positive participation in music activities through singing, playing instruments, moving, listening, and creating
9.05   Using computer technology to enhance instruction

---

* NOTE: Some schools or school districts may opt to include band and/or chorus for sixth graders.

9.06   Mastering the music curriculum through frequent use of reading, writing, speaking, and listening skills

9.07   Providing nine-week music experience for 6th grade

10.0 Physical Education: The physical education program develops in students an understanding of the importance of living a healthful life, as well as a mastery of individual motor skills, sportsmanship, and physical fitness. In each grade the program consists of a minimum of 45 instructional days of comprehensive health education, which is an integral part of the physical education middle school program. In the sixth grade, these 45 days consist of both an orientation to physical education to discuss the importance of physical education and a comprehensive health education study. Each comprehensive health unit is taught by instructors who have received either health certification or adequate health inservice instruction. The remainder of each year is devoted to participation in a team-sports and life-sports program.

10.01   Health and safety instruction provided initially in the 6th grade, continuing through the middle school years

10.02   Development of motor skills stressed throughout the entire middle school physical education program

10.03   Life sports such as table tennis, badminton, and horseshoes, based on student demand and available facilities

10.04   Opportunities for students to demonstrate skills in individual and team sports

10.05   Emphasis on sportsmanship and healthy, less stressful competition

10.06   Individual student assessment of fitness development strategies for self-improvement

10.07   Intramurals conducted both during and after the school day

10.08   Provisions for students with physical limitations and disabilities, such as adaptive physical education programs

10.09   The use of technology to enhance instruction

10.10   Mastery of the physical education curriculum through frequent use of reading, writing, speaking, and listening skills

11.0 Science: A strong instructional program that emphasizes critical thinking skills and problem-solving skills in science and mathematics is essential. Whereas a general science course structure may not prove as challenging to the middle school student as a focused, content-specific structure, students in the sixth grade will receive yearlong instruction in general science with an emphasis on earth science in order to provide instructional continuity from the elementary grades. However, the science curriculum for students in grades seven and eight will consist of yearlong courses in life science at the seventh-grade level and physical science at the eighth-grade level. The course content at both of those grade levels will be based on inquiry, problem solving, and process skills.

11.01   Specifically scheduled hands-on laboratory experiences on at least a weekly basis

11.02   Instruction in basic and integrated process skills (e.g., observing, comparing, analyzing, classifying, communicating, and experimenting)

11.03   Social implications of technological advancements

11.04   Current environmental issues and concerns

11.05   The use of technology to enhance instruction

11.06   Mastery of the science curriculum through frequent use of reading, writing, listening, and speaking skills

12.0   Social Studies: The primary purpose of the middle school social studies program is to enable students to develop those skills needed to function as productive citizens in a democratic society. Because a general social studies course structure may not prove as challenging to the student as a focused, content-specific structure, students in the sixth grade will receive yearlong instruction in world history; seventh-grade students will be taught geography; the emphasis in eighth-grade social studies will be U.S. history.

12.01   Provision for reasoned, logical, and critical thought

12.02   Stimulation of career awareness

12.03   Promotion of positive personal development

12.04   The use of technology to enhance instruction

12.05   Mastery of the social studies curriculum through frequent use of reading, writing, listening, and speaking skills

13.0   Special-Needs Programs: Some middle school students face more than the usual number of developmental, economic, and social problems. Special-needs programs heterogeneously group students so that self-worth is realized and opportunities for positive interaction with other students are provided. Programs are also designed to meet individual academic and social needs and to monitor the progress of each student.

Dropout Prevention

Dropout prevention programs target students who are "at risk" due to apathy, poor motivation, underachievement, and who are overage for their grade level. Special programs that provide a positive environment for social, emotional, and cognitive growth give these students an opportunity to become contributing and participating members of society.

Compensatory Education

Compensatory programs in mathematics and communication will be offered to all students on an as-needed basis.

English Speakers of Other Languages (ESOL)

Students with limited English-speaking capabilities require special sensitivity to their unique experiences and needs. These students are provided the opportunity to learn new ways of behaving, learning, and thinking. Opportunities are also provided for discussing, examining, and evaluating conflicting values and norms presented to them by their home and school environments. Proper guidance is available for understanding the differences in expectations and values in order to find a balance between the two cultures so that smooth adjustments can be made to their newly adopted American society.

Program Design: A Model for Setting Standards

1.0 Adviser/Advisee Program: Designed to give each student the opportunity to develop a positive relationship with an adult member of the school staff. An environment is created in which faculty and staff respond to the needs of, and take a personal interest in, each student. With the help of parents, teachers, counselors, and advisers, students learn to monitor their academic progress and accept the consequences of their decisions and behavior. Advisers serve as positive role models and provide opportunities for students to develop positive relationships with peers and adults. The program is particularly designed to include topics in health education instruction.

1.01   All certificated staff is included as part of the program.
1.02   Inservice is provided to all advisers prior to their participation in the program.
1.03   The program includes, but is not limited to, these topics:
  □ Study skills
  □ Substance abuse
  □ Self-concept
  □ Decision making
  □ Goal setting
  □ Career education
  □ Interpersonal relationships
  □ Family relationships
1.04   Daily uninterrupted adviser/advisee sessions are at least 25 minutes in length.
1.05   Scheduling and organization are flexible enough to meet the needs of each school.
1.06   A standard curriculum base is developed within each school according to the needs of the student population, from which advisers have the option to select activities that best meet students' needs.
1.07   An annual review is conducted at each school to monitor program effectiveness in meeting students' needs, input for which is sought from students, advisers, parents, and school administrators.
1.08   A specific designee within the school (preferably a guidance counselor) coordinates the adviser-advisee program's activities/functions.

2.0 Intramural Athletics Program: Designed to be an outgrowth of the physical education program, the intramural program is meant to assist the student in physical, mental, and social development. The program, which may include interscholastic competition in non–contact sports, provides recreational activities, physical fitness, group loyalty, success, and a permanent interest in leisure-time activities. The program is structured so that *all* students may take part.*

Whatever program is developed, it should be limited to seventh-grade and eighth-grade students and should be scheduled only in the afternoons and without postseason play.

---

* Some schools or school districts may choose to eliminate all interscholastic sports.

2.01   The interscholastic athletic program for boys does not include football. Basketball, soccer, baseball, track, volleyball, and swimming will be offered depending on student demand and available facilities.

2.02   The interscholastic athletic program for girls includes volleyball, basketball, soccer, softball, track, and swimming, depending on student demand and available facilities.

2.03   An intramural program exists for all three middle school grades.

2.04   Based on student interest, intramural activities include those that parallel the interscholastic athletic program and any other sports/activities that the school chooses to offer.

2.05   Based on student demand and available facilities, a lifetime sports intramural program includes activities such as badminton, table tennis, chess, and horseshoes.

2.06   Intramural activities are offered during and after school.

3.0 Facilities: Ideally, new schools would be designed and constructed to reflect middle school philosophy. Because this is impractical, however, most "new" middle school buildings are housed in older facilities already in operation. Consequently, most make do, keeping in mind that it is the program, not the building, that is the essence of the middle school. Even so, facilities must provide enough flexibility to accommodate interdisciplinary teaming and intramural activities.

3.01   School facilities are pleasant and attractive.

3.02   Space is provided for counselor-student conferences.

3.03   Furniture is appropriate for each learning area.

3.04   Accommodations are made for teaming, including considerations such as close proximity of teamed classes, available space for team planning, and available spaces (large and small) for varied activities.

3.05   A sufficient number of rooms is provided both for academic and exploratory/elective classes.

3.06   Space and facilities are adequate for physical education, intramurals, and athletics.

3.07   Adequate space is available for students' social interaction.

3.08   Larger schools are divided into houses to create a "small school" atmosphere.

3.09   Annual reviews are conducted to determine the most efficient and effective uses of the facilities in matching the structural design with the middle school's program design.

4.0 Flexible Block Scheduling: The goal of scheduling is to provide teachers with flexibility in instructional time so as to satisfy students' academic needs. This goal is best achieved by using flexible block scheduling, which involves allocating an amount of time for each area of study. Within each interdisciplinary team, blocks of time are designed for the study of academic subjects (reading/language arts, mathematics, science, and social studies) and separate times for electives/exploratory programs and physical education/health. Teams shift blocks of time to accommodate additional instructional activities as necessary.

The degree of flexibility in blocking areas of time for the study of academic subjects provides progressively higher levels of independence and variety as students progress from sixth to eighth grade. The eighth-grade schedule more closely resembles a traditional junior high school schedule than does the block schedule of the sixth and seventh grades.

4.01   Provision is adequate for a flexible daily time schedule.
4.02   A block of time (minimum of 225 minutes) is assigned to the interdisciplinary team for academic instruction.
4.03   Provision is made for a block of time for exploration and physical education (minimum of 45 minutes for each area).
4.04   The daily schedule is sufficiently variable to allow for athletic competition between inhouse student groups or intramural teams during an extended physical education class or for planned activities by an interdisciplinary team of teachers.
4.05   Provision is made for daily interdisciplinary team planning and concerns.

5.0 Guidance and Support Services: Providing a strong guidance service is key for middle grade students in coping with their specific (and diverse) problems, which involve self-esteem, peer relations, and the students' own physical changes.

Guidance counseling services are not limited to counselors; they also include support personnel—psychologists, psychiatrists, house administrators, social workers, teacher-advisers, adviser/advisee groups, and community programs and resources.

5.01   Guidance staff members participate in team planning sessions and assume a leadership role in all guidance-related aspects of the learning program.
5.02   Each school has access to Multi-Agency Community Council (MACC) resources.
5.03   Administrators play an active part as support personnel, in addition to accepting discipline responsibilities.
5.04   Teachers are familiar with the results of testing programs and receive assistance in the use of test results as an instructional tool.
5.05   Guidance and support staff assists in orienting the student to the new school, its purposes, facilities, rules, and activities in order to facilitate adjustment to the middle school environment.
5.06   Staff provides assistance with small and/or large group instruction.
5.07   Communication occurs with all service personnel within the school for the maximum benefit to students.

6.0 Instructional Strategies: The teacher must examine classroom methodology for, and demonstrate a variety of, instructional strategies that are designed to meet the specific needs of the middle school student. Such variety encourages student learning and participation.

6.01   Inservice opportunities are provided for teachers to examine various teaching and learning styles.
6.02   Teachers assess their individual teaching styles.

6.03   Teachers assess their own students' learning styles.

6.04   Students are provided opportunities to learn at different proficiency levels.

6.05   A variety of delivery methods is used to accommodate different learning styles.

6.06   A balance in strategies allows students some experience in cooperative learning and independent study.

6.07   Broad use is made of the competitive nature of the middle school child to enhance the student's self-concept through formal and informal competitive learning.

6.08   Media and concrete demonstrations are used regularly in classroom instruction.

6.09   An active mechanism exists through which teachers and administrators can share ideas and activities.

6.10   Program improvement feedback is elicited from the instructional staff.

7.0 Integrated Curriculum: The purpose of an integrated curriculum is to ensure that middle school students will perceive the relationships among the disciplines, develop a holistic knowledge structure, and transfer learning among disciplines.

7.01   Each team prepares and implements at least one interdisciplinary unit during each nine-week period in which each discipline's application to a common theme is taught.

7.02   Core skills in each discipline are reinforced by all other teachers.

7.03   Provisions are made for the display of students' work to show integration of disciplines for a unit of work.

7.04   Teams coordinate instructional activities with specialists in an area of study (e.g., speakers, demonstrations, field trips).

7.05   Team and cross-subject goals are established.

7.06   Homework and testing are coordinated.

7.07   Common difficulties are remedied.

8.0 Interdisciplinary Teams: Middle school students are organized into interdisciplinary teams. The teaming concept provides for integrated instruction in the core subjects of language arts/communication skills, math, science, and social studies. It also provides a smooth transition from the self-contained classroom of the elementary schools to the departmentalization of the high school setting.

Sharing a common group of students facilitates the extension of educational involvement from the classroom to the home and community. The team becomes thoroughly familiar with each student and therefore is better prepared to address the needs of the whole child and to help guide the student through his or her own life experiences.

Interdisciplinary teaming and block scheduling further provide for the flexible scheduling of students within the team area. The following are standards for team *organization*.

8.01   Teams consist of a balance of 2–5 teachers selected according to experience, age, race, sex, and special talents and who represent the core academic areas of mathematics, language arts, social studies, and science.

8.02   Team assignments are made for elective teachers, ESE teachers, and other resource personnel.

8.03   A common group of students is shared by each team with a ratio of 25–35 students per teacher per time block.

8.04   Common planning times are provided for all teachers on the same team.

8.05   When feasible, additional individual planning time or resource assignment time is provided for each team member.

8.06   Classrooms for team teachers are in proximity to each other, depending on available facilities.

8.07   A team leader is designated to coordinate each team and act as a representative for the team.

8.08   The interdisciplinary team controls a block of time.

8.09   The interdisciplinary team is responsible for the coordination of curriculum and for the delivery of instruction to the students on its team.

As the basic organizational unit in the middle school, the interdisciplinary team is responsible for the coordination of curriculum and for the delivery of instruction to the students on its team. The following are standards for the team *functions*.

8.10   Members of the team plan cooperatively.

8.11   Methods are developed to enhance the instructional delivery system.

8.12   Common pools of information about students are shared among team members.

8.13   Teams meet with parents to discuss individual students' academic and developmental progress.

8.14   Team members participate in a team meeting at least once each week.

8.15   Team members provide support for each other.

8.16   Uniform procedures for middle school instruction and classroom management are developed and consistently implemented within the team.

8.17   Activities are planned to foster a sense of team identity and pride among teachers and students.

8.18   The school's adviser/advisee program is implemented.

8.19   Members of each team interact cooperatively with other members of the school staff (guidance counselors, resource teachers, administrators).

8.20   Interdisciplinary units of instruction are developed and implemented.

8.21   Action plans are developed for individual students who are experiencing difficulties.

8.22   The team operates on a consensus basis so that when a decision must be made and agreement has not been reached, the team leader will make the decision based on available input.

9.0 *Parent-Community Involvement:* Because of the total-child educational philosophy of the middle schools, parent involvement is essential in defining goals, in educational decision making, and in monitoring their children's studies. In addition, middle schools should have an active public relations program to promote the school within the community and to maintain good community relations. Communities share with parents and middle school staff the responsibility for each student's success by serving as a learning environment and source of instructional resources, by providing opportunities for constructive afterschool activities, and by ensuring that students have access to health and social services.

9.01   An annual report of staff, parents, and students is conducted to evaluate and study the progress of the entire school through PTSA, LSAC,* program improvement committees, or other avenues.

9.02   Parents have the opportunity to support the learning process at home and at school by involvement in school activities, instructional support roles in the classroom, curriculum planning, disciplinary procedures, and incentive planning.

9.03   Open and frequent communication exists between school and parents about the school program and the students' progress, as evidenced by the following:
   □ Parents' handbook that explains the middle school program
   □ Individual report cards that are sent to each student's home
   □ Parent-student-teacher conferences
   □ Regular communication updating school activities (e.g., newsletters, calendars)
   □ Progress reports
   □ Group activities for parents, including seminars, parents' night, and open house

9.04   Each middle school has a PTA/PTSA program.

9.05   Each school has a lay advisory committee representative of various community organizations and businesses (LSAC) to maintain parent and community awareness of educational changes and to provide channels for parental and community input.

9.06   The middle school provides service-learning opportunities for students such as visiting a nursing home, helping at a day-care center, or cleaning a park. These activities are designed to enhance and supplement classroom learning, foster meaningful participation in the community, and encourage self-exploration.

9.07   Each school establishes a business partnership with at least one business organization in the community.

10.0 Shared Decision Making: Decisions that have an impact on the overall school program must involve input from those who are affected. Established by a committee of principals and teachers, the following guidelines are used for schoolwide decision making. (The following are district guidelines, not standards.)

10.01   A committee that is representative of the total school staff will be established at each pilot school and will consist of members selected by a democratic process within areas of responsibility (departments, teams, grade levels, or as otherwise stated).

---

* PTSA—Parent-Teacher-Student Association
LSAC—Local School Advisory Committee

10.02   Parent and student participation is strongly encouraged when deemed appropriate by the committee.

10.03   The purpose of the committee is to develop the philosophy and to establish and evaluate the goals and policies of the school.

10.04   The committee's areas of responsibility may include, but will not be limited to, the following:

- □ Departmental or local school programs
- □ Development of master schedule
- □ Recommendation and evaluation of instructional materials
- □ Development of curriculum
- □ Facilities and equipment
- □ Disciplinary plans
- □ Student activities
- □ Budget preparation
- □ Staffing
- □ Staff development

Many of these areas are already provided for in School Board Rule 10-201.

10.05   The committee will strive to reach consensus on all decisions; otherwise, the principal will make the decision utilizing the committee's input. Daily operational decisions are the responsibility of the principal or designee(s) and will be made within the spirit of this program.

10.06   If a school committee requests an instructional delivery system that is at odds with school board policy or collective-bargaining agreements, the school may petition the appropriate agency for a waiver of policy to implement the desired program.

11.0 Staff Development: A middle school staff is effective only if each employee possesses special understandings, skills, and attitudes in working with middle school students, parents, and community members so as to implement the middle school concept. These personnel see the middle school as neither elementary nor secondary but as an institution designed to meet the special needs of emerging adolescents. In that the schoolwide philosophy is student-centered and not subject-centered, each staff member's role is to help all students develop emotionally, socially, and academically.

To ensure that educators work effectively with the emerging adolescent, inservice education is essential. The decision to teach the whole child and attend to the developmental needs of the middle school student means that teachers and other staff will be seeking an expansion of their skills.

11.01   All teachers are trained in characteristics of the middle school child, interdisciplinary team organization, adviser/advisee strategies and techniques, and curriculum planning and evaluation.

11.02   Inservice training is available in the areas of learning styles, teaching strategies, interdisciplinary units, team leader training, and special training for middle school administrators.

12.0 Transition and Articulation: The movement of students into, out of, and within the middle school program requires communication and the cooperative effort of all staff. This movement may be between schools, teams, or special education programs. The curriculum requires not only horizontal, interdisciplinary coordination but vertical articulation within the K–12 continuum.

Flexible two-way communication is essential, and opportunities for parental involvement are more frequent and more participatory than in the junior high school model.

12.01   Orientation programs exist for students, teachers, staff, and parents.
12.02   Special strengths and talents are utilized through a Teachers Teaching Teachers (TTT) program.
12.03   Guidance programs facilitate transition for students and staff.
12.04   Teachers and staff schedule interschool meetings on a regular basis with feeder school staffs.
12.05   An operative plan exists to facilitate communication between school and parents.
12.06   Positive communication occurs in addition to communication that is punitive in nature.
12.07   School visitations are available for feeder schools for students who are entering as well as exiting the middle school program.

13.0 Evaluation: Whereas planning and organization set the stage for the change process, evaluation ensures that change has taken place to the extent desired. The evaluation process therefore will monitor and assess the implementation of the standards in the design.

13.01   Achievement/academic records
13.02   Staff/student attendance
13.03   Parent/student/staff attitudes

SUMMARY

The effective middle school program is balanced, comprehensive, and success-oriented. It differs from the traditional junior high program in that the middle school curriculum is developmentally centered; that is, it moves in tandem with the growth and developmental dynamics of the age group it serves.

The balanced curriculum includes three major components: subject content, personal development, and essential learning skills.

The curriculum design of the middle school includes a wide variety of course offerings and experiences, both in core cognitive areas and in the affective and psychomotor domain. This chapter described those program elements found in the middle school and standards used to measure each one.

The program must include a planned sequence of concepts, emphasize skills and interests needed for continuous learning, provide exploratory experiences, stress development of values, and give special attention to personal development of adolescent students.

The key feature of the chapter was a design prototype for a comprehensive and balanced middle school curriculum.

SUGGESTED LEARNING ACTIVITIES

1. Develop an outline of a program design for the middle school.
2. What courses and activities would you include in a special-interest program?
3. Prepare a statement for a school board on the need for a skills program in the middle school.
4. Develop a rationale for a balanced program in the middle school.
5. Design an adviser-advisee program for your middle school.

NOTES

1. Association for Supervision and Curriculum Development, Working Group on the Emerging Adolescent Learner, Joseph Bondi, chairman, *The Middle School We Need* (Washington, DC: ASCD, 1975).
2. Charles Cline, Betty White, Michael Walker, et al., *A Middle School Design*, Duval County (Florida) School District, 1990.
3. The authors wish to acknowledge the Duval County school district for their permission to use the material in this chapter. (The authors served as chief consultants in the middle school conversion development.)

SELECTED REFERENCES

Dade County School Board, *Recommended Literature: An Annotated Bibliography of Outstanding Books for Reading Aloud, Class Study, and Independent Reading.* Grades PK–12 (Miami: Dade County, Florida Public Schools, 1991). *Note:* This list contains many multiethnic, multicultural selections.

Middle School Task Force, *Caught in the Middle* (Sacramento: California State Department of Education, 1988).

National Association of Secondary School Principals, *Schools in the Middle: A Report on Trends and Practices* (Washington: DC: NASSP, 1990).

National Science Teachers Association, *Science Education for Middle Level Students* (Washington, DC: NSTA, 1991).

Wiles, Jon, and Bondi, Joseph, *The Middle School America Needs* (Tampa: Wiles, Bondi and Associates, Inc., 1990).

_____, *The Book of Learning Skills and Objectives for Middle Schools* (Tampa: Wiles, Bondi and Associates, Inc., 1991).

5

Organizing for Instruction

*You can either knock down walls
or go around them.*

INTRODUCTION

As discussed in Chapter 1, the regimented ("corrective") approach to instruction used formerly in the junior high setting has been replaced with student-centered teaching techniques in the middle school setting. This change is the result of research findings on early childhood development—particularly the unique physical, emotional, social, and intellectual needs of ten- to fourteen-year-olds. Consequently, middle school teachers, administrators, and support staff are applying new strategies tailored specifically for emerging adolescents.

Efforts are under way to structure broader and more relevant programs for the diverse student population found in the middle grades. To ensure continued movement in this direction, middle schools are becoming more flexible in terms of how they teach and where they teach.

All middle schools consist of five variables—students, teachers, time, space, and media/curriculum[1]—and skillful manipulation of these variables allows staff to provide flexible curriculums and organizational structures. The result is more individualized ("student-centered") instruction, which leaves room for each student to exercise his or her growing independence *while at the same time* satisfying state mandates regarding core subjects to be learned.

Prior to this change, traditional intermediate schools operated on a principle of uniformity, a principle based on certain assumptions about how all students learn. For example:

□ *Uniformity of students:* Once a group was formed, that same group remained unchanged for a wide range of learning activities.

□ *Uniformity of teachers:* The same teacher was qualified to teach all aspects of a subject during the same school year. All students required the same kind and level of supervision.

□ *Uniformity of time:* Appropriate time for learning a subject was always forty to sixty minutes per day, six or seven periods per day, or thirty-six weeks out of the school year. All learners were capable of mastering the same subject matter in the same length of time—for example, everyone was given the same test on the same material on the same day, or everyone was passed from level one to level two in June.

□ *Uniformity of space:* The same classroom was equally suitable for a spectrum of learning activities—no conference rooms for teacher-student conferences, no large group facilities for mass dissemination of materials. A group of thirty to thirty-five students was most appropriate for a wide variety of learning experiences.

□ *Uniformity of media/curriculum:* The same learning media were appropriate for all members of a group—for example, the same assignment from the same workbook was given to the entire group.

However, research has shown there to be nothing "magical" about rigid class size, fixed classroom space, or repetitive schedules. Therefore, emphasis is on designing facilities and schedules that allow for a variety of group sizes based on individual learning needs and the activities to be performed. The effect is that a child's learning progress is defined by his or her unique mastery of skill levels or competencies *at the child's own pace.*

"Ideal" school buildings do not guarantee flexibility. For example, a number of good middle schools operate effectively in buildings originally designed for conventional high school or junior high programs. They do so either by knocking down walls (symbolically and literally) or going around them. Conversely, some highly rigid structures remain in place despite new, open-space "classrooms" designed specifically for middle graders. All of which is to say that flexibility of *physical space* does not guarantee flexibility (or effectiveness) of *instruction*.

This chapter discusses four innovations geared toward breaking down this organizational lockstep: team teaching, interdisciplinary teaming, flexible modular scheduling, and nongraded structure. Appendix 5 at the back of the book provides a sample comprehensive proposal for organizing a middle school. Components of the sample are referred to as part of specific discussions throughout the chapter.

TEAM TEACHING

What Teaming Is

Team teaching (or teaming) is a type of instructional organization in which two or more teachers pool their resources, interests, expertise, and knowledge of students and take joint responsibility for meeting a significant part of the instructional needs of the same group of students.

In terms of organization and facilities, many middle schools have accommodated team teaching by clustering teachers and students in designated sections of the building and by providing a common instructional block of time and common teacher planning time. Newly constructed facilities have been built with open-space areas and movable walls, whereas older buildings have been renovated for this purpose.

Teaming makes maximum use of teacher strengths and allows teachers to work flexibly with individuals, small groups, and large groups. In the middle school this strategy involves two types of skills: ability to facilitate student academic and social growth, and ability to work cooperatively and/or collaboratively with other adults. For example, in terms of promoting academic and social growth, teaming offers support and aid in attempts to provide better instruction and classroom management; gives students and teachers the feeling of belonging to a small group that has common goals and whose members are supportive of each other; permits correlation of subject-matter content and concepts through planned repetition and reinforcement; and provides opportunity to share ideas, plans, student information, and classroom observations. In terms of students learning to work with other adults, team teaching requires a common group of students who are assigned to a common group of teachers who share a common planning time, which results in a more productive classroom/school environment. Consequently, this student-teacher interaction fosters students' sense of human interdependence, responsibility, and citizenship. These areas have particular import at this stage of child development.

Aside from contributing to the overall quality of education, team teaching is intended to serve a number of organizational purposes in the middle school. Among these are improving staff utilization, serving diverse student populations, presenting more sophisticated instructional media as a result of scientific and technological advances, providing more varied educational experiences, and treating students as individuals.

In fulfilling these purposes, many middle schools have clustered teachers and students in certain sections of the building and provided for a common instructional block of time and teacher planning time. Whereas new middle schools are constructed with open-space areas and movable walls, older buildings may be renovated to accommodate this instructional approach.

Some Advantages of Team Teaching

Students benefit from team teaching in a number of ways:

□ Superior teachers are shared by *all* students.
□ The effect of the "poor" teacher is neutralized.
□ Students receive more individualized attention.
□ Pupils can be grouped based on shared interests.
□ Students can enjoy independence and broaden their boundaries while retaining security/nurturing as they learn responsibility.
□ Students can work across grade lines with subject-matter specialists.
□ Pupils have access to more than one image/role model.

Teachers benefit from the team approach in the following ways:

□ Their professional talents and interests are used more effectively.
□ They can share information and ideas that help solve problems and improve their professional backgrounds.
□ Team teaching provides inservice education opportunities.

Generally speaking, both students and teachers benefit from the flexible scheduling, which makes for better correlation of school work, homework, and field experiences. The wider range of grouping possibilities (e.g., small groups, large groups, independent study teams) also facilitates a wider resource of talent, knowledge, skills, and experience from which students *and* teachers derive new educational opportunities. Finally, the fact that the "whole" of the participants working together will be more productive than the "sum" of individuals working in isolation can only further the primary goal—improved quality of education.

Some Disadvantages of Team Teaching

This discussion would not be complete without also looking at certain problems that can arise with the team approach. For example:

□ Teachers may not always agree on how to evaluate or discipline individual students.
□ Unless a facility has provided blocks of common time, teachers may find it difficult to plan lessons, activities, and study during the day.
□ Conflicts may arise as a result of differing teaching styles.
□ Unless teachers are trained specifically for the middle school environment, they may lack confidence in this unique setting.

- The need for a designated leader, the danger of pupil detachment in a large group (if this is the case), or the tendency toward restriction of a teacher's freedom of action can create further conflict.
- Sometimes teams tend to "gang up" on certain students.
- Unhealthy competition may emerge among teams.

What Teaming is *Not*

Teaming is not "turn" teaching; that is, it is not a large group situation in which teachers take turns conducting classes. Nor does teaming imply homogenization of teaching styles, which probably is not desirable in any case.

Teaming is not comprised of daily coordination of interdisciplinary subject matter, but it does permit opportunity for teachers to coordinate and reinforce subject matter when doing so is convenient, desirable, or advantageous to the students. This coordination need not involve all of the usual subject areas—language arts, math, science, and social studies—every time. Occasional interdisciplinary units (defined below) are a very desirable aspect of teaming and will be discussed later in this chapter. Although teaming does not mean "anything goes," it does give students enrichment experiences (independent study/exploration) while keeping sight of subject content as the primary goal. Whereas the clustering of rooms is desirable, it is not essential. Finally, team teaching is not a panacea but a strategy for identifying problems and working for improvement in a combined supportive setting rather than in an isolated one.

INTERDISCIPLINARY TEAMING

As its name suggests, an interdisciplinary team is made up of teachers from different subject areas who plan and conduct instruction for particular groups of pupils.

Designing Interdisciplinary Units

Over the past thirty years, middle schools in the United States have attempted to integrate subject matter for students through the interdisciplinary unit. As an outgrowth of the core curriculum in the 1940s and 1950s (and earlier), in "unified studies" and "common learnings," the interdisciplinary unit attempts to interrelate subject matter from various disciplines through a central topic or theme. Rather than fuse disciplines together such as core subjects did with language arts, social studies, math, or science, the interdisciplinary unit is conceptually flexible. Rather than a central body of knowledge to be communicated, the interdisciplinary unit allows teachers to weave together many subjects into a creative pattern. (Examples of interdisciplinary topics are included in Appendix 5 of this book.)

In schools that have highly developed units, the vertical curriculum is first mapped and then unit topics identified. Topics or themes are broad enough to encompass teachings in the four basic subjects commonly found in the middle school—language arts, social studies, science, and mathematics. The topics are also broad enough to include other areas such as guidance, music, art vocational areas, and physical education. Figure 5.1 illustrates themes by nine-week grading periods (6-1 is first nine weeks, 6-2 is second nine weeks, and so on).

The interdisciplinary approach is based on at least five premises:

1. This approach is a way of organizing the school in terms of curriculum, instruction, and human and material resources.
2. Disciplines do not lose their integrity because of a team approach; rather, each discipline's unique contribution to problem solving is demonstrated.
3. The interdisciplinary approach is compatible with team teaching; in addition, it is compatible with flexible scheduling and nongrading (to be discussed later in this chapter).
4. The approach is ideally suited to the middle school student because it provides many and varied opportunities for success, exploration, and growth.
5. All disciplines need not combine for all interdisciplinary teaming; only teachers of complementary skills may combine. Moreover, some areas of instruction may best be taught in the discipline to which they belong.

FIGURE 5.1   Interdisciplinary (thematic) unit titles

6-1	**7-1**	**8-1**
Ancient Civilizations	Plants of the Earth	Decision Making
People and Environment	Dependence	Problem Solving
World Cultures	Population	Class/Cultures
Family	Disease Prevention	Exploration
	Around the World	
	Contraptions	
6-2	**7-2**	**8-2**
Our Physical World	Structures of World	Safety
Weather	People's Habits/Customs	Atomic World
Personal Health	Microscopic World	Change
6-3	**7-3**	**8-3**
Ecology	Life Cycles	People and Machines
Communication	Our Neighbors	Exploration
Endangered Species	Metrics	Milestones in Human History
	Changes	
6-4	**7-4**	**8-4**
Consumerism	Pollution	Recycling
Values and Self	Money	Life-styles
Water and People	Exotic Cultures	Technology
People and Laws	Leisure	
	Conservation	

Factors that are essential to interdisciplinary team teaching are a staff committed to this particular approach as a means of serving students' needs, positive interpersonal and professional relationships among all staff members, and a sufficient amount of common team planning time.

The aim of interdisciplinary teaming is to promote communication, coordination, and cooperation among subject-matter specialists (guidance counselor, art teacher, music teacher, and such) so that students benefit from instruction planned by specialists while escaping the fragmentation that characterizes many departmentalized plans. Working together, interdisciplinary team teachers deal with individual student problems, consult with specialists, integrate subject areas, and consider other school-related topics.

The Wiles-Bondi Curriculum Mapping Model

Because interdisciplinary (thematic) units of instruction interrelate what is taught in each subject area of an interdisciplinary team, the authors, in their consulting work with middle schools, have developed a vertical mapping model of the middle school curriculum. The Wiles-Bondi model includes a sequenced set of middle school content or topics in a subject area, a list of major concepts or generalizations taught in that subject, and a list of intended outcomes and specific skills to be mastered.[2] Logical connectors from either content or concepts are identified, and they form the theme for an interdisciplinary unit. (Remember, not all disciplines need combine for an interdisciplinary unit.) Units may vary in length from two days to two weeks.

Too many middle school teams pick topics "out of the hat." Those topics may be interesting to students and teachers but may not "fit" what is being taught during the grading period (either nine-week or six-week grading periods are most common in middle schools). Teaching an interdisciplinary unit that fails to take into consideration what is being taught during a grading period further disjoints an already unrelated curriculum. There must be continuity and cohesion within a program.

Team teachers are also content-focused and in most school districts each delivers his or her curriculum 180 days a year. If comfortable with delivery of their content, teachers will be more willing to find connectors that reinforce learning from one discipline to another and reduce isolation of one subject area from another.

The mapping process (usually a grading period is mapped on one sheet for ease of communication among teachers on an interdisciplinary team) is a simple way to provide instant communication about what each team member is teaching in his or her own discipline. (A sample of the curriculum mapping process is shown in Appendix 5.)

Much emphasis has been on affective (e.g., arousing feelings, emotions) education in middle schools, and rightfully so. This sense of "feelingness" is present in the concept of "Family" teams that spend much of their time talking about student needs, discipline, parent conferences, and reward activities—and this is what should be happening. What was missing, before schools adopted the Wiles-Bondi process, was daily or weekly discussion about what was being taught in the subject areas. Upon visiting team meetings, we found teachers heavily engaged in discussions about student rewards or discipline problems—except that after the bell these teachers would return to their classrooms and teach their subject matter in isolation. Once every few months, a team would teach an interdisciplinary unit (often borrowed from another school and unrelated to what was being taught) and then return to affective discussions. With a mapped curriculum, teams can discuss student needs *and* content, concepts *and* skills that are being taught to the same students the team shares. Interdisciplinary units have become natural outgrowths of those discussions, and students find teachers often relating their course topics to what was taught in the students' previous class period. For instance, students are more attentive when the language arts teacher uses vocabulary from social studies and science and the science teacher talks about the climate of the Egyptian desert along with the social studies teacher's teaching about the country of Egypt.

It must be pointed out here that the authors are not minimizing the affective approach of middle school teams but are attempting to make teams more functional and eliminate the conflict of middle school teachers being either student-centered *or* subject-centered; they must be both. In addition, interdisciplinary units of instruction include many affective activities, and when combined with cognitive activities they present a holistic approach to learning. Figure 5.2 is an example of a curriculum map for a subject area for one grading period.

Distinct from team teaching, interdisciplinary team organization is a way of structuring teachers, students, resources, and facilities. Even if a middle school does not utilize a team approach, interdisciplinary team organization when used to its fullest extent will provide benefits tantamount to teamed instruction.

Three Functions of Interdisciplinary Teams

In its commitment to promote communication, coordination, and cooperation among specialists, interdisciplinary team teaching has three major functions: instruction, organization, and establishment of team identity/climate.

Instruction

A team of teachers with common students and common planning time can provide many innovative instructional opportunities. On a practical level it is the classroom teachers who best assess the academic needs of their students. Agreement among team members will allow teachers to move students about in the most appropriate groupings for instruction. The new student may then be assigned a schedule based on teacher recommendation rather than on having the class filled with the least number of students.

Common planning time provides an opportunity for teachers to meet to correlate subject matter into integrated messages for students. For example: Instead of merely *assuming* that every seventh-grade student should become proficient in the use of metrics, why not introduce metrics in mathematics, reinforce its vocabulary in language arts, and practice its usage in science and social studies activities?

Finally, if students are the focus of a common team meeting, constant check may be kept on their educational progress. Teachers may compare notes on frequency of homework completions, rising or falling test scores, absenteeism, and excessive tardiness. Student learning problems can be identified earlier and addressed with consistent effort from all team teachers.

FIGURE 5.2 Curriculum Mapping

Curriculum Area/Subject: Middle School/Jr. High
Gen. Science

Grade Level: 6th

Grading Period: 5th
and 6th weeks

Major Topics	Generalizations/Concepts	Intended Outcomes (Specific Skills/Standards)*	CAT**	SE**	MSPS***
1. *Earth's Resources:* Living Renewable Resources	1. Natural resources are valuable materials found in nature and are used by people to meet their needs.	1. Recognize the interactions among science, technology, and society. The student will			
Nonliving Renewable Resources		7.01 describe specific ways by which an individual can conserve energy.			G211
Recycling	2. Because the earth's population is increasing faster than some resources are being replaced, knowledge of resource use, recycling, and conservation is important to our survival on earth.	7.02 describe how one is a consumer of the various natural resources.			K280
Fossil Fuel Resources		7.03 identify those factors that contribute to or harm environmental quality.			K281
Ocean Resources		7.04 explain how population growth affects Florida's environment.			K285
Cycles: Oxygen Carbon Water		7.05 explain how water quality and quantity affect Florida's environment.			K284
2. *Changes in the Earth's Crust:* Floating Crust	1. The earth's surface is experiencing dynamic change. Studying the two forces acting on the earth help us to understand "how and why" violent change occurs (earthquakes, volcanoes).	7.06 describe how heat influences our everyday lives (i.e., food, cooking and refrigeration, heat, air-conditioning, and weather).			F183
Earthquakes Plate Tectonics Volcanoes Mountain Building		2. Describe major earth/space science concepts and facts from the following topics: meteorology, astronomy, geology, oceanography. The student will			
Fossil Records	2. This understanding can help us prepare for future change, predict future events, and explain our past.	5.21 identify the natural resources found in the ocean.			G221
		3. Describe major earth/space science concepts from the following topics: meteorology, astronomy, geology, oceanography. The student will			
		5.01 name the most common gases that make up the earth's atmosphere.			

*Review the model for standards in Chapter 4.
**CAT—California Achievement Test
SE—Standards of Excellence
MSPS—Michigan Student Progress Standards

A team teacher's instructional responsibilities fall into three categories:

1. *Subject area:* A teacher has been given an assignment in his or her area of certification, along with a course description as mandated by state regulations. Most of the instruction in this area will be done independently of what the other team members are doing.
2. *Interdisciplinary activities:* Many concepts and skills taught in the assigned subject area can be coordinated with or reinforced in other subject areas. When teachers share their course content and lesson planning with other team members, interdisciplinary activities can be developed as feasibility allows. This may involve anywhere from two teachers to all members of the team.
3. *Thematic units:* These units of study are carefully planned around a central theme. Research indicates that thematic units are especially important to the middle school age group in that they can foster an understanding of the interrelationship of all subjects. Consequently, thematic units must involve the entire team and therefore require a great deal of advance planning. It is recommended that two or three projects that involve thematic units be undertaken during the school year.

Organization

In addition to improving instruction delivery, team teachers may agree to set team rules, grading and homework policies, headings for assignments, and the like. Such organizational planning provides students with the guidelines and consistency they need at this stage of their development.

Teachers are able to work together to ensure the most appropriate uses of resources. For example: Why impose on a guest speaker to appear five different times when one appearance at a team assembly would serve? Why not reinforce media skills through subject content along with the language arts curriculum? Why not schedule lessons so that students do not have an overabundance of homework assignments and major tests?

Parent conferencing can become more effective if a team of teachers meets with parents to discuss the educational and social progress of each child. This structured approach makes it easier to pinpoint patterns of learning difficulties and/or behavioral problems.

Teachers working cooperatively often leads to discovery of new insights into school policies and procedures that may help administrators improve schools.

Team Building.   When organizing a team, a number of factors must be taken into consideration. Because each team is comprised of different personalities, personality scales may be used to identify personality types. Other instruments give indications of teaching styles or ability to function in small group planning. Additional factors to be considered include balancing "weaker" teachers with "stronger" teachers and achieving a racial and gender balance on each team. Not all teachers are "team players" and those who are not should be counseled into other school organizations. Figure 5.3 shows some guidelines for team building; others will be presented in Chapter 9.

Team components include a team leader, a team leader council, team principal, other team members, and support personnel. Working together is a foreign notion

FIGURE 5.3 Team building: A worksheet

1. What do we expect from each other as team members?
   _____
2. How will the team make decisions?
   Subgroups?
   Majority-minority?
   Consensus?
   Other?
3. What kind of attendance is expected?
   Regularity?
   Lateness?
   Leaving early?
   Absenteeism?
4. How frequently will we meet?_____
5. How long will meetings last?_____
   Will we start and end on time?   Yes   Not necessarily
6. How will meeting records/reports be kept (e.g., what format)?
   _____
   Who will maintain records/reports?_____
7. How will team communicate with absentees?_____
8. How are members expected to participate in meetings?
   Active listening?
   Paraphrasing?
   Identifying similarities and differences?
   Asking questions?
   Saying the same things *in* meetings as are said *between* meetings?
   Other?
9. How will team assess itself?_____ When?_____
10. How will a team leader be chosen? _____
11. What is expected of the chairperson? _____
    _____
12. How will team exchange feedback?_____
    _____
13. What functions/activities does the team need to plan in order to accomplish its purpose?_____
14. What is the team reporting protocol (e.g., when? to whom?)?_____
15. What specific information will be reported?_____
    _____
16. What work schedule will enable the team to accomplish its functions/activities?_____
    (Include meetings, topics for each meeting, person responsible for planning each meeting, and resources needed—persons, materials, and the like.)

for many teachers who are used to working in their own classrooms with their own group of students. Once a team is in place, questions may arise as to who is responsible for what with regard to team activities. Thus, most administrators either appoint or allow teams to elect a *team leader*. Whereas some principals select team leaders in consultation with teachers or allow teachers to select their own leaders, other schools rotate leaders each year. No matter how he or she is chosen, the team leader is in a unique position to ensure that the information, ideas, and concerns of the team are channeled to the appropriate groups. Following are some key responsibilities of the team leader.

□ *Coordination:* Call, conduct, and preplan meetings (curriculum, student scheduling, discipline, parent conferences, and so forth); techniques for effective team meetings shown in Appendix 5

□ *Administration:* Prepare reports, assist in inventory control (requisition and distribute supplies and equipment), disseminate information to team members, evaluate team program and recommend changes, and the like; sample critique shown in Appendix 5

□ *Leadership:* Orient and assist new teachers; assist substitute teachers; energize and mobilize other team members; communicate effectively and tactfully with parents, faculty, and administration; sample letter to parents shown in Appendix 5

A team meeting agenda might include the following:

□ Making announcements
□ Establishing and evaluating team goals and expectations
□ Solving educational and behavioral problems cooperatively
□ Discussing student grouping and scheduling
□ Discussing school progress reports
□ Planning interdisciplinary units and sharing information
□ Coordinating parent-team and student-team conferences
□ Coordinating field trips and speakers
□ Delegating responsibilities

Finally, the team leader acts as liaison between team and administration and serves as a member on the grade-level steering committee. Team leaders should be compensated for all extra time spent on team business.

The *team leader council* consists of building administrators, team leaders, and other staff members as needed. The council meets weekly to coordinate building activities, provide consistency in building policy and programs, help resolve conflicts between opposing teams, evaluate team performance, organize task forces as needed, and facilitate communication. Team leader council minutes are distributed to all staff members and district supervisors.

Principals ensure that the team building model (Figure 5.3) is implemented in a manner that is consistent with district guidelines. They support teams by providing common time for teams to meet, screening new teachers (with the help of team teachers if possible), and preparing a weekly agenda for the team leader council. In addition, a principal chairs a weekly meeting where, among a multitude of other functions, he or she provides opportunity for staff input; facilitates building goals; assesses and monitors for continuous improvement of staff, students, and curriculum; and troubleshoots problems.

Whereas the team leader is responsible for communicating with the administrative staff, *team members* must work together to keep the group operational. Toward this end, members should share in all decisions, be on time for scheduled meetings, bear equal responsibility for the team's well-being, be open to innovation, and ask for help when needed.

Support personnel are often overlooked in the team's effort to provide optimal instruction to middle graders. Team leaders should invite occupational specialists, guidance counselors, and media specialists (for example) to attend team meetings on a regular basis. These visitors can save hours of work and prove to be (or provide) valuable resources. For example, an occupational specialist can plan field trips, correlate career opportunities with current unit theme, facilitate a "Mini Career Day," or help set up a career resource center. A guidance counselor can work with the team to identify students who have special emotional needs, provide individual or group counseling, or provide peer tutors and peer counselors. A media specialist might provide bibliographies of print and/or nonprint materials, conduct workshops for teachers and students on better use of library materials, or videotape projects and presentations related to a current theme.

Team Goal Setting.   The team must agree on a common set of goals and actions. Although individual teacher requirements will still exist, common areas of concern will benefit students and teachers alike. Possible goal-setting areas include courtesy and respect, preparedness, punctuality, classroom discussion, and quality of work.

Students will also benefit from procedural goals set by the team, such as devising a grading scale, exam schedule, homework schedule, special projects, field trips, guest speakers, and audiovisual coordination.

Team Planning Activities.   As noted earlier, common planning time should be provided daily so that team members can review, plan, and evaluate operations. Specific issues might include:

- Student behavior and/or emotional problems
- Individual progress (e.g., parent–teacher conferences)
- Compatibility of team schedule and student needs
- Curriculum changes throughout the school and within the team
- Advisement activities and home–school communication
- Space utilization
- Specific information to be kept in student folders
- How to translate student needs into course designs
- How to get feedback from students
- Enrichment activities (e.g., career days, speakers)
- Consultation with specialists (e.g., guidance counselor, speech teacher, psychologist)
- Correlation of subject areas
- Other school-related issues (e.g., student council, field trips, assemblies, cafeteria)

One very important team activity is the parent-teacher conference. Whether initiated by parents or teachers, whether to inform or inquire, conferences result in better understanding and improved home-school relationships. Also, parents see that their children are being instructed by an organized teachers group driven by specific goals and strategies.

Prior to the conference the team should agree on specific objectives to be accomplished, discuss each student, and establish a conference time limit. During the conference teachers should encourage parent responses and suggestions, be clear about areas of a child's progress that need improvement, and end each conference on a note of hope.

At no time during a conference should a teacher "label" a child's character traits, focus on past misdeeds, urge or cajole or moralize, discuss himself or herself or his or her children, play psychologist, or use "ganging-up" tactics.

Grouping.   Flexible organization in the middle school means that different student grouping patterns are used in instruction. Some of these patterns include the following:

□ Large group: Consists of up to 120–150 students in a team (or "house"); used to present introductory material, speakers, or to administer standardized tests
□ Medium or class-size group: Consists of twenty to thirty-five students; the most common class grouping
□ Small group: Operates within a class-size group; can be very effective when students have common interests or skill levels
□ One-to-one group: May be teacher-to-student or student-to-student
□ Independent study group: May be a part of classwork, homework, or community study

Figure 5.4 illustrates various student groupings commonly found in the middle school.

One question that often arises is whether there should be homogeneous or heterogeneous grouping in the middle school. The answer is both. Skills groups should be homogeneous but not static; that is, students should be able to move from group to group as they progress along a skills continuum. Students grouped heterogeneously in teams may be grouped and regrouped according to interests, tasks to be accomplished, and skill levels.

School-based Management: Shared Decision Making.   After two decades of top-down management, accompanied by numerous legislative and school board mandates, schools in the 1990s are undergoing a radical transformation where teachers have become full partners in making curricular and organizational decisions.[3]

The middle school, with its team approach, is a perfect vehicle for shared decision making, a model for which is shown in Figure 5.5 on page 116. In this model, directive management and facilitative management work in harmony to meet the needs of those who provide and receive services in the organization.

The norms of the organization have been stated in the goals, characteristics, and expectations. The basic structure of the organization calls for an instructional team formation with a representative on the facilitative management team, which directs the school's resources in response to program change and development within the organization.

Directive management coordinates the concerns of school law, board policy, and policies from the area office. The staff facilitates directive management, and directive management moves into a facilitative role in support of team management.

Clearly, the staff will require extensive training in order to learn the skills necessary to make the model work.

FIGURE 5.4 Sample student groupings

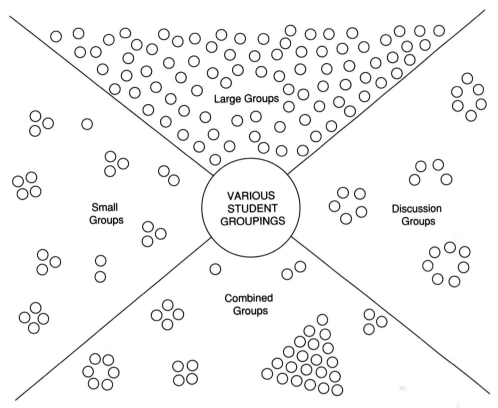

Team Identity and Team Climate

Interdisciplinary team organization promotes within students a healthy sense of belonging. It is generally agreed that students who enjoy school perform better academically. Furthermore, building team identity and team pride will endow students with ownership—a stake—in their school, improve attendance, have a positive effect on behavior, and further nurture their commitment to study.

Some activities a team might undertake to create group identity are discussed below.

Bring team members together. Share time as a large group to present team goals and expectations and to discuss concerns of the total team community. Assemblies are especially effective for speakers, demonstrations, entertainment, or team awards.

Discuss team responsibilities. Some teams involve their students in creating the team's list of expectations. Allow students to take some ownership in identifying team rules and responsibilities. The fewer rules needed to achieve the desired results, the better.

Involve teams in the total school. Help student group function as a catalyst for positive school involvement. For example, one team provided the principal

FIGURE 5.5 Shared decision management model

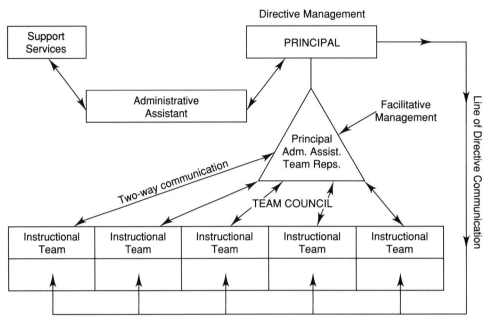

with its own list of fact and opinion questions to be read over the intercom to help prepare for the eighth-grade assessment test. Still other schools allow for team involvement in activities such as student councils and special teacher-student committees such as library or energy committees.

Acknowledge academic achievement. Display lists of honor-roll students by team in prominent areas. A little interteam competition—not too much—may be fruitful. Promote academic recognition ("student of the month") as well as athletic recognition.

Explore new worlds. Field trips can become more meaningful when four teachers pool their resources to provide activities that reinforce the purpose of the field trip. For example: During a trip to Cape Canaveral, students may be given a booklet that requires them to calculate the average miles per gallon the bus gets on the trip (math); rank in chronological order the historical events that led to the flights of the space shuttles (history); complete a crossword puzzle based on a vocabulary list prepared for the trip (science/English); or create a paragraph, that begins "if I could take the space shuttle anywhere in the universe, I would. . ." (writing). Pages of this booklet can be taken apart easily and graded by the assigning teacher.

Expand student's community awareness. Thanksgiving and Christmas baskets for needy families from team members can promote social responsibility. Some teams have adopted a community service organization to support. Still others have become ecologically aware, helping to fight pollution by collecting and recycling aluminum cans. Each of these projects reminds the student of the larger world beyond his or her own.

Spread the word. Many teams publish their own team newsletters highlighting team activities and individual members (hobbies, interests, pets, and awards). Puzzles or contests can incorporate names of students or teachers, vocabulary, or common math problems. A section entitled "from teachers to parents" can facilitate home-school communication.

Celebrate birthdays. Announcements, displays, or cupcake giveaways can make one day very special for each student in the group. Behavior can be improved by the child who feels valued.

Locate a team bulletin board. Make students responsible for decorating a bulletin board (preferably in a hallway) to celebrate holidays, interdisciplinary and thematic projects, and special activities.

Choose a logo. Choose a symbol to represent team spirit and incorporate it onto bulletin boards, wall murals, clothing, and reproducible materials.

Design a t-sheet or team banners. Use logo and school colors to create team identity for special occasions. Some schools have graphic arts departments that can produce t-shirts at minimal cost.

Note: Although team spirit is desirable and important, students must maintain a sense of grade-level and schoolwide identity. Teams should be encouraged to share successful experiences and work together toward improving the total school climate.

The team should not be isolated from other school programs and may be a vehicle through which special-area teachers can lend support, communicate program goals, and monitor student progress.

Planning Cycle for an Interdisciplinary Unit

The following outline is suggested for developing an interdisciplinary unit.[4,5] (An alternate format is suggested in Appendix 5.)

1. Select a theme.
   □ Brainstorm possible themes for your unit.
     —Look for a theme that relates to a district/school/team goal and fits the curriculum map.
     —Possibly survey students' interests before you begin brainstorming. Or, you might want to suggest several possible themes and have your students vote for the one that appeals to them.
   □ Define (expand or narrow) the theme so that it:
     —justifies the time you will put into it.
     —fits within the time you will allot to it.
     —can be mastered by your students in the time you will schedule for it.
   □ Perhaps appoint one teacher on your team to be the leader for the development and implementation of the unit.

2. Work independently.
   - □ Develop *topics* that can be addressed within your individual subjects that relate to the theme you have agreed on.
   - □ Develop one or two *objectives* for your subject-area topic.
   - □ Identify *skills* that your subject can address within the topic.
   - □ Think of specific *activities* that you might like to use. However, do not set these in concrete; the activities for the unit should ultimately be planned jointly with your team.
3. Meet together to define objectives for the unit.
   - □ Discuss each of your topics, objectives, and skills areas.
   - □ Combine each of these into a manageable package for your unit.
   - □ Develop a (suggested) maximum of four objectives and six to eight skill areas. *Note:* Do not think of this step as four separate subject units but one combined unit that must be perceived by your students as something they can accomplish.
4. Meet together to select activities.
   - □ Match activities to your goals.
   - □ Match activities to your subjects. *Note:* Be flexible here!! If you are devoting time to a unit your team has developed, your activity may not match your course description for a few times. Try not to think of this as detracting from your content teaching. Visualize it as "going beyond" your stated curriculum.
   - □ Consider providing student options within the unit. You may have a certain number of required activities combined with optional ones from which the students are expected to select an established number.
   - □ Think about including some open-ended, exploratory activities.
5. Brainstorm resources.

   Media specialists   Field trips
   Electives teachers   Reference books
   Physical education teachers   Commercial kits
   Occupational specialists   Learning center ideas
   Guidance counselors   Community service agencies
   Guest speakers   Parents
   Films/filmstrips/tapes

6. Develop your activities (individually and collectively).
   - □ Order materials if necessary.
   - □ Prepare materials.
   - □ Contact resource people.
   - □ *Divide Tasks.* Determine who is responsible for what. No one person could possibly do all of this. If each person is responsible for one area, the process becomes manageable. *The process will fall apart at this point if everything is put on the shoulders of one person.*
7. Schedule your unit.
   - □ Put the activities and events on a calendar.
   - □ Reserve the library, stage, gymnasium, etc., if needed.
   - □ Schedule guest speakers.

☐ Schedule field trips.

☐ Schedule large group and individual classroom activities.

8. Advertise your unit.

☐ Distribute teasers!! Make your students eager for the unit.

☐ Decorate your bulletin boards with "Coming Attractions."

☐ Send a letter home to parents explaining the theme and objectives of your unit. This would be a good vehicle to get parent permission for field trips or solicit financial support, for example.

☐ Wear slogans on your lapel or collar that relate to the upcoming unit.

☐ Advertise over the public address system.

☐ Announce it in the PTA or team newsletter.

9. Implement your unit.

☐ Do not expect everything to go perfectly.

☐ Have fun with it!!

10. Evaluate your unit.

☐ Posttest your students if desired.

☐ Survey your students' attitudes about the unit.

☐ Analyze the experience from your perspective.

☐ Maintain a resource file. Decide which activities, speakers, events, etc., were beneficial. Which ones would you want to use again? Keep this evaluation on file; it can save time should you decide to repeat the unit next year. You can also share this information with other teachers.

The inspiration for an interdisciplinary unit can come from a current event, a school or team goal, a current curriculum focus, a passage from a textbook, an understanding for the characteristics and the needs of early adolescents, or any number of ideas or comments expressed by a teacher or a student. The realm of possibilities is endless, limited only by your imagination.

FLEXIBLE MODULAR SCHEDULING

A *module* in a school schedule simply refers to a period of time. Many middle schools have adopted flexible modular (block) scheduling, which means that the school day is arranged in modules of varying length. Modules may be fifteen, twenty, twenty-five, or thirty minutes or longer. The smaller the module, the more flexibility in grouping patterns. For example, operating under a fifteen-minute module plan, an hour can be broken into one, two, three, or four time periods. A thirty-minute module plan can allow for two.

Most middle schools operate blocks of time during the school day where the core academic disciplines (science, mathematics, language arts, and social studies) can be taught in longer time periods than those afforded by a single class period. Such blocks consist of a number of modules grouped together (for instance, seven modules, each of which is thirty minutes) where four-member teams teach a group of 120–135 students. Blocks of time allow for correlation among the participating disciplines and permit teachers to utilize instruction for small or large groups with varying lengths of time depending on the needs of students. An example of flexible

FIGURE 5.6   Parts of a block schedule

6th	7th	8th	
			8:30 ①
ADVISORY	ADVISORY	ADVISORY ◄	
			8:50
BASICS	EXPLORATORY/ PHYSICAL EDUCATION		
90*	90	BASICS— ◄ English Math Reading Science Social Studies	②
EXPLORATORY/ PHYSICAL EDUCATION	BASICS 60		
90	LUNCH 30		
LUNCH 30		210	12:20
		LUNCH 30 ◄	③
BASICS	BASICS		12:50
		EXPLORATORY/ ◄ PHYSICAL EDUCATION	④
120	150	90	2:20
ENRICHMENT AND REMEDIATION 40	ENRICHMENT AND REMEDIATION 40	ENRICHMENT ◄ AND REMEDIATION 40	⑤ 3:00

* Indicates number of minutes

modular scheduling appears in Figure 5.6, and ideas on how to develop flexible scheduling appear in Figure 5.7 and 5.8.

Variables That Affect Scheduling

A number of variables affect attempts to develop a block schedule, any one of which will cause deviation in the traditional rotating pattern (in which the same students move as a group during the school day). Among these variables are:

Size of school: Schools with populations of eight hundred to twelve hundred students have enough teachers who do not teach core subjects to take up the student slack while core teachers are otherwise engaged (planning, at lunch). Smaller schools (fewer than six hundred) occasionally will need to have core

FIGURE 5.7   Scheduling: A step-by-step process

1. Determine total number of students.
2. Identify total number of teaching and support staff.
3. Identify all teaching, planning, guidance, administrative spaces.
4. Examine bus schedule.
5. Identify school day for students and teachers.
6. Identify all shared or itinerant staff.
7. Identify all special-needs students.
8. Schedule lunches.
9. Determine team planning periods—during student day or before or after school.
10. Schedule electives and physical education classes to cover planning periods for core teachers.
11. Block core courses together in as large a block of time as possible (e.g., common students, common teachers, common planning time).
12. Schedule teachers in common areas of the building (e.g., four rooms side-by-side for English, math, science, and social studies). *Note:* Science facilities sometimes must be moved to accommodate clustering of rooms.
13. Keep grade levels in one wing or area of the building, if possible.
14. Determine traffic patterns for students exiting core areas to lunch, electives, physical education. Find the shortest straight line for students to travel.

FIGURE 5.8   Some hints on flexible scheduling

- *Manipulate time.* Shorten school days for intramurals, advisement programs, field days, etc.
- *Create a six-day schedule if desired.* Who said five is a magic number?
- *Schedule music three days a week and art two days a week during fifth period.* This gets in more electives.
- *Try a forty-five-minute period.* Must bells ring every fifty-five minutes? Must there be periods at all?
- *Vary period length.* A period can be thirty, forty, or ninety minutes if desired.
- *Manipulate grade terms.* Why not a split grade term?
- *Avoid letting the tail wag the dog.* Neither high school, band director, nor coach should dictate scheduling (although their input is welcome).
- *Barter.* Talk the superintendent into changing the bus schedule if you'll take on more kids.
- *Barter some more.* Do not hesitate to trade teaching positions if doing so means getting a balanced program and schedule. (Will one more English teacher and one less art teacher make the schedule work?)
- *Look into certification areas.* Are there "sleepers" on the staff who are fully certified to teach in areas other than those they cover currently?

teachers serve in multiple roles so that a rotation works. Regardless of school size, the objective is to create blocks of students who share common teachers, common blocks of time, and, hopefully, common spaces.

Number of teachers: Each middle school needs a certain number of teachers in order to offer a broad curriculum (physical education, fine arts, related arts, guidance services, for example). Without a sufficient number of specialists, the school must rely on regular teachers to assume more diverse responsibilities.

Teacher sharing: If located in a high school, a middle school might have to share teachers with the high school (or junior high). One scheduling task is to break the pattern where the middle school gets its "share" of a teacher only *after* the high school (or junior high) is done.

Student/teacher ratio: Efforts to maintain a uniform student/teacher ratio in all classes during all periods complicate scheduling efforts. With team and other cooperative teaching, students can be grouped according to the current activity (sixty for a field trip, ten for reading review, for example). Being able to break standardized patterns will make for easier scheduling.

Nonspecialist teachers: Teachers who do not teach core subjects (or who do not have special credentials) need to be more diverse in their instruction. Few departments of education have objected to a teacher's being "out of field" for a period—particularly when the school occasionally uses an interdisciplinary curricular design.

Number of rooms: Teachers who feel they "own" their classrooms and are indignant if "their" space sits idle while they are otherwise engaged create major scheduling headaches. Use of "team" spaces, coupled with use of "community" spaces (lunchroom, auditorium, library) scheduled by the team leader council helps remedy space shortage *and* makes more efficient use of available space.

Lunchroom capacity: Due to multiple lunch shifts, middle school principals (or other schedulers) are concerned about lunchroom capacity. But because it is deemed community space, the lunchroom should be put to other use when meals are not being served.

Daily time requirements: Usually, middle schools follow a state-mandated requirement or a districtwide schedule that defers to bus schedules. Requesting extra minutes in the school day should not be overlooked as an option if this will facilitate scheduling.

Pull-out programs: Special programs (ESE, ESOL) may present unique problems. A joint effort between "special" teachers and team teachers can alleviate scheduling crunches.

Grouping prerequisites: Middle schools group heterogeneously when forming groups and homogeneously within teams as conditions dictate. A schedule that begins with all the special groups found in a traditional setting will surely end up being a "traditional"—and ineffective—schedule.

Length of periods: Periods do not have to be a certain length, and there is no Carnegie requirement (as with high schools).

Scheduling Priorities

Principals, teachers, and counselors should draw on a carefully defined school philosophy in determining scheduling priorities, which should be program-driven. Priorities include:

☐ Extended time blocks for selected core curriculum classes

☐ Differentiated assignments of instructional time based on the nature of the subject (e.g., laboratory versus expository instruction)

☐ Alternated time to allow a broader range of learning experiences within fixed time constraints (e.g., classes that meet every day, alternate days, alternate weeks, alternate semesters, or other variations, as appropriate)

☐ Elective/exploratory course options

☐ Shared planning time for teachers who team or collaborate

☐ Scheduled planning time for all teachers

☐ Allocated time for counseling and guidance programs; options to be accommodated within a common alternating time block include adviser/advisee programs; group guidance activities; tutorials and mentoring sessions for special groups of students (e.g., underrepresented minorities, gifted; basic skills–deficient; limited–English proficient, and others)

☐ Shortened or otherwise modified activity schedules to allow for assemblies or other special events without canceling regularly scheduled classes

Principals, teachers, and counselors should view the schedule as dynamic and always subordinate to changing program requirements.

All middle school schedules contain five essential sections:

1. Advisory guidance/homeroom
2. Basics/core instruction
3. Lunch
4. Exploratory/physical education
5. Enrichment/remediation

Figure 5.6 illustrates those five sections in a typical middle school schedule. (Another sample schedule is found in Appendix 5.)

GRADED VERSUS NONGRADED ORGANIZATION

If educators want to do more than give lip service to the idea of individualized instruction in the middle school, then **nongraded organization**—that is, dropping grade-level barriers—must be considered.

Although for accounting purposes many middle schools retain grade levels, they nevertheless devise a curriculum that allows pupils to work at school levels in subject areas. In other words, there is a continuum of learning objectives to be

TABLE 5.1 Some Characteristics of Graded Versus Nongraded Structure

Graded Organization	Nongraded Organization
Each year's progress in subject matter deemed roughly comparable to each year student spends in school.	Each year's school life valued in direct proportion to each year's progress in subject matter.
Each current year's progress deemed comparable to each past or each successive year.	Progress deemed dynamic (e.g., student may advance rapidly one year, slowly the next).
Progress deemed unified, advancing in lock-step with all areas of development, and probably close to grade level in most subjects.	Progress deemed dynamic across studies (e.g., student may leap ahead in one area, lag in another).
Certain content deemed appropriate—and so labeled—for successive grade levels (e.g., subject matter "packaged" by grade).	Certain content deemed appropriate over a span of years (e.g., learning viewed vertically or longitudinally rather than horizontally).
Student's progress measured based on coverage deemed appropriate to the grade.	Adequacy of progress measured by comparing student's attainment to ability and both to long-term accomplishment desired.
Progress deemed inadequate penalized by grade failure; progress deemed satisfactory or better rewarded through enrichment; horizontal expansion encouraged over vertical advancement in work.	Slower progress accommodated by longer time for given blocks of work without grade repetition; rapid progress accommodated vertically and horizontally, with encouragement to move ahead regardless of grade level of work.
Inflexible grade-to-grade advancement, usually at end of year.	Flexible pupil movement whenever indicated (e.g., innovative semester systems).

mastered in each academic area and some students, although classified as seventh graders for example, are actually doing work that should have been mastered in the third or fourth grade.

Other middle schools may cut across grade lines in grouping students, whereas still others have progressed to nongraded organization after being developed initially in a graded format. Table 5.1 summarizes the respective features of graded versus nongraded structures.

SUMMARY

Flexibility enhances the instructional program of middle schools, which have used a number of organizational patterns to break the regimentation found in traditional school programs.

This chapter highlighted four such innovations: team teaching, interdisciplinary teaming, flexible scheduling, and nongraded structure.

Team teaching involves multiple teachers who pool their respective resources, interests, and professional expertise to instruct the same group of students. Interdisciplinary teaming correlates different subject-matter areas so as to complement and reinforce instruction within the same group (e.g., across disciplinary lines). Flexible scheduling breaks the traditional mold of a set arrangement in terms of classroom period length by creating fifteen-, twenty-, thirty-minute modules. Nongraded organization has to do with dropping grade-level barriers so that each student can move from group to group on the basis of his or her unique mastery of skill levels.

Accompanying factors that contribute to organizational flexibility include team building (components of which are a team leader, team leader council, team principals, other team members, and support personnel); team goal setting (there must be consensus of objectives and actions); team planning (a common block of time must be made available for the team to plan, review, and evaluate its activities); grouping (creating large, medium-size, small, one-to-one, or independent study groups); and, finally, shared decision making (a move from top–down management of the past to teacher-participative/partnership management).

Organizational patterns, schedules, and staff usage of selected middle schools illustrate the many creative ways in which time, space, and instructional media have been structured to provide diverse experiences for middle graders. Appendix 5 provides a rich variety of team and interdisciplinary materials as well as a comprehensive proposal for middle school organization.

SUGGESTED LEARNING ACTIVITIES

1. Prepare an organizational plan for your school that would include block scheduling and team teaching.
2. Discuss the advantages and disadvantages of team teaching in the middle school.
3. Prepare a talk to a parent group about flexible scheduling in the middle school.
4. Interdisciplinary instruction has been proposed for your school. What subject areas would you include in interdisciplinary teams? Why?
5. What is the role of fine arts and practical arts teachers in interdisciplinary instruction? Suggest ways they could work with other academic teams in preparing an interdisciplinary unit of instruction.

NOTES

1. Jon Wiles and Joseph Bondi, *Teaming in the Middle School* (Tampa: Wiles, Bondi and Associates, Inc., 1990).
2. _____, *Subject Area Curriculum Maps for the Middle Grades 6, 7, 8* (Tampa: Wiles, Bondi and Associates, Inc., 1991).
3. See *Focus,* Board Reports of the Dade County (Miami, Florida) middle school conversion project, 1989, 1990, 1991, for positive results of the school-based management/shared decision-making process. Each of the 52 middle schools involved in the conversion process (the largest middle school conversion in the history of the middle school) uses the school-based/shared decision-making model. The reader is also referred to the Dade County evaluation document of the middle school program, the first longitudinal-comparative study of progress of middle school students compared with junior high students.
4. _____, *Designing Interdisciplinary Units* (Tampa: Wiles, Bondi and Associates, Inc., 1990).
5. _____, *The Interdisciplinary Unit Sampler* (Tampa: Wiles, Bondi, and Associates, Inc., 1990).

SELECTED REFERENCES

Association for Supervision and Curriculum Development, Commission on Secondary Curriculum, *The Junior High We Need* (Washington, DC: ASCD, 1961).

———, Working Group on the Emerging Adolescent Learner, Joseph Bondi, chairman, *The Middle School We Need* (Washington, DC: ASCD, 1975).

Dade County School Board, Joseph Gomez, principal evaluator; Jon Wiles and Joseph Bondi, chief consultants, *Evaluation of the Middle School Project* (Miami: Dade County School Board, 1991, 1992).

Wiles, Jon, and Bondi, Joseph, *Making Middle Schools Work* (Alexandria, VA: Association for Supervision and Curriculum Development, 1986).

6

Identifying Instructional Leadership

*Instructional leadership in the essential
middle school is everyone's business.*

INTRODUCTION

Instructional leadership is a vital building block in the middle school and cannot be delegated to others by the principal. As the key instructional leader, the principal must possess the skills necessary (see Figure 6.1) to ensure that the program fits the needs of adolescent learners. He or she is assisted in this process by assistant principals, curriculum directors, instructional associates, team leaders, department chairpersons, and classroom teachers. This group functions as a team under the principal's direction to develop, implement, and evaluate the curriculum; articulate the program within the school and among other middle schools; and articulate the program with the elementary and high schools. To carry out these responsibilities, the leadership team must understand patterns of instruction, know how to organize learning experiences, and be able to develop new designs for learning.

However, no body of philosophies, goal statements, administrative policies, or fiscal resources can lend the creative spark that fuels a *successful* middle school program of instruction. Only dynamic classroom teaching can do that; without it, the curriculum will assume the same dull and insipid routine of traditional intermediate programs.

This chapter addresses questions about middle school instructional leadership that must be answered *before* staff development can be successful: Who are the most

FIGURE 6.1   The principal as an instructional leader

To be an effective instructional leader, the principal must—

1. Understand the nature of the transescent learner.
2. Be proficient in new instructional programs in the various disciplines.
3. Be able to develop organizational structures (teaming, interdisciplinary instruction, block scheduling, activity periods, and flexible time arrangements).
4. Be creative, dynamic, and able to communicate well with students, teachers, and parents.
5. Bring in resources to support the instructional program (speakers, consultants, district instructional leaders, and materials).
6. Orchestrate the various resources, both human and material, within a school to support the teaching staff and articulate the instructional program within the school.
7. Possess group leadership skills to work with teams and support personnel (instructional aides, parents, and parent groups such as PTAs and booster groups).
8. Be active in the community and able to tap community resources to help develop the instructional program.
9. Interpret the program to parents, other principals, instructional leaders in the district, and school board members.
10. See the middle school not as an isolated program but part of the school district's total K–12 curriculum.
11. Work closely with elementary and senior high school instructional leaders to articulate the total instructional program of the district.
12. Welcome every opportunity to be in the classroom and teach.
13. Understand various patterns of instruction and develop new designs for learning.
14. Organize a warm and nurturing learning environment.

likely candidates for instructional leaders among teachers? How can they be inspired to come forward? What kinds of teacher involvement can be expected? Who can benefit from teacher involvement?

The chapter also examines instructional patterns, taxonomies of learning, and key learning designs including the process-patterned curriculum.

Appendix 6 provides an instructional checklist, which can serve as an evaluation tool to measure the quality of classroom teaching.

THE TEACHER AS AN INSTRUCTIONAL LEADER

An essential question is how are teacher involvement and enthusiasm kindled in middle school program development? Unfortunately, common responses to this inquiry are predictable and discouraging. Some leaders, doubtful of the need for substantial teacher involvement, erect administrative sand castles. Others, under the misguided assumption that qualified teachers are easy to find, search their staffs for those who fit certain "profiles." Even administrators who recognize the need to groom teacher-leaders may promote staff development—but without considering *why* a teacher may or may not respond; their hope is that these leaders will simply "emerge."

Who Are Likely Candidates?

The past decade of middle school experience has shown that teachers of all backgrounds are potential instructional leaders and that age, sex, race, and other social variables appear democratic in their distribution. However, a common denominator among most teachers who become influential in middle schools seems to be their pattern of professional development.

In studies of teacher professional development, it has been found that classroom teachers go through a regular and predictable sequence of development. The first year of teaching, for instance, is an adjustment period where the teacher becomes familiar with the routine and the environment. The second, third, and fourth years are devoted to perfecting delivery technique and experimenting with instructional style. Somewhere between the fourth and eighth years, teachers reach a plateau and teaching becomes dominated by routine. At this point, teachers must find a new challenge or look outside the profession for personal stimulation. Middle schools must capitalize on this need for professional challenge by identifying and engaging those experienced (often, "take-charge") teachers who are ready for increased responsibility and challenge.

Several signs are helpful in identifying the teacher in search of professional fulfillment. Generally, these teachers have experimented with new techniques in their classrooms over the past several years. They often appear as high-energy individuals whose personal lives may be fulfilled by experiencing activities like art classes or yoga. Many times they have become somewhat argumentative in meetings in an attempt to vent their personal frustration. A very important indicator is that they have not yet dichotomized their "school lives" from their "other lives," and that there is still a flow back and forth between these interest areas.

How Can Candidates Be Motivated to Come Forward?

During this century, social science research has shown considerable interest in the question, "What motivates individuals to participate in organizations?" A number of recent studies support the idea that people expend their energy in situations in which they feel their needs will be met. In short, if environments or tasks are perceived as unrewarding or unfulfilling, people will not volunteer to be active participants. In the campaign for teacher involvement in middle schools, we must encourage those who can perceive the middle school instructional format as potentially rewarding.

Three major types of motivation needs might be met by the middle school curriculum: the need for achievement, the need for affiliation, and the need for power. The search for personal achievement can be an outgrowth of the creativity called for in curriculum materials development. The need for affiliation or belonging can be met through counseling roles and interpersonal aspects of team teaching. Power or status needs can often be met by task leadership opportunities or team leadership roles.

It seems certain that the key to involving those teachers singled out as desirable candidates is to determine what their needs are and match those with middle school development tasks.

What Level of Teacher Involvement Is Necessary?

As instructional leadership in the middle school is identified and encouraged, the type of involvement desired must be clear. Although the middle school presents an opportunity for teachers of extraordinary caliber to surface, it would be a disservice to promote involvement without sincerity. The degree of involvement required and the opportunities available should be spelled out concisely.

In truth, it is necessary to decentralize both decision making and participation in order to have a fully functioning middle school. The flexibility of the program in terms of planning resource allocation, instructional delivery, and evaluation calls for on-the-spot operations. Such irregularity, while troublesome from the administrative vantage point, is also the strength of a highly individualized instructional program.

If we encourage teachers to become involved in instructional leadership, we must be willing to alter traditional administrative patterns to accommodate that involvement. To the degree that good classroom teachers can assume additional responsibilities commensurate with their needs for personal growth, the middle school program will be energized and move forward. Such involvement is the key to a top-quality middle school program.

Who Will Benefit from Teacher Involvement?

In addition to a creative instructional program that is designed, implemented, and evaluated by the same individuals, at least two major payoffs can be anticipated when instructional leadership comes from teachers.

First, energized and involved middle school teachers will teach each other. Rather than a pattern of growth symbolized by scheduled interaction with outside consultants, staff development will occur naturally. The growing, experimenting motif of the individual teacher will be multiplied as teachers "grow on" each other. This interaction of talents and skills will lead to a stronger total staff in the school.

Second, it can be anticipated that the behavior of the teachers will rub off on students. Teacher enthusiasm and energy will encourage student growth; a climate of involvement in organizations is self-reinforcing.

Involved teachers are the key to vibrant middle school programs. Certain teachers are more promising candidates for instructional leadership than others, but they must be encouraged to meet the challenge of leadership. Understanding the professional needs of classroom teachers and helping them see the middle school as a means of satisfying those needs is the beginning point for involvement. A better instructional program and improved human relations can be anticipated from these acts of encouragement.

INSTRUCTIONAL PATTERNS IN THE MIDDLE SCHOOL

In that the goals of a middle school are unique, so too are its instructional patterns. Teaching in such an environment, then, presents a startling contrast to other, more traditional intermediate programs. Primary differences in the instructional pattern of the middle school comes more from the *orientation* of instructional activity than from the *substance* of instruction. Thus, the middle school represents a new way of educating preadolescents as well as a new form of education. Middle school instruction and traditional approaches are compared in Table 6.1.

From Table 6.1 it can be seen that instruction in the middle school represents a new definition of the teaching/learning process. The new instructional roles are drawn from the philosophy and goals of middle school education and differ from traditional instructional patterns in the following six categories:

1. The purpose of the instructional process
2. Beliefs about students learning capacities
3. Roles of teachers and students in the learning process
4. The way knowledge/information is utilized in formal learning
5. The means by which learning experiences are organized
6. The ways in which pupil progress is to be evaluated

Study the instructional checklist in Appendix 6.

THE ORGANIZATION OF LEARNING

In developing learning experiences in the middle school, two major concepts are important: continuous progress and guaranteed progress. Whereas the ideal condition for any student is continuous growth and development in a number of dimensions of growth, the middle school also must ascertain that all students do in fact grow and develop. The middle school represents the last general education the student will experience.

Previous educational programs in the intermediate grades have been content to pursue learner growth on a plane, being concerned more with rate of development

TABLE 6.1 Middle Schools and Traditional Intermediate Patterns of Instruction

Middle School Patterns	Traditional Patterns
Recognize and respond to the uniqueness of each learner	Treat learners in a uniform manner
Involve the student in the learning process as an active partner	Give the teacher all responsibility for the learning process
Provide an instructional balance in the emphasis given different realms of development	Possess an overriding concern with intellectual capacity
Integrate information/knowledge bases in instruction	Emphasize the distinctiveness of subjects/disciplines
Present learning opportunities in many forms through many media	Present the learning opportunities in standard didactic forms
Emphasize the application of information and skill development	Provide little opportunity to deal with meaning or application
Teach through student interests and needs	Teach according to predetermined organization of information
Define the purpose of instruction in terms of pupil growth	Define the purpose of instruction according to organizational/administrative criteria such as units of credit and graduation requirements
View teachers as guides or facilitators of the learning process	View teachers as subject-matter specialists
Utilize support staff as trainers of instructional personnel	View support staff as specialists in narrowly defined roles
Use an exploratory, inquiry, individualized approach to learning and evaluation	Use standardized patterns of instruction and evaluation

than with order of development. Although a student's rate of development is a legitimate concern, to assume a sequence of learning based on uniform materials is to totally ignore learner growth patterns. In the middle school, it is believed that the learner growth pattern is a more logical organizer for curricular sequence than for materials.

The middle school seeks to build in continuous instructional progress by focusing on learner developmental growth. The essential thought of a continuous progress plan is that learner development is never static but always ascending to higher levels of complexity. If the instructional program in the middle school is to keep pace with the learner, and serve all students, learning design must match learner growth. The learning design must allow for individuality, and it must be multidimensional to reflect depth of learning as well as rate of learning.

During the past thirty years, educators have been at work developing "taxonomies" of learning. These taxonomies, or hierarchies, of learning have sought to communicate that all modes of learning progress from the simple to the complex. This is true whether the learning is of an intellectual, socioemotional, or physical nature. Learning taxonomies are useful in program planning because they allow us to design learning activities for students at a level that corresponds to their development.

An example of developing a continuous progress learning program based on learner growth patterns can be given using two well-known learning taxonomies and sample objectives from the area of academic adequacy.

Two taxonomies of learning, Bloom's Cognitive Domain and Krathwohl's Affective Domain,[1] are attempts to show a rising complexity of learner responses to stimuli. At the lowest level of response, the learner possesses knowledge after having received it. At the highest level of learning, the learner evaluates the meaning of the knowledge and internalizes that knowledge by acting on it. Between these extremes are various stages of dealing with the stimuli mentally or emotionally.

Bloom's Cognitive Taxonomy	Krathwohl's Affective Taxonomy
Evaluation	Internalizing
Synthesis	Organizing
Analysis	Valuing
Application	Responding
Comprehension	Receiving
Knowledge	

As we look at sample objectives of learning in the area of academic adequacy, it is recognized that the objectives are not of equal complexity on these scales.

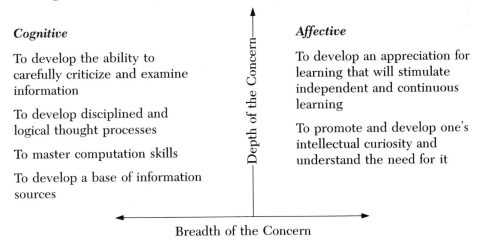

Cognitive

To develop the ability to carefully criticize and examine information

To develop disciplined and logical thought processes

To master computation skills

To develop a base of information sources

Affective

To develop an appreciation for learning that will stimulate independent and continuous learning

To promote and develop one's intellectual curiosity and understand the need for it

Depth of the Concern

Breadth of the Concern

The value of taxonomies and other indexes of learning responses to instructional planners in the middle school is in their demonstration of how learning objectives and activities can be inappropriate. Students have a pattern of readiness for learning, a pattern determined by development in the middle grades, and that pattern is a crucial factor in planning learning experiences. Students cannot analyze what they do not comprehend. Students cannot internalize what they are not receiving.

For each student in the middle school there is an optimal sequence of learning and an optimal degree of complexity for any activity. Instructional leaders must view their curriculum in terms of its increasing complexity and sequence the experiences for each student in terms of his or her development and readiness for that activity. The sequence of the curriculum is focused on the learner, not on the material.

It is particularly important that instructional planners correlate the cognitive and affective dimensions in school. This correlation can be thought of as a diagonal track (see Figure 6.2).

Continuums of learning in the middle grades can be thought of in terms of information, skills, attitudes, and a host of other concerns of program planners. What is crucial for planning purposes, however, is that the program design recognize the range of learners present and make arrangements for the development of learners within that range.

Because of the immense range of development during the preadolescent period, it is believed that no single standard program can adequately serve all learners. A rule of thumb for the range of intellectual development in school has been said to be one year for each year in school. According to this formula (which is probably conservative), there may be up to an eight-year range of achievement among students in the middle grades. A comparable range probably exists in terms of physical, social, and emotional development.

Obviously, any responsible middle school program must acknowledge and provide for such diversity. One possibility to be considered by instructional leaders is the adoption of a minimum-maximum concept of "acceptable progress." The commitment of an educational program with such a perspective is to ensure that all students achieve minimal levels of development while aspiring to assist all learners in achieving their maximum potential development.

The minimum end of the growth continuum recognizes that not all students who enter the middle school will be ready to benefit from its programs. This absence of readiness may be a function of readiness, of environment, or of poor previous educational experience.

Regardless of the reason, instructional planners can expect to meet incoming students who possess identifiable learning problems—those who do not have primary

FIGURE 6.2 "Diagonal track"

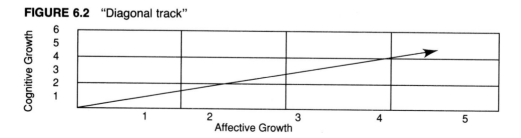

learning skills and/or basal knowledge; those who have inadequate social maturity; those who possess physical defects; and those who have had severely deprived aesthetic experiences. Such students will be excluded, by an absence of readiness, from full participation in the programs offered in the middle grades.

The minimum growth expectation for such a problem student would be a curricular experience that would foster a readiness to benefit from later educational experiences. (Participation in school experiences is a minimal goal.) Whereas each school would have to develop its own expectations, a sample of a minimal commitment to all learners might be the following:

☐ Learning deficiencies (sight, hearing, emotion) will be corrected, if possible, and learning problems confronted.
☐ Primary learning skills (reading, computation) will be mastered, basal knowledge learned, and primary attitudes toward learning developed.
☐ Socially acceptable behavior will be encouraged and rewarded, and each learner will be assisted in forming significant relationships with others.
☐ Each learner will be given an opportunity to discover his own personal identity, to explore adult roles, and to develop personal interests.
☐ Each learner will be given an opportunity to experience sensory discovery and to uncover latent talents.

These goals may seem modest for a student emerging from a program of education in the middle school, but they are in fact ambitious. Our present intermediate programs house thousands of preadolescents who possess none of these minimal capacities.

Discrimination in many school curriculums is not limited to students who are academically or socially delayed in their development. We also often fail to accommodate pupils who are, because of superior educational preparation, maturity, or environment, far advanced in their development. Such students—literate, healthy, socially mature, talented, and self-confident—also must be properly served by the middle school curriculum.

An adequate school program must provide for advanced study opportunities, career exploration, values clarification, talent development, and for the pursuit of individual health-related activity. Although each school must assess and develop individually its commitment to a program of development for learners, sample maximum goals might be these:

☐ To allow for advanced study in academic areas of interest, and for the specialization and development of academic talents
☐ To provide opportunities for increasing learner independence and autonomy, and to assist in the exploration of adult roles
☐ To assist learners in the development of skills and interests pursuant to better health
☐ To assist learners in values clarification activities leading to greater self-awareness, career possibilities, and the expansion of interests
☐ To allow for the development and advanced study of aesthetic talents and for the exploration of individual leisure-time activities.

FIGURE 6.3 Hypothetical profile of student growth

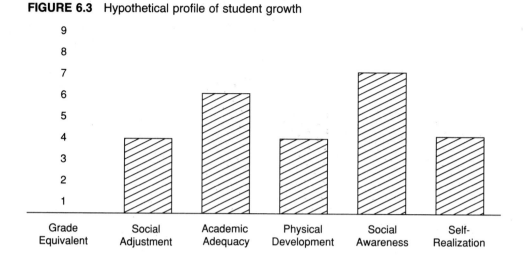

The concept of a minimum and maximum thrust in the middle school curriculum is an attempt to develop learning activities that can benefit all learners. Such a design would span remediation on the one hand, to expansion of potential on the other.

It would be incorrect for the middle school instructional leader to think of any one student as being completely on either end of such a continuum because growth and development patterns in this age group are simply too unpredictable. It is probable, rather, that an individual student would present a mixed profile of development for any planning of classroom experience. The individual student may be concerned with minimal achievement in one dimension of development and with maximum achievement in another. A hypothetical profile of student growth might resemble the bar graph in Figure 6.3.

LEARNING DESIGNS

Building Blocks, Branching, Spirals

In addition to providing a multidimensional instructional program that will serve all learners, middle school instructional leaders must develop new designs for learning that will tie the school to the needs of the individual student. As already established, traditional learning designs will *not* serve the middle school adequately.

In schools throughout the United States, fairly standard learning designs can be found at the classroom level. Even though many such designs are not the result of deliberate planning by teachers, they often are the product of established philosophical positions regarding the purpose of education.

Three well-known designs often found in the middle grades are knowledge-based. That is, they gain their rationale or order from the assumption that education exists to transmit knowledge. Although these designs have been given many names, we can refer to them by their design function—building blocks, branching, and spiral curriculums.

The *building blocks design* takes a clearly defined body of knowledge and orders it into a pyramidlike arrangement. Students are taught foundational material that leads to more complex and specialized knowledge. Deviations from this prescribed course are not allowed because the end product of the learning design is known in advance. Equally, activities that do not contribute directly to this directed path are not allowed due to the "efficiency" of the model. Such designs represent the most traditional knowledge-based design.

Another very common learning design is the *branching design*. Branching is a variation of the building blocks design but incorporates limited choice in terms of what is to be learned. This plan, too, recognizes the value of foundational material that must be mastered by all but allows choice within prescribed areas beyond that common experience. Like the building blocks design, branching prescribes the eventual outcomes of the learning experience, although the prescription is multiple rather than uniform. In terms of classroom activities, this design allows for some variation, but again within tightly defined boundaries of acceptance.

A third common knowledge-based design is the *spiral* configuration. According to this design, learning in specified areas is continually revisited at higher and higher levels of complexity. Whereas the "tightness" of this design is more difficult to observe, it controls what is taught and even predetermines the timing of the delivery to the student Classroom activity is, of course, developed to fit the topics being "uncovered."

In visiting a classroom in the middle grades, an observer might see any of the three described designs in operation. In the building blocks design, all students would be experiencing nearly the same program of learning, at the same time, with the same outcome expectations, and with few if any distracting extracurricular learning activities. In the branching classroom, students might be grouped according to academic destination and engaged in different activities within the room. The activities nonetheless would be predetermined and directed toward future learning experiences. In the spiral classroom, learning would appear like the building blocks design, but would use increasingly diverse and sophisticated "methods" to achieve the planned outcome.

All three of these common intermediate learning designs operate from the assumption that education is the act of becoming schooled in specified bodies of knowledge. Because of this basic assumption, these designs are restricted in their ability to gear learning to the needs of the individual student. They cannot individualize the instructional process because they cannot significantly deviate from predetermined learning expectations.

Knowledge-based learning designs are characterized by set bodies of knowledge to be mastered, universal experiences for students, standardized learning environments, and tightly defined learning outcome expectations. They do not exist to serve the learner, but rather to serve tradition and the hierarchy of knowledge-based learning.

Throughout this book, the assumption has been made that the curriculum for the middle school should be designed to serve the learner who is engaged in experiencing the program. Because of this assumption, we have looked at philosophic possibilities, ways of assessing common needs of learners, theories of individualized learning, and arrangements that schools can make at the building level to prepare for such a personalized approach to learning. If we are to develop a program of education that is significant for students in the middle school, we must abandon knowledge-based designs and refocus our perspective of the learning experience.

Process-Pattern Designs

An alternative design to traditional knowledge-based designs is what will be called the process-pattern learning design which, as the name implies, seeks to define education as a process, and school as a medium for learning. *It is a design that attempts to focus learning on each student and her experience, rather than on a predetermined body of information.* It is a design concerned with *how* learning occurs more than *what* knowledge is mastered. As such, the process-pattern design seeks to redefine the purpose of schooling in a philosophical sense by making education serve the learner as an individual.

The essential concept underlying the process-pattern instructional program is that, in terms of ultimate objectives, the purpose of education is to enable each learner to understand herself, to become whatever she is capable of as an individual, and to find ways to allow those capacities and talents to serve society as a whole. Schools, as institutions of society, are mediums for that process.

It is believed that, by this definition, the process of becoming educated must be an individual phenomenon. *To design a learning environment relevant to all students, we must have a highly individualized environment characterized by flexibility and open-ended outcomes.* In terms of design, the process-pattern curriculum seeks to set up learning opportunities, to guide the "delivery" or medium of learning, and to emphasize the meaning of the experience.

The process-pattern design, then, is a series of repeating arrangements designed to teach skills, foundational concepts, and meet needs of individual learners.

The process-pattern design can use data about the learners, such as knowledge of the developmental tasks of preadolescents, to focus learning activity. Such student concerns and needs are linked to school-identified learning skills and processes by carefully designed thematic units, as illustrated in Figure 6.4.

Of course, thematic learning is nothing new. It can be found in many intermediate schools across the country. *What is different about the process-pattern curriculum in the middle school, however, is the rationale for the design.* The thematic approach is used to bring the learning activity closer to the student so that learning may be personalized and therefore meaningful to the individual.

Thematic learning that is knowledge-based is generally wasteful in terms of time and resources. If the essential knowledge can be clearly identified, then the efficiency of mastery becomes the only variable in the process of learning design.

FIGURE 6.4   Thematic learning

Many "teaching teams" formed in the middle grades along subject-matter lines have made this painful discovery. In the middle school process-pattern design, however, there is no such concern with efficiency; the concern is only with the effectiveness of the design in promoting individual growth, development, and skill acquisition in predetermined ways.

Of course, the familiar knowledge bases do play a role in the process-pattern curriculum of the middle school. These subject disciplines are time-tested ways of ordering perspectives of the surrounding world. The use of these informational frameworks, however, is incidental rather than predetermined. Subjects in the middle school program are perceived as a means rather than an end of learning. As such, they simply represent one more factor to be incorporated into the learning design in the classroom.

It is important to remember that the planning of classroom learning in the middle school should be an extension of previous planning. The middle school philosophy suggests a student-focused learning plan. The arrangements of environmental variables build in planning flexibility. Finally, a classroom level plan is developed to enable teachers to work with students in many desired ways.

Constructing Process-Pattern Units

The process-pattern unit is similar to units taught in intermediate schools each day except that the primary organizers of the unit are based on the developmental needs of students and recurrent academic processes rather than on predetermined subject matter.

In the process-pattern design, teachers in the classroom construct units of learning activity by manipulating a number of ever-present variables. Included among these are things known about learner needs and interests, skills and processes identified by the school as essential during this period, and manipulative instructional factors that make up the medium of delivery in the classroom.

Chapter 1 presented the needs and interests of the preadolescent under the generic title of developmental tasks. It was noted that all students of this age have similar concerns related to growing up (see Table 1.2).

These developmental needs and interests of students in the middle grades were grouped into five broad categories from which points of intersection by the school can be used in the instructional program:

Physical development, promoting physical and mental health, physical conditioning and coordination; understanding hygiene, sexual functioning, nutrition

Academic adequacy, developing basic literacy, skills for continued learning, learning autonomy; introduction to primary knowledge areas; refinement of critical thinking; exploring career potential

Aesthetic expression, stimulating aesthetic interests, aesthetic appreciation; developing latent artistic talents, leisure-time activities

Social awareness, refining social skills; accepting responsibility; understanding interdependence of individuals; exploring social values; promoting human relations; developing interpersonal communication skills

TABLE 6.2 Process-Pattern Curriculum Choices

Length of Unit	**Unit Objective**
Daily	Exposure
Weekly	Familiarity
Monthly	Mastery
Quarterly	Analysis
	Application
Unit Location	
Classroom	**Unit Grouping Patterns**
Learning resource center (LRC)	Individual study
School grounds	Paired study
Immediate community	Team study (3–6 students)
Beyond community	Small group study (7–20 students)
	Large group study (21 + students)
Unit Interaction Pattern	
LRC research/individual exploration	**Unit Medium of Delivery**
Question/answer inquiry	Lecture
Group question	Individual reading
Team problem solving	Programmed materials
Creative projection	Film, videotape, audiocassette
	Debate/theatrics
Unit Student Evaluation	Outside speaker
Standardized tests/measures	Field trip/visitation
Teacher-made tests/measures	Simulation
Student "sample work" folders	
Narrative diaries	
Student-teacher contract	
Progress conferences—project products	
Criterion-referenced demonstrations	

Self-realization, promoting self-understanding and self-acceptance; identifying and accentuating personal strengths; exploring individual values; expanding personal interests

As teachers plan classroom learning activities, these student needs and interests serve as "connectors" or "intersectors" into the lives of the learners by suggesting themes or interests that allow communication with each preadolescent.

Another category of variables essential in planning learning design in the middle school are those skills and processes that teachers feel must be mastered at this level of schooling. Although this category of planning variables is totally dependent on local educational conditions and expectations, identification of these items can be best achieved by viewing the educational system as a continuum. By the time the student has reached the middle school, which skills does he possess? What skills are essential, and what skills are desired? Beyond the middle school, what skills and processes must the student possess to benefit fully from learning opportunity? Which of these skills and processes are essential and which are desired?

An example of the kinds of skills and processes a teacher might deal with in the middle grades can be extracted from the language arts. Five major skill areas might be reading, spelling, speaking, writing, and listening. These areas might be made up of the following specific skills:

Reading	**Spelling**	**Writing**
Developmental—word analysis, comprehension, structural analysis, phonetic analysis	Familiarity Utilization/application	Creative writing Note taking Outlining Letter writing
Functional—locating, organizing, interpreting, evaluating information	**Speaking** Informal Dramatization Story telling Reporting	**Listening** Appreciation and enjoyment Critical and evaluative Application

As teachers or groups of teachers seek to identify and order those skills and processes they believe need to be mastered in the middle grades, it is helpful to think initially of them holistically as skills needed for particular experiences in the future. Perceiving the skills holistically will assist the teacher in planning units that integrate skills into a "whole" approach to learning.

Finally, planning units for a process-pattern curriculum means choosing among a host of manipulative instructional variables that are possible in the classroom. Decisions as to which arrangement to employ in a given unit should be made on the basis of the unit's composition. Some of these choices are found in Table 6.2.[2]

As teachers or teams of teachers ponder these choices and place emphasis in any given unit, a pattern emerges that is unique in composition but uniform in underlying processes. Although the format of units avoids monotony, the essence of the learning experience is regular.

According to the schedule and administrative order of the school district, the teacher-planner should arrive at a number of units to be developed for the coming school year. (Somewhere between four and six units is probably a workable number for the middle grades.)

The task for the curriculum planners is to weave a design, a multidimensional organizational structure, made up of a variety of learning activities, learning approaches, learning skills, learning levels, learning objectives, and so on, that will facilitate classroom interaction.[3] It is important, given the need to have a balance between the many expectations of the teacher and the needs of the students, to see that greater emphasis is given to certain areas in different units. One unit, for instance, might be focused on the development of learning skills, be dominated by a mastery orientation, and take place primarily in conventional learning areas. Another unit might be more concerned with the development of individual values and perceptions and could occur outside the traditional learning locations.

In planning the year as a whole, the essential concept, is to build in diversity and balance in the design. All of those areas deemed important by the planner should be given sufficient attention sometime during the year so that program is comprehensive.

In developing units, it will be necessary to identify unifying themes, which will give an overall cohesion to the varied activities of the unit and will fit the mapped curriculum. Possibilities for such themes are infinite. Keeping in mind the transescent student and observing interaction patterns between students will assist the teacher in identifying the best themes for a particular classroom. Examples are advertising, effects of technology, pollution, transportation, nostalgia, communication, the future, and comedy.

In the sample calendar shown, five units use five general themes:

Sept	Oct	Nov	Dec	Jan	Feb	Mar	Apr	May	June
Effects of Technology									
		Advertising							
				Pollution					
						Nostalgia			
								The Future	

Once the major themes for the year have been selected, the planner constructs a learning experience that will achieve educational objectives and match the learners' needs. From each major list of variables, the planner seeks key ingredients:

Technology Unit

Developing skills for continued
    learning
Refinement of critical thinking   } Student Needs
Exploration of career potential

Utilization of library resources
Creative writing
Note taking
Spelling familiarity
Data analysis   } Skills and Processes
Hypothesizing
Synthesizing information
Charting and graphing

Eight-week Unit

Familiarity, analysis, application
Classroom, learning resource
    center, community
Individual and small group study
Individual reading, simulation,   } Instruction
    field trips
Inquiry technique, problem
    solving
Contracts and project products

Following the selection of the key ingredients for the unit, the planner then begins to construct the learning activities that will produce the desired outcomes. For each unit there should be a general plan and then unifying activities that tie all classroom activity together. The following is an example of a technology general plan.

TECHNOLOGY GENERAL PLAN

For this unit the students will become a community of people during a period of great technological change (mechanization of America 1800–1840), and will assume an occupation or trade that is representative of the period.

Unifying Activity Week I:

All students will investigate life during this period of our national history by attempting to identify an occupation that existed during the era. Attention can be directed to the task of identifying those jobs extending from a previous era, those jobs originating during the era of study due to technological change, and those occupations existing today that date from this period.

Subactivity:

Reading biographies for overview of period

Limited historical research of period

Writing short descriptive essays about occupations of age

Build list of unusual words discovered in research

Identify occupational counterparts in community

Gather comparative statistical data on era under study

Unifying Activity Week II:

Each student will participate in the production of a product or the offering of a service that exemplifies a trade of the period of study. The student may wish to choose an early form of the occupation now held by a parent. Occupational activities may be of three kinds: the realistic production of a commodity, the construction of simulated models, or theoretical treatments of technological questions. (Example: Why was transportation during this era limited to foot, horse, and sail?)

Subactivity:

Discussion about the interrelatedness of work

Students become "reporters" and interview workers about jobs

Field trips to industry altered by technology

Scheduling parents as guest speakers about interesting jobs

Conduct "efficiency studies" of workers

Introduce an assembly line in class—make analysis

Charting and graphing of classroom-generated data

Introduce the computer as a tool for people

Unifying Activity Week III:

Students will be asked to draw conclusions about life during this age of change and the effects of technology on their own occupational specialty. The objective of the week will be to develop a set of hypotheses (statements), which each student will individually formulate about work and the effects of technology. These hypotheses will assist the student in clarifying his values and feelings about work. Three major relationships are to be emphasized: the effect of technology on work itself, the ways technological developments can affect community development, and the effects of technological change on the worker.

Subactivity:

Set up assembly-line manufacturing, dealing with issues of quality control, overstaffing, strikes within sections, monotony, efficiency, advantages, disadvantages

Develop a list of "vanishing" jobs in America

Ask students to develop a "scale of trade" among their jobs based on analysis of the merits of their work.

Unifying Activity Week IV:

Students will explore the effects of technological life on a worker. Students will look at such things as specialization in work, degrees of education required, on-the-job independence versus dependence decision-making autonomy, etc. The objective of the week will be to stimulate student thinking about the nature of work, its complexity, its moral implications, and the student's personal preferences toward work.

It may be that during this week the teacher will want to introduce some case studies in order to challenge students to personalize their observations. For example:

George Sterns is a master electrician working in Chicago for Local Union 1440. The union has assigned George to work on a two-year project constructing a high-rise apartment on Michigan Avenue.

George has always loved electricity. In high school, he constructed a miniature relay station unassisted. After graduation, he became an apprentice electrician and seventeen months later an electrician journeyman. Later, George was awarded the title Master Electrician after much study. His wife and family are proud of him.

When George reported to the apartment project, the union representative met him at the gate and walked him to the assigned workstation. Located at this site were two small generators run by gasoline engines that were about the size of lawn mowers. George was puzzled about what he was supposed to do at the site.

The foreman soon came along to explain the job to George. His sole responsibility, the foreman said, was to start the two small engines and be sure they remained running all day. There must be a mistake, George thought. Why pay a man $15.80 per hour to handle a job a child could do?

Later that afternoon, George stopped the union representative to ask him about the assigned work. The representative, surprised at George's attitude, replied that the position was written into the contract months ago. What's more, he added, an operating engineer and a pipefitter would join George tomorrow at the station.

Seeing that George was still uneasy, the representative smiled and, nudging George, said, "Take it easy, Sterns, the union is looking out for you. After all, where else can you get $15.80 for this kind of work?"

Questions:

1. What do you think is bothering George Sterns?
2. How would you feel if this happened to you?
3. Is there anything George can do about the job?

Subactivity:

Ask students to interview their parents about their own jobs.

Try to develop categories of things that separate jobs.

Develop a vocabulary list of words relating to work.

The sample unit could be expanded or contracted in its scope to fit the pattern of the school. It is important to note that in the unit, traditional learning skills such as note taking, graphing, hypothesizing, spelling, and so forth, are all taught through the medium of participatory activity. The interest of the student provides the motivational force for more traditional intellectual exercise. Learning ceases to be an artificial product but rather becomes a process strongly related to the real world.

It can also be noted that in this sample unit on the theme of technology, activities progress through a hierarchy from the simple to the complex. First-week activities were concerned with reading, word building, and gathering simple data, whereas the last week was concerned with the synthesis, analysis, and applications of learning.

As the teacher-planner looks at a number of thematic units during the school year, balance among objectives is important. A unit objectives grid can assist in ensuring balance (see Figure 6.5).

Teachers constructing such units work through twelve simple steps prior to unit commencement that become routine with practice:

1. Identify themes from student interest inventories.
2. Cross themes with existing traditional subject areas (mapped curriculum).
3. Develop broad goals for the unit.
4. Assess these goals in terms of general school objectives.
5. Brainstorm (with students) activities for the unit.
6. Select activities that fit school objectives and unit goals.

FIGURE 6.5   Unit objectives grid

	Unit I	Unit II	Unit III	Unit IV	Unit V	Unit VI	Unit VII
Student Needs							
1	X		X			X	
2		X		X			X
3	X			X	X		
Skills and Processes							
1		X	X			X	
2	X	X		X	X		
3				X		X	X
Instructional Arrangements							
1	X		X		X		
2		X		X			X
3					X	X	

7. Match activities with planning variables, such as group size.
8. Choose overall teaching strategies for activities (inquiry approach).
9. Project (with students) activity "outcomes."
10. Gather materials and other resources for activities in unit.
11. Assign individual learning responsibilities for activities.
12. Order and schedule activities.

In summary, the process-pattern design represents a curricular arrangement allowing for flexibility and creativity in teacher planning. Because the design focuses on interaction and on processes as well as products of learning, it can individualize the instructional process. The process-pattern can incorporate the needs, interests, and tasks of preadolescent development. A complex educational design fitted to the learner, it is philosophically aligned with the goals of education in the middle grades.

Instructional Delivery

The process-pattern unit will not be effective as a learning medium until both teacher and student recognize that they each have new roles and responsibilities in the learning process. Instructional leaders can begin to build this awareness and understanding by doing the following:

1. Recognize the crucial role of the affective dimension in learning.
2. Begin learning activities in areas familiar to the learner.
3. Place instructional emphasis on learning patterns that will have academic application at a later time.

4. Actively stimulate intellectual growth through varied experience.
5. Accept many kinds of intelligence, especially creative thought.
6. Recognize the social quality of school motivation and utilize self-interests and peer interests to school's ends.
7. Tap ever-present sources of motivation by knowing the needs and interests of individuals.
8. Accept many language patterns, recognizing their cultural emphasis.
9. Emphasize *how* to communicate and allow teachers to be seen as people.
10. Realize that groups can aid in the socioemotional growth of students.
11. Realize that values are not easily taught but that values formation is promoted by exposing value alternatives.
12. Understand the importance of out-of-school activity on classroom learning.
13. Acknowledge the power of peer influence and plan accordingly.
14. Capitalize on the potential of media as alternative sources of learning.

SUMMARY

Instructional leadership is essential in the middle school if it is to accomplish its goals. The key instructional leader in the middle school is the principal, who must be able to design an instructional program that will accommodate the diverse group of students found in the middle grades.

The principal is assisted in planning an instructional program by an instructional leadership team whose role is to expedite the program by developing, implementing, and evaluating the instructional plan.

Instruction seeks to set up learning opportunities, guide the delivery of instruction in meaningful ways, and place emphasis on the meaning of learning experiences. Developmental needs of learners and recurrent academic pro-

cesses serve as primary organizers for learning. Taxonomies of learning and a minimum-maximum orientation can assist in providing depth and breadth to instructional planning.

Process-pattern learning units should be developed by teachers by weaving an interaction design from student needs, academic processes, instructional variables, and knowledge bases. In that the focus of instruction is on student growth, outcomes for such units are largely open-ended.

Teachers in the middle school must come to perceive the teaching-learning process in different ways if the middle school program is to succeed. Instructional leadership is the key to achieving that goal.

SUGGESTED LEARNING ACTIVITIES

1. Develop a position paper on the role of the principal as the key instructional leader in the middle school.
2. Discuss the three learning designs discussed in this chapter.
3. Outline the role of each member of the middle school instructional leadership team.
4. Prepare a presentation for your school board on the need for a continuous progress learning program based on learner growth patterns.
5. Design a unit of instruction based on the process-pattern discussed in this chapter.

NOTES

1. Benjamin Bloom, ed., *Taxonomy of Educational Objectives: Handbook I* (New York: David McKay Co., 1956). David Krathwohl, et al, *Taxonomy of Educational Objectives: Handbook I* (New York: David McKay Co., 1964).
2. Jon Wiles and Joseph Bondi, *Designing Interdisciplinary Units* (Tampa: Wiles, Bondi and Associates, 1990).
3. *Motivation Techniques for Middle School Students* (Tampa: Wiles, Bondi and Associates, 1991).
4. *Cooperative/Peer Learning in Middle Schools* (Tampa: Wiles, Bondi and Associates, 1991).

SELECTED REFERENCES

Wiles, Jon, and Bondi, Joseph, *Curriculum Development: A Guide to Practice*, 4th ed. (New York: Merrill/Macmillan, 1993).

_____, *Supervision: A Guide to Practice*, 3rd ed. (New York: Merrill/Macmillan, 1991).

7

Developing Creative Instructional Activities, Materials, and Learning Environments

I hear and I forget;
I see and I remember;
I do and I understand.
   —*Chinese Proverb*

INTRODUCTION

In that its program design focuses on developmental characteristics of emerging adolescent youth, the middle school suggests a need for instructional activities, materials, and learning environments that meet the wide range of achievement levels and interests of those youth.

With this fact in mind, imaginative teachers and support personnel have developed learning activities that embrace a broad range of modes—reading, listening, writing, making, and doing. Similarly, learning materials encompass a wide variety of media—laser discs, videodiscs, DAT (digital audiotape), interactive video, computers, cable access, books, teacher-made and commercial materials, print, wire services, audiotapes, videotapes, audiocassettes, and videocassettes. The interactive nature of materials developed by today's high-tech companies allows the learner access to information that reaches all learning styles, teaching styles, and student abilities.

To accommodate pupils' varying attention and interest spans, the middle school learning environment provides many opportunities for an assortment of activity-oriented and short- and long-term learning experiences.

This chapter, supplemented by Appendix 7, presents samples of creative instructional activities, materials, and learning environments found in innovative middle schools in the United States.

DESIGNING CREATIVE INSTRUCTIONAL ACTIVITIES

Middle school instructional activities are designed to allow students maximum opportunity to interact with peers, teachers, and outside resources in a "real-world" atmosphere. Activities are centered around the three major programs—subject matter, personal development, and essential learning skills. A wide variety of cognitive, psychomotor, and affective learning activities are necessary to account for the full range of students found in the middle grades.

The focus of instruction is on learning by doing, higher-order thinking, and individual and/or group projects. Projects especially offer many advantages, including an emphasis on complex higher-order learning, alternative evaluation over paper-and-pencil tests, allowance for differences in learning styles and learning skills, and development of leadership skills. By means of a learning pyramid, Figure 7.1 illustrates the value of the types of active learning activities inherent in projects.

Teaching and Learning Styles

Instructional methods may include *whole class assignments,* in which all students receive the same assignment, with each student completing it individually; *cooperative learning,* whereby students work in structured teams to achieve a common goal; *interdisciplinary instruction,* through which teachers design assignments that link one discipline to another; and *differentiated* (or *theme*) assignments, made up of two or more assignments that address the same topic but vary in level of difficulty.

FIGURE 7.1   Learning activities (projects)

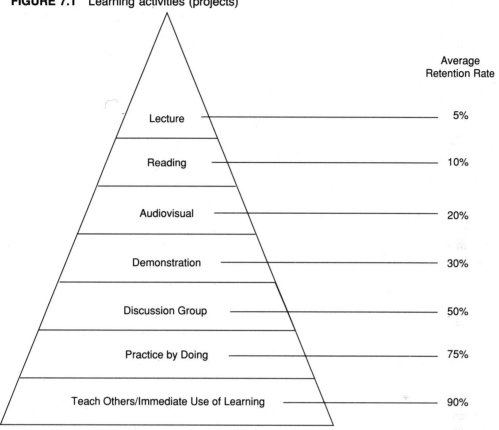

Average
Retention Rate

Lecture	5%
Reading	10%
Audiovisual	20%
Demonstration	30%
Discussion Group	50%
Practice by Doing	75%
Teach Others/Immediate Use of Learning	90%

The 1980s and 1990s have witnessed a number of research studies about how students learn, and middle school educators should be aware of this body of research, which includes findings about cooperative learning, problem solving, decision making, critical thinking, and creative thinking. Some of the findings on learning styles is based on Jung's theory of psychological types (1921), which inventories various instruments that help identify a learning profile based on learner preferences for how information is collected and makes judgments about its significance. All learners are different, of course, so knowing whether a student learns best by working alone, in groups, in an interactive environment, or in a quiet one will help teachers vary their methods, materials, and activities.

Research also indicates that, compared with competitive and individual-oriented learning, cooperative learning promotes higher levels of comprehension for most middle school pupils. Furthermore, it promotes greater acceptance of differences among students and higher levels of self-esteem. Both advantages contribute to resolving the socialization crisis that is part of transescence.

Cooperative learning procedures may be used successfully with other teaching approaches. Johnson and Johnson[1] have contributed much information about the

FIGURE 7.2 Left brain and right brain activities

Left Brain Functions:	Right Brain Functions:
Speech	Awareness without description
Reading	Seeing whole things at once
Writing	Recognizing similarities
Analyzing and linking ideas	Understanding analogies and metaphors
Abstracting	Intuition
Categorizing	Insight
Logic	Gut-level feeling
Reasoning	Synthesizing
Judgment	Visualizing
Counting and mathematical ability	Spatial perception
Verbal memory	Visual memory
Symbols usage	Recognizing patterns
Time management	"Feeling" the way
	Relating things to the present

benefits of cooperative learning; because cooperative/collaborative skills should be a part of every teacher's repertoire, the interested reader is referred to their work.

One way to understand how the mind functions (and thus how learning occurs) is to look at what functions are controlled by the left brain and right brain (summarized in Figure 7.2).

Ways to Improve Thinking Skills

Following are eight steps a teacher can use routinely to improve students' thinking skills:

1. Ensure that students *process* information.
2. Ask broad, open questions.
3. Pause before calling on students.
4. Follow up student responses by asking for clarification, elaboration, evidence, the thought process by which response was arrived at.
5. Have a clear purpose, and plan a sequence of activities to accomplish it.
6. Make students conscious of their own thinking processes.
7. Model thinking processes.
8. Have students ask their own questions.

Four strategies for improving thinking skills are used extensively in the middle school setting: problem solving, decision making, critical thinking, and creative thinking.

Problem solving is the process of defining a problem and selecting a solution. Five steps are identified in the process: identify the problem; assemble facts and information; hypothesize, that is, make an educated guess as to the solution; test the hypothesis through experimentation; and accept or reject the hypothesis. Key words, then, are *describe, identify, state, select, compile, solve, find,* and *assimilate.* (Sample assignment: *Identify* problems posed by the need to evacuate massive numbers of people.)

Decision making is the act of comparing alternatives and justifying a selected response. Five steps can be identified in making a decision: assemble information, determine alternative solutions, compare advantages and disadvantages, choose the most effective action, and justify the choice. Cue words here are *explain, distinguish, categorize, compare, contrast, determine, justify,* and *discriminate.* (Sample assignment: When a disaster of this magnitude occurs, *determine* whether government should publish full details.)

Critical thinking encompasses analysis of differing points of view so as to arrive at a credible opinion. Three stages make up the process: analysis of differing points of view, interpretation of meanings (developing logical relationships and understanding assumptions and biases made), and attainment of a credible point of view. Key words are *analyze, interpret, appraise, disseminate, modify, infer, conclude, explain, justify, support,* and *criticize.* (Sample assignment: Who should be evacuated first? *Justify* your answer.)

The fourth strategy that is popular for enhancing thinking skills among middle school students is *creative thinking,* that is, putting things together in new ways. Four steps make up the creative thinking process: assemble known information, build on that perspective, devise possible solutions, and invent novel ideas. Prompts here are *invent, devise, modify, rearrange, enrich, reconstruct, generate, illustrate, compose, create,* and *manipulate.* (Sample assignment: *Devise* a feasible means of evacuating and relocating the population.)

Each of these teaching strategies, combined with the eight-step routine outlined earlier, can serve to improve thinking skills and thereby facilitate the learning process.

RESPONDING TO SPECIAL NEEDS

At a time when our society begs for creative solutions to pressing social problems (discussed in Chapter 2), a schooling process that champions standardization and structure over creativity is taking its toll on today's youth. Within the schooling continuum, the intermediate grades are probably best suited to encourage creative thought because the student at this level is undergoing a transformation of mind and body that allows for a renewed outlook on the world. Acceptance of body change, realignment of social relationships, emotional adjustments, and new intellectual capacities all suggest a basic malleability in the learner. The preadolescent's and early adolescent's need to reconstruct reality, as it were, is regularly characterized by his or her occupational projections, moral reasoning, role exploration, and plain fantasizing. In addition, many preadolescents exhibit creativity or "flash insights" during this period; creativity which, if not reinforced, is soon dimmed or submerged by conventional patterns of thought and action. Middle schools that recognize this special quality in preadolescents can capitalize on the opportunity to restructure student thinking along creative pathways.[2]

The gifted program in many middle schools runs head-on with new concepts of grouping. Heterogeneous grouping, for instance, does not fit the homogeneous grouping pattern found in gifted classes. Cooperative learning also involves students of differing abilities working together. In addition, homogeneous grouping of advanced classes for science and mathematics isolates gifted students from needed social and academic interaction with other students. Allowing for some grouping of gifted students—but not static grouping—appears to be the approach many middle schools are taking when planning instruction. Gifted students may be a part of a heterogeneously grouped team but be homogeneously grouped for certain classes or lessons part of the day or week.

"Giftedness" is multidimensional; it can include superiority in general intellectual ability, a specific ability, physical ability, leadership, visual and/or performing arts, or creative thinking.

Encouraging creativity among gifted students through use of innovative activities and media will continue to be a challenge to middle school educators.

Guidance and Affective Activities

Guidance specialists or counselors should be assigned to every middle school, with a minimum ratio of 1 specialist per 250 students. Unfortunately, that ratio is much higher in many middle schools, where guidance counselors must participate in group and individual guidance and work closely with teacher teams and specialists in instructional exercises. In addition, it falls to the guidance specialist to coordinate the adviser/advisee program. Following are fourteen important functions of the guidance counselor in the middle school:

1. Providing individual and group student counseling for problems relating to educational, personal, social, and vocational development and adjustment.
2. Familiarizing teachers with the results of varied testing programs and assisting and counseling them in the use of test results.
3. Assisting in orientation so that new students become familiar with the school, its purposes, facilities, rules, and activities in order to adjust better and further their development.
4. Assisting with small or large group instruction, both in subject areas and in group counseling situations. As a part of coordinating the adviser/advisee program, the counselor should model advisory lessons on class size and smaller groups.
5. Securing the testing, interpretation, and subsequent therapy for students with speech, hearing, or health difficulties.
6. Referring students with family problems to the social worker for help.
7. Evaluating special needs for underachievers or slow learners.
8. Assisting in determining the appropriate level of learning for each student.
9. Communicating with all service personnel within the school for the maximum benefit to students.
10. Participating in team planning sessions and assuming a leadership role in all guidance-related aspects of the learning program.
11. Assisting in determining appropriate diagnostic tests for use in a particular discipline and then being involved in its administration and follow-up.

12. Initiating and facilitating parent-team-counselor conferences.
13. Relating students' needs and progress to parents (not necessarily a group conference), thus acting as a liaison between home and school.
14. Preparing reports and collecting information to be used in team-parent conferences, which will facilitate communication.

Support personnel such as psychologists, psychiatrists, and social workers must be available to middle school staff. The complex socioemotional problems of emerging adolescent youth (caused by breakdown of the family, for example) have resulted in increased numbers of youths in need of specialized services.

Family teams are interdisciplinary teams of teachers with common planning time who teach students in a flexible frame of time. Family teams provide family counseling, help develop group affective activities, and encourage a group or family identity among students and teachers.

Homebase refers to the time during which a common group of students can interact with a single teacher over a long period. The homebase (or homeroom) teacher works with students in a number of schoolwide activities and serves as a teacher-counselor to students.

A *teacher/adviser* may be any adult at school who functions in an advisory role with a small group of students. The teacher/adviser meets periodically with a small multiage group. Both structured and unstructured guidance activities are carried out with the group or with individuals within the group. The focus is on social and emotional growth of students.

Community agencies and resource persons (e.g., drug abuse centers, mental health agencies, county health departments, and medical personnel) can be utilized to provide services to middle school youth. In many instances, pediatricians are used as resource persons to help emerging adolescents understand the changes their bodies undergo during transescence. Middle schools cannot possibly meet all the physical, social, or emotional needs of students and therefore must be able to tap the valuable reservoir of community resources available in most school districts.

Alternative Programs

By the time they reach middle school, many students have been "turned off" by school programs. To remedy the situation, many middle schools offer alternative school programs. Such programs usually are supported by special funds (federal, state, or local) and are designed to provide a positive environment for cognitive and socioemotional growth. Examples of alternative programs include the following:

☐ Work/study programs—Students go to school in the morning and are employed in the community part of the afternoon.

☐ Time-out rooms—In lieu of suspension, students attend a time-out room that is highly structured. Counseling and remedial work is provided, and students have no contact with classmates during the days spent in the time-out room. Inschool suspension is a similar program but often does not provide the counseling services.

☐ Crisis intervention centers—A place for students to get immediate psychological help for severe problems.

□ Special learning centers—In lieu of regular classes, special learning centers provide structured skills programs and affective activities. Students are placed back in regular classes once their academic and social goals have been met.

Physical Education

Daily PE activities should be offered to all students, with programs tailored and adaptable for each student so as to accommodate bodily changes typical in this age group. The curriculum should be designed to help students cope with maturational problems—awkwardness, underdeveloped psychomotor skills, weight gain or loss, and so forth. Physically disabled students should be given instruction that will help them attain maximum growth and development.

For the most part, intramurals have replaced interscholastic programs, but where the latter still exist they have been restructured to operate much like intramurals. For example, contests are scheduled during school time or in the afternoon, and all students who choose to are allowed to play. (With the loss of the ninth grade to the high school, middle schools wisely have dropped contact sports in favor of lifetime sports such as golf, tennis, bicycling, and swimming.)

Law Education

As a result of alarming increases in youth crime, a growing number of middle schools are introducing law education programs in the curriculum to acquaint their students with the functions of law in our society. Several states have mandated law education through legislation.

Health Education

Health education helps ten- to fourteen-year-olds understand the human body and how it works as a system. The increased incidence of drug and alcohol abuse, as well as AIDS and other sexually transmitted disease, makes it imperative that transescents develop a desire to take care of their bodies and minds.

To help accomplish this objective, middle school health programs may be scheduled as independent courses or incorporated into science or PE programs. Key topics should cover proper use of birth-control and safe-sex products; health information services; how to identify community social service resources; and family issues.

Students with Disabilities

Based on current populations in the middle grades, it can be expected that a school having 720 students will have the following breakdown of disabled youth:[3]

Speech and hearing impaired	36
Educable mentally impaired	14–15
Emotionally disturbed	7–8
Diagnosed learning disabled	7–8

Socially maladjusted	7–8
Visually impaired	1–2
Physically impaired	1–2

Obviously, the characteristics of school population vary from school to school, but the foregoing figures clearly indicate that students with special needs (gifted and disabled) cannot be ignored. The nature of the exceptionality mandates an individualized approach to instruction—reinforcing the guideline that each child must have a tailor-made program that provides for continuous progress.

Middle school years are important to building self-concept. Students faced with more than the usual number of developmental problems need to feel wanted and capable. Mainstreaming and heterogeneous grouping help build an awareness of the worth of all students and, likewise, provide an opportunity for students with special needs to interact positively with other students.

Exploratory Courses

To supplement the required exploration in such areas as art, music, industrial arts, and home economics, it is desirable for the middle school to offer a series of short-interest–centered courses. Also known as enrichment or special-interest courses, *minicourses*, or electives, these are an outgrowth of clubs in the junior high school and an expansion of elementary exploratory experiences. Exploratory courses are unique to the middle school and are offered in a variety of patterns. Nevertheless, they have the common goal of offering a variety of affective, psychomotor, and cognitive exploratory experiences beyond those found in the regular program.

Students can elect to take special-interest courses that are taught by teachers with special talents. The courses can run three, six, or nine weeks in length; some may be taught on a semester or yearly basis. Teachers, administrative personnel, and, frequently, community volunteers, help teach electives which, combined with other activity programs (intramurals, school assemblies, and play days) enhance student interest in school as well as provide valuable exploratory experiences. In that they participate on a nongraded basis, students are provided an opportunity to interact with other students of varying age levels.

The following sampling illustrates the variety of special-interest courses a middle school might offer. See Appendix 7 for additional program possibilities.

Aerobics—"exerdance" for fitness

Animal science—care and training

Holiday crafts—keep what you make

Barbells—weight lifting

Cake decorating and uncooked snacks—eat what you make

Computer club—basic literacy

Cooking—eat what you make

Drama—practice techniques

Fantastic flicks—watch movies for fun

Bingo—play for prizes

Grooming—hair care, makeup, hygiene

Ping pong—table tennis

Pottery—keep what you make

Skateboard videos—watch exhibitions, competitions

Soccer—practice basics

Spanish—conversational

Surfing—basics, water safety

Team sports—baseball, basketball, etc.

Tennis—build skills

Yoga—posture, breathing, relaxation

Colorizing—dress to flatter complexion, hair coloring

Art—acrylic painting

Art—collage, monoprinting

Fishing—freshwater, saltwater game-fishing basics

Model making—construct a rubber-band-propelled airplane

Needlework—cross-stitch projects to take home

Golf—learn and practice basics

Babysitting—practice safe, effective skills

Bike safety/repair—basic construction, tools

Basket making—keep what you weave

First aid—basics

I do not wish to participate in enrichment activities; please assign me to a study hall.

USING BROAD THEMES IN CURRICULUM DESIGN

During the early years of the middle school movement, sixth-grade courses of study were not articulated with those in the seventh and eighth grades. Also, the sixth-grade courses were designated as elementary, and the seventh and eighth as secondary. In recent years, educators have tried to design middle school courses of study that have an identity of their own. Following are samples of content that might be incorporated into the basic studies courses. Samples 7.1, 7.2, and 7.3 use the topic "Man" as a unifying broad theme. A math continuum is presented in Appendix 7.

Sample 7.1: Language Arts   Following are proposed broad-unit topics agreed on by a middle school language arts committee. The units will be developed to include activities in the *grammatical and nongrammatical aspects of language, literature, oral and written composition.*

I. *Man, a World Citizen*
   A. Responsibility
   B. Values
   C. Citizenship
   D. Heritage
   E. Myths, Legends, Tall Tales, Folk Tales

II. *Man, Communicator of Ideas*
   A. Languages
   B. Art through the Ages
   C. Mass Media
   D. Creative Expression—Drama

III. *Man, a Problem Solver*
   A. Growing up
   B. Prejudices
   C. Family
   D. Drugs
   E. Animals

IV. *Man, an Explorer*
   A. Space, Oceanography, Land
   B. Medicine
   C. Sports and Recreation
   D. Tools
   E. Foods
   F. Fashions and Fads

V. *Man Alone in a Crowd*
   A. Who Am I?
   B. Mysticism
   C. Ethics

Sample 7.2: Social Studies   In moving toward social competence, the middle school student must deal with the social dimension of personal growth, which involves a widening understanding of how people behave in today's world. Students are defining themselves, in part, in terms of a relationship to a broader stream of human development. By examining the realities of man's social and historical environment, middle school students can better understand their role in an increasingly interdependent society.

I. *Man as an Individual*
   A. Attitude toward Self
   B. Attitude toward and Relationship with Others
      1. Family and friends
      2. Town, state, country, world
      3. Prejudices

II. *Man Learns about Others*
   A. People in Other States
      1. How do they differ from his way of life?
      2. How are they alike?
   B. People in Other Countries
      1. How do they differ from him?
      2. What makes them different from him?
      3. How are they alike?
   C. Man as an Explorer
      1. Explorations yesterday and today
      2. The importance of explorations
      3. Changes brought about because of explorations and findings

D. Important Makers of History
   1. World history
   2. American history
   3. Their effects on us today
   4. Current events
E. Man's Geographical Relation to the World and to the Rest of the Country
   1. Geography influences ways of living and means of survival
F. Man as an Inventor
   1. Research goes on today
   2. Man in early civilizations
      a. Stone Age man and his inventions
      b. Greek and Roman civilizations and their innovations
G. Man as a Creator
   1. Arts
   2. Music
   3. Crafts

III. *Man as a Lawmaker*
A. Reasons for Laws
   1. Crimes
   2. To ensure justice
   3. To ensure freedom
B. Rights and Responsibilities of All Citizens
   1. All are responsible for making and upholding laws
C. Comparing the Structure and Organization of Local, State, and Federal Governments
   1. Similarities
   2. Differences
D. Governments Different from Ours
   1. Communism
   2. Socialism
   3. Monarchy

IV. *Man in Conflict*
A. Man at War
   1. Reasons for wars
   2. Aftereffects of wars
   3. Advantages and disadvantages of wars
B. Man against Nature
   1. Pollution
   2. Natural disasters
   3. Extinction of some animals
      a. Man-made extinction
      b. Natural extinction

V. *Man and His Needs for the Future*
A. Individual Needs for the Future
   1. More education will be needed
      a. College
   2. Other types of schools
      a. Mechanical, etc.
   3. Jobs
      a. Finding a suitable job

B. Physical Needs
   1. Food
   2. How to fill more leisure time
C. Social Needs
   1. How to deal with poverty
   2. How to deal with overpopulation
D. Helping to Strive for Peace
   1. In one's own country
   2. In the world

Sample 7.3: Science

MAN AND HIS WORLD

FIRST LEVEL

I. *Man and His World*
   A. How Man Learns about His World
      1. Five senses
         a. Observational skills
         b. Bias
         c. Recurrence
         d. Discrepancy
         e. Sense extensions (e.g., microscope)
      2. Graphics and quantifying
         a. Probability
         b. Development of patterns
         c. Science attitudes—news, UFO, ESP
      Suggested Unit Titles:
         Using Five Senses
         Discovering Problems
         Cycle of Proof
         Cultivating Scientific Attitudes
         Patterns and Natural Law
   B. How Man Behaves toward His World
      1. Categorizing
         a. Keys
         b. Identification
         c. Recurring properties
      2. Measurement
         a. Precision
         b. Accuracy
         c. Length
         d. Capacity and weight
         e. Time
         f. Problems in measurements
      3. Model Building
         a. Atom
         b. Carbon chains
         c. DNA
         d. Crystals
         e. Math models

      f. Probability model—heredity

      g. Solar system

    4. Communication of Data

      a. Language

      b. Scientific terminology

      c. Words

    Suggested Unit Titles:

    Similarities and Differences

    Units of Measurement Are Man-made

    Making and Using Models

    Need to Name Things

C. How Man Expects His World to Behave

    1. Consistency and Uniformity

      a. Projecting expectations

      b. Moon and stars

      c. Relationship among different kinds of change—daily, monthly, annual

    2. Cause and Effect

      a. Force and motion

      b. Chemical reactions

      c. Superstitions

    Suggested Unit Titles:

    Dependable and Predictable World

    Why Do Things Happen?

    How to Resolve Dilemmas

SECOND LEVEL

  II. *The Kind of World Man Thinks He Has Found*

    D. Man Assumes the Existence of Variation and Change

      1. Normal Curves

        a. Normal curves show variation

        b. Measuring leaves

        c. Success depends on variability

        d. Which Way Does Wind Blow?

      2. Directional Variation

        a. Color gradients

        b. Taste gradients

        c. A gradient in heating H_2O

        d. Topographical maps

      3. Extrapolation and Interpolation

        a. Predicting from a gradient

        b. Clockface

        c. Growth of corn

        d. Alternate hypothesis

      4. Time—Gradient

        a. Natural selection

        b. Variation of human hands and feet

        c. Competition

        d. Species—competition quantitative

        e. Protective coloration

        f. Selection—gene pool

5. Repeating Sequences
    a. Animal life cycle—fruit fly
    b. Simple plant cycles—mold, bacteria
    c. Growth cycles in higher plants
    d. Water cycle
    e. Rock cycle
6. Interacting Changes That Result in Balance
    a. Internal equilibrium: weight balance in humans
    b. Chemical indicators
    c. Equilibrium in landscape
    d. Balanced aquarium

Suggested Unit Titles:
    Norms and Averages
    Variation Can Be Continuous
    Judging the Future by the Past
    Response to the Challenge of the Environment
    Cycles in Nature
    An "Almost" Balance That Constantly Approaches Balance

E. Man Thinks in Terms of Relationships Rather Than Absolutes
    1. Measurements Express Relationships
        a. Balance
        b. Depth and pressure
        c. Calories and degrees
        d. Speed
    2. Patterns Govern Relationships
        a. Replication
        b. Communication
        c. We are what we are because . . .
    3. Frames of Reference Determine Relationships
        a. What do we mean by "where"?
        b. Illusions
        c. Earth coordinates
    4. Interdependence Consists of Relationships
        a. Pond infusion culture
        b. Lab field trip
        c. Relationship of acidity and alkalinity to yeast activity
        d. Evaporation
        e. Forest edge communities
        f. Interrelationships on school grounds
        g. City birds
    5. Heredity and Environment Are Related
        a. Plants and soil nutrients
        b. Plants and light
        c. Human characteristics—heredity or environment
    6. Changes and Rates Are Related
        a. Development of chick embryo
        b. Development of bean plant
        c. Differential growth rate in humans
        d. Developing stream patterns
    7. Man and His Tools Are Related
        a. Extending body with tools

     b. Work
     c. Simple machines
     d. Complex machines and utilization of outside energy
     e. Extension of man's body—how it has evolved
    Suggested Unit Titles:
     Quantifying Our Relationships Rather Than Absolutes
     We Use Patterns All the Time, So Does Nature
     Relativity and Common Sense
     Everything Is Dependent on Something Else
     Heredity and/or Environment
     Changes That Depend on Rates
     We Sharpen a Word to Express an Area of Man's Relationships

THIRD LEVEL

  III. *Man Finds That His World Has Limits*
    F. Science Is Limited by How We Feel about the World
     1. We Can Look at Our World Two Ways
      a. Problems of conflict
      b. Poetry and real world
      c. Painting and pictures
      d. Music and sound
     2. Complementarity
      a. Structure and function
      b. Nature of light
      c. Science and religion
    G. Continuous Discovery
     a. Prognosis of science inquiry
     b. Limitations
     c. Moral obligations
      1. Social Limitations
       a. Political limitations
       b. Cultural limitations

DEVELOPING MATERIALS AND RESOURCES

Communications to Parents

Parent messages are another resource for teaching parents and students. The messages in Samples 7.4 and 7.5 illustrate an affective approach.

Sample 7.4: How to Help Your Child Succeed in School

□ Send him in a good frame of mind.
□ Build up confidence: "I'm proud of you. I know you'll do well. You're a hard worker."
□ Praise her for doing something well, especially if not usually her strong point.

- ☐ Do not praise unsatisfactory work. Do not criticize; just do not praise.
- ☐ Expect to see samples of schoolwork regularly. Ask for them.
- ☐ Support the teacher and the school. If you have a complaint, take it up with the teacher. Do not mention it to the child. (We certainly would not criticize *you!*)
- ☐ Take in what you hear objectively.
- ☐ Keep books around the house, either the library's or your own. Keep a dictionary for sure, other references if possible.
- ☐ Keep your child well stocked with school supplies, even if he must go without treats. All workers must have tools; the nicer the tools, the better they work—usually.
- ☐ Show real interest in school. Attend PTA meetings, class functions, etc. Teachers take more interest in children whose parents they know personally. This is not "favoritism," it's just that knowing the parent makes the child more "real" to the teacher.
- ☐ Encourage your child to inquire. Do not put him off. If you do not know the answer, encourage him to look it up or figure it out. Then check to see how he did.
- ☐ Encourage your child to do homework carefully. Look it over. In the end, though, it is her responsibility—not yours or mine. She must remember to complete homework and to bring the book in each day.

Thanks for taking the time to read this message. If you made it all the way through, you are a *terrific parent!* And if I haven't told you lately, let me tell you now . . . *you have a really nice child!*

The Individual Summer Plan (ISP) illustrated (in part) in Sample 7.5 is used to help students continue their learning during summer months. The form includes a student contract; a conference among the teacher, student, and parents; and a packet of materials and activities to be completed during the summer. Packet materials and activities are used to reinforce skills but are also designed to be fun and interesting to students. Sample 7.6 is a suggestions list for improving communications among parent, child, and school.

Sample 7.5: Individual Summer Plan

Dear Parent of _____ Date:_____

It is very important that your child review during the summer. It is easy for a student to forget math computation skills. Please review items I through V.

It is possible for me to order workbooks for review purposes. I have the opportunity to purchase these workbooks at a 25% reduction from the retail price (see attached price list). If you are interested in purchasing one of these workbooks, please send your check by April 6. The check should be made payable to Morgan Fitzgerald.

Sincerely,

Morgan Fitzgerald
Math Department

I. *TEST RESULTS*

	Beginning Test Scores	Ending Test Scores
Math		
Reading		
Social Studies		
Science		

II. *PROGRESS*

Dear _____ :

_____

_____

_____

_____

_____

To continue your progress your Individual Summer Plan is listed below.

III. *INDIVIDUAL SUMMER PLAN*
   1.
   2.
   3.
   4.
   5.

IV. Your summer resource contact persons: Mrs. Smith or Mr. Jones (phone number).

V. Review materials (attached).

Sample 7.6: Improving Communications—Some Suggestions

What Parents Can Do!

□ Call teachers for information about why student received failing grade.
   Look up planning period for best time to call. Call (phone number) and leave a message with a number where you can be reached during the day.
□ Make sure student has necessary materials (books, paper, pencil, notebooks, and such).
□ Provide student with a separate notebook for homework assignments.
□ Make sure homework is done—all teachers assign homework at least three times per week.
□ Provide student with a regular time and place to do homework.
□ Ask student to bring home notebooks to show you what work is being done in each class.
□ Write a note to teachers every couple of weeks to check whether student's work is satisfactory or unsatisfactory.
□ Encourage student to use tutoring, either at school or at home.

What Students Can Do!

- □ Ask teacher for help during or before class or after school.
- □ Ask teacher to assign another student to help you before or after school.
- □ Sign up for tutoring through the community school.
  Sign up for NIKE program, which uses computers to work on basic skills.
- □ Come to class prepared with book, paper, pencil, notebook, and so forth.
- □ Do your class work!
- □ Ask questions when you do not understand.
- □ Write down homework assignments, carry books home, and complete assignments on time.
- □ Find out from teacher exactly why your grade was failing for first nine weeks.

Student Recognition

Middle school staffs have designed both formal and informal guidance and affective activities for middle school students. The certificate in Sample 7.7 illustrates a student reward system used by many middle schools. Such certificates are awarded daily (or in some cases during a special-activities week) to students who excel in grades, school service, politeness, helping others, and so on. Other samples are found in Appendix 7.

Sample 7.7: Student Award Certificate

```
★ ★ ★ ★ ★ ★ ★ ★ ★ ★ ★ ★ ★ ★ ★ ★ ★ ★ ★ ★ ★ ★ ★ ★
★                                                  ★
★              CERTIFICATE                         ★
★                  OF                              ★
★              APPRECIATION                        ★
★                                                  ★
★          This is to Certify that                 ★
★                                                  ★
★        _____          ★
★                                                  ★
★        has been Awarded this Certificate in      ★
★      Recognition of the Excellent Service Rendered ★
★                                                  ★
★          RIVIERA MIDDLE SCHOOL                   ★
★                                                  ★
★   Given this _____ day of _____ 19__ _____  ★
★                                      Principal    ★
★ ★ ★ ★ ★ ★ ★ ★ ★ ★ ★ ★ ★ ★ ★ ★ ★ ★ ★ ★ ★ ★ ★ ★
```

Learning Units That Appeal to Student Interests

Many middle school teachers and teacher teams use learning units to teach concepts of specific interest to students. For example, topics like "Dating and Etiquette" can teach social graces (e.g., how to ask for a date, good manners in a group); "Why Don't Teachers" allows students a chance to discuss characteristics of teachers; and "Who Am I?" used at the beginning of school by many teacher teams can examine physical and social characteristics of emerging adolescents. (For the latter unit, students often compile a Who's Who booklet, which lists students' names, hobbies, phone numbers, and interests.)

Disciplinary Resources

As discussed in Chapter 3 and earlier in this chapter, middle schools use a number of techniques and activities to deal with disciplinary issues. Teacher/advisers, team members, guidance, administrative, and school support personnel all aid the classroom teacher in solving discipline problems. One innovative technique mentioned earlier is the Time-Out Room, which is usually staffed by a teacher who accepts those students whom other teachers feel they can no longer deal with effectively.

Oftentimes, with the guidance and direction given by the teacher in the Time-Out Room, the student can return to the regular classroom without being sent to the office or suspended from school. Sample 7.8 shows a Time-Out Room Referral Form.

Sample 7.8: Time-Out Room Referral Form

Student _____   Teacher _____

Date _____   Time In _____   Time Out _____

Reason for Referral
_____ 1. Student request (has a problem)   _____ 4. Peer conflict
_____ 2. Classroom disruption   _____ 5. Emotional problem
_____ 3. Refuses to work   _____ 6. Other

Has student completed his work? _____
Have you sent work to be done? _____
Feedback from Time-Out Room if requested _____
_____
_____

Other disciplinary resources include student-faculty planning committees to discuss problems, behavior modification procedures (like earning free time for good behavior), and parent calls by team members who volunteer on a weekly basis to call parents to notify them that their child is involved in a disciplinary incident.

The behavior referral form in Sample 7.9 demonstrates the many procedures followed by middle school staff members before a student is referred to a counselor or administrator. Another approach is shown in Appendix 7.

Sample 7.9: Behavior Referral Form

BEHAVIOR REFERRAL   Student   Date

_____

Class-Grade   Date of Incident   Time   Teacher

_____   _____   _____   _____

_____

Notice to Parents

1. The purpose of this report is to inform you of a behavior incident involving the student named above.
2. You are urged both to appreciate the action taken by the teacher and to cooperate with the corrective action initiated today.

_____

REFERRING TEACHER HAS EXPLORED AT LEAST THREE ITEMS LISTED:

___ Held team conference	___ Telephoned parent
___ Made change in curriculum	___ Held conference with parent
___ Checked student's folder	___ Sent previous report home
___ Held conference with student	___ Other _____
___ Consulted counselor	_____
___ Changed student's seat	_____

_____

REASON(S) FOR REFERRAL:

___ Five or more tardies	___ Rude, discourteous behavior
___ Continuous annoyance to class- mates	___ Destructive to school property
___ Inappropriate dress	___ Other _____
	_____

_____

PRESENT ACTION AND RECOMMENDATION(S):

___ Time out—isolation	___ Student placed on probation
___ Referral to Guidance Counselor	___ Student suspended
___ Student will make up time	___ Parents notified
___ Student regrets incident, is cooper- ative	___ Other _____
	_____

_____

COMMENTS

_____

_____

_____

Parent's Signature   Office Signature

_____

Guidance counselors can assist teachers in developing a system for monitoring student behaviors. Sample 7.10 is an example of this resource:

Sample 7.10: Classroom Learning-Behavior Inventory

CONFIDENTIAL

Student _____ Grade _____ Semester 1 2
Subject _____ Teacher _____
Counselor _____ Information needed for:
Return to _____   _____ Staffing
by _____   _____ Parent
                                                 _____ Other

Please rate the learning behavior characteristics of the above student on a scale of 1–4. Please circle the appropriate number.

Scale Code: 1—Always applies   3—Sometimes applies
             2—Frequently applies 4—Never applies

Rating				Behavior	Description
1	2	3	4	Hyperactive	Restless, unable to sit still
1	2	3	4	Impulsiveness	Reacts without thinking, demands immediate attention
1	2	3	4	Excessive reaction	Responds too quickly and too much to stimuli
1	2	3	4	Anxiety	Overly worried, upset by failures
1	2	3	4	Excitability	Another type of overresponse; extreme reaction to normal situations
1	2	3	4	Daydreaming	Withdraws from reality and problem situations
1	2	3	4	Irritability	Touchy, cross, out of sorts
1	2	3	4	Insecurity	Constantly in need of attention, encouragement
1	2	3	4	Emotional instability	Reactions unpredictable, inconsistent
1	2	3	4	Distractibility	All items have equal value; cannot concentrate on one thing
1	2	3	4	Short attention span	Cannot work at anything for long; often does not finish tasks
1	2	3	4	High motivation	Tries very hard despite failure
1	2	3	4	Confusion	Misses total concepts; often cannot figure out what is wanted or needed
1	2	3	4	Retention	Poor memory
1	2	3	4	Perseveration	Tendency to repeat activity or phrase after meaning and purpose have ceased
1	2	3	4	Visual perceptual	Cannot see wholes against a distracting background
1	2	3	4	Auditory perception	Cannot distinguish sounds against background noises

1 2 3 4   Speech   Hesitant, slow, stuttering, substitution of
                                       gestures
1 2 3 4   Reading and writing   Reverses letters and words
1 2 3 4   Talkativeness   Constant chattering, irrelevant conversa-
                                       tions
1 2 3 4   Flightiness   Lack of steadiness
1 2 3 4   Explosive laughter   Sudden, loud, uncontrollable
1 2 3 4   Annoying, teasing   Disturbing others to gain attention

Describe the student's attitude toward the subject you teach:

                ATTENDANCE: Cumulative number of days present this semester_____
                             Cumulative number of days absent this semester_____

ADDITIONAL COMMENTS:

                Teacher _____ Date _____

Why Students Fail Courses: An Analytical Tool

Counselors can uncover why students fail middle school courses by providing teachers with relevant data. Sample 7.11 illustrates grading practices in a seventh- to
ninth-grade junior high.

Sample 7.11: Grading Practices

6876 Student Courses
626 Student/Course Failures   GRADING PERIOD 1
9.1 Percent Failures

Student Course Failures by Department and Grade

Department	7th	8th	9th	Total
English	39	19	54	112
Math	31	29	14	74
Science	57	33	47	137
Social Studies	56	30	38	124
Physical Education	8	15	—	23
Electives	*45	*19	*92	*156
	236	145	245	626
Percentage of Grade	9.5	7.1	10.5	9.1

Reasons for Failure

1. Excessive absences
2. Failure to do homework
3. Failure to make up work missed
4. Inability to do classwork

5. Incomplete classwork
6. Apathy
7. Other _____

Reason	English	Math	Science	Soc. Studies	P.E.	Electives	Total
1	33	22	25	25	9	40	154
2	57	56	64	43	—	74	294
3	45	35	38	33	4	59	214
4	30	33	21	46	2	12	144
5	113	86	120	89	—	80	488
6	23	8	20	17	6	65	139
7	74	75	74	7	18	17	265*

*Teachers indicated "Poor study skills."

Other Creative Activities

Other instructional guidance and affective activities in the middle school include student government, student assistant projects, and (as mentioned earlier in the chapter) work-study programs. Unlike the junior high model, where a few select students are elected to school or class office, middle school teams (or "houses") often elect their own officers. These offices frequently are made up of a panel of students instead of simply a class president, a vice-president, and a secretary.

Student assistant programs include activities such as a "meeters and greeters" group involved with a school's public relations functions, team assistants, peer tutors, and office assistants.

Work-study programs allow certain students to work outside or within the school for one or more class periods daily. This way students can earn a salary while receiving class credit for their work. In addition, work-study students learn to fill out job applications and to participate in real job interviews. Vocational guidance is also provided.

A list of special-interest (or enrichment) activities is presented in Appendix 7.

Mentor Program

Mentor programs provide students access to caring adults—grandparents, retirees, business executives, parents—from whose life experiences students can benefit. Some programs offer tutorial support; for example, engineers at a local company may offer help in mathematics and/or computer classes, or a local naval base may provide volunteers as teacher aides. Local executives may spend quality time with a student at lunch, a sports or cultural event, or even an at-home visit. In all of these cases, the time is well spent discussing career options, sharing motivational exchanges, and entering into "first-hand" experiential observations.

Independent Study

Whether it be an individual project undertaken by class members or a plan of study developed for children judged by a teacher to be exceptional and in need of further exposure, independent study is an integral part of the middle school experience. Some schools use activity-specific contracts between teacher and student (see Sample 7.12) to spell out what is expected by both parties to an independent study activity.

Sample 7.12: Study Skills Contract

_____ promises to spend one (1) hour of "Study Time" each evening during the Study Skills Week, beginning March 18. _____ will study Monday, Tuesday, and Wednesday evenings for one hour and have this contract signed by a parent stating that the requirements of this contract have been met.

Complying with the terms stated above will entitle _____ to a special treat during 4th period lunch on Thursday, March 21.

I sign this contract willingly and will do my best to adhere to the requirements stated above.

_____
             (Student's signature)   (Date)

My child has met the contractual requirements as stated above, and deserves a special treat at lunch.

_____
             (Parent's signature)   (Date)

Outdoor Classrooms

In the continued move toward removing real and imaginary walls, many middle schools use a number of creative activities designed to link each content or subject area to the study of nature. For example, to apply math to the outdoors, assignments may include doing scale drawings in the form of maps, figuring the percentage of slopes, pacing distance on a hiking trip, or estimating and checking distance between trees. Or, in applying language arts, activities may include creating ecology commercials, writing a story about a drop of water's journey through the water cycle, or listing adjectives that describe a specimen found in nature.

PLANNING CREATIVE LEARNING ENVIRONMENTS

Clearly environment—real and perceived—sets a tone for learning. The traditional intermediate schools characterized by a solitary, sedate, and rigid atmosphere emerged from many forces: a narrow definition of formal education, limited public access to knowledge, and a didactic (telling-listening) learning format.

By contrast, the essential middle school is an innovative organizational opposite. In an environment that is open and sometimes noisy, there is structure in the numerous activity centers planned by teachers and students. A new understanding of the environmental conditions that enhance learning has resulted in the establishment of creative learning centers. The rest of this chapter reviews building and classroom conditions that affect pupil attitudes and self-concept (summarized in Table 7.1) and examines the effects of spatial properties that characterize progressive middle school facilities and their effect on students' learning process.

Classroom Climate

Once an instructional learning area has been established, its effectiveness depends on a number of factors. The "set" of the instructional learning environment, commonly referred to as *classroom climate*, directly affects learning. Table 7.2 on page 176 identifies some of the important variables that affect classroom climate.

A distinct classroom climate can be created by a distinct teacher leadership style. Once created, these climates have a significant effect on motivation and performance: *Climate determines motivation; teachers determine climate; therefore, teachers determine motivation.*

Classroom Space: Implications, Functions, Effects

The organization, movement, and ownership of physical space in the classroom is often indicative of school philosophy.

One way of viewing classroom spaces is in terms of the organization for instructional effectiveness. In the traditional layout, where all lines of vision and attention were on the teacher, there was little opportunity for lateral communication.

Another classroom space organization creates multipurpose spaces with the focus of attention generally in the center of the classroom. This configuration permits increased student involvement, mobility, and simultaneous learning activities. It avoids focusing solely on the teacher but still can be controlled easily in terms of noise or lateral communication among students.

The spatial distance maintained between teachers and students during interaction was found to affect students' listening comprehension and their own distance behavior. For example, teacher-to-student distances from five feet down to one foot between the teacher and student resulted in improved listening comprehension.

According to Hall, "The use of space (proximics) is a subtle component of nonverbal communication that indicates territory to which we allow or deny access to other people or objects." Hall identified three types of space:[4]

1. Fixed-feature space (immovable walls or partitions and objects)
2. Semi-fixed-feature space (big objects, such as chairs and tables)
3. Informal space (personal space around individuals)

Straight-row seating, originally evolved to make optimum use of natural lighting from windows, greatly affects student involvement in the process of communication. The location of students in typical straight-row seating is a major factor in determining which students the teacher talks with and which students respond to the teacher.

The major reason for the greater participation from the center-front area is the fact that 77 percent of classroom interaction is directly or indirectly facilitated by the

TABLE 7.1   Learning Environments Affect Pupil's Self-concept

High-Growth Conditions	Low-Growth Conditions
1. Pupil ideas are frequently accepted by the teacher, who listens to and incorporates them in discussion and other learning situations.	1. Pupil ideas are rarely encouraged or accepted. When discussion occurs, it is highly controlled and seeks *recall* of information previously learned. Pupil contributions are frequently criticized.
2. Pupil feelings and emotions are acknowledged by the teacher as long as harm to others is avoided.	2. Pupil feelings are ignored or minimized. The teacher disallows expressions and discussions of feelings.
3. Pupils are encouraged to explore, make suggestions, etc. An atmosphere of "try it and tell us what happens" pervades the classroom.	3. Pupils are discouraged from exploration. Only the teacher has the "one right way" of doing things. Alternatives are not discussed or tested.
4. The teacher is willing to "get off the subject" when an interesting event or question is raised. Sometimes the question unfolds as the topic.	4. The teacher controls the subject at all times. Penetrating philosophical questions are discouraged. The principal aim is to teach the lesson and complete it.
5. The teacher, attempting to understand and respond to each child's psychological needs, recognizes that some children may need more direction and control while others may need to exercise more choice. Therefore, students are encouraged to learn and explore in ways that each child is comfortable with.	5. The teacher denies individual differences and needs and demands conformity. The teacher who demands that every child participate in an "open" classroom may produce the same low-growth conditions as the teacher who provides a "lock-step" atmosphere. Both strategies are authoritarian and demand conformity at the possible expense of pupil's esteem, control, and connectedness.
6. A continuing dialogue with pupils is maintained to involve children in making decisions about their learning (e.g., individual and small group projects, work contracts, etc.), and to help children further clarify what they are learning.	6. The teacher always dictates what and how students are to learn. Little room is left for pupil choice and expression.
7. The teacher is genuine—willing to express ideas, feelings, experiences and be real rather than play a role. Where appropriate, the teacher allows students entry into his/her private world of feelings, ideas, needs, and concerns.	7. The teacher plays a role, masks feelings, and reveals little of own uniqueness and inner thoughts. An emotional gulf separates teacher and pupil, denying common bonds, needs, and feelings the two might have explored.

TABLE 7.2 Variables Affecting Classroom Climate

Variable	Effect
Structure	The feeling students have about constraints on the group: rules, regulations, "red tape"
Responsibility	The feeling of "being your own boss," not having to double-check all decisions, freedom to do the job
Reward	The feeling of being rewarded for a job well done, an emphasis on positive reward rather than punishment, perceived fairness in rewards given
Risk	The feeling that taking calculated risks (asking a "foolish" question) is all right, that you don't have to play it safe to succeed
Warmth	The feeling of general good fellowship, the prevalence of friendly and informal social groups
Support	The perceived helpfulness of the teacher, emphasis on support from both above and below
Standards	The perceived importance of performance standards, the emphasis on doing a good job
Conflict	The feeling that the teacher and other students want to hear different opinions, the emphasis placed on getting problems out in the open
Identity	The feeling of belonging, of being a valuable member of a working team, the importance of team spirit

teacher, who habitually occupies that location and selectively attends to students in that immediate vicinity.

Space in the classroom may also serve to indicate status, dominance, and leadership. A teacher's desk may act as a barricade to prevent students from entering her or his space and thus inhibit interaction. (Students frequently use space to send a message about their interest or preparation in a course by sitting in the front or back of the classroom.)

To foster productive communication in the classroom, teachers must allow for flexible changes that are beneficial for group interaction.

The implications concerning fixed-feature spatial environments for today's classrooms are obviously important, considering that students spend about six hours a day, five days a week, forty weeks a year in these learning environments. Clearly, the physical classroom environment can create moods and establish how much interaction (communication) takes place.

Pupil movement within the classroom is a strong indicator of the structure or flexibility in the learning environment. Movement in stationary classrooms is totally dependent upon the teacher, and students in this type of classroom must request permission to talk, go to the washroom, or approach the teacher. Stationary structure usually minimizes noise and confusion but restricts activity to verbal exchange only. When movement does occur, it is generally forward and aft from the teacher's locale.

In a controlled classroom, movement is possible within prescribed patterns monitored by the teacher. Movement usually depends on the activity engaged in.

FIGURE 7.3 Pupil movement patterns

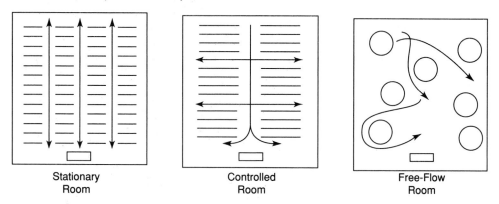

Stationary Room	Controlled Room	Free-Flow Room

During teacher talk, for instance, movement may not be allowed, whereas at other times students may be permitted to sharpen pencils, get supplies, or leave the room for a drink of water without teacher approval.

Pupil movement is sometimes left to the complete discretion of the student. In open-space buildings with high program flexibility, students are often seen moving unsupervised from one learning area to the next. Parents accustomed to more structured, traditional programs often view such *free-flow* movement as questionable, believing that the teacher must be in direct contact with students for learning to occur. Yet, self-directed, unsupervised movement is an integral part of any open, activity-centered curriculum. The three movement patterns are illustrated in Figure 7.3.

Figure 7.4 describes the continuum suggested by the potential range of classroom spatial alternatives.

Learning Centers

A learning center (or station) is an area organized such that middle school pupils can be responsible for much of their own learning. A learning *station* implies *how* a student learns (auditory, visual, kinesthetic), whereas a learning *center* implies *what* a student will learn (grammar, fractions). A learning center/station is generally characterized by the following:

□ Clear directions that help a student proceed through a learning activity without constant reliance on the teacher
□ Clearly stated objectives
□ Choice of activities so students can use a variety of learning modes
□ Multilevel activities so that learning activities are appropriate for each student
□ Evaluation activities that allow students to check their work at the center
□ Opportunities to work in small groups so that students can assist each other and learn together

Every learning center/station should contain multimedia materials to support the topic, theme, concept, or skill being explored. The teacher needs to "introduce"

FIGURE 7.4   Potential classroom alternatives

Classroom Organization

| Uniform seating arrangement dominates room | Classroom furniture uniform but not symmetrical | Furniture arranged for each activity | Multipurpose spaces in room | Space outside classroom used for instruction |

S _____ F

Classroom Movement

| Movement totally restricted by teacher | Total teacher control with noted exception | Pupil movement contextual | Pupil has freedom of movement within limit | Movement totally at pupil's discretion |

S _____ F

Classroom Ownership

| Classroom space is dominated by teacher | Teacher dominates some student zones | Classroom has areas of mutual free access | Territory only at symbolic level—open to all | All classroom spaces totally accessible to all persons |

S _____ F

S—Stationary
F—Free flow

the center—what it contains and how it can be used. A flexible organizational pattern in the classroom and school must be planned so that pupils can have easy access to these facilities.

Middle school learning centers/stations may be housed in classrooms or in specially designed media rooms. Learning resource rooms for reading or mathematics are often structured around teaching machines that include computer terminals and a variety of learning stations that include hardware and software. Middle schools with multiple learning centers can call on parent and community volunteers to assist at those centers.

As mentioned in the introduction to this chapter, middle school instructional materials reflect a wide variety of media—from books and newspapers to satellite images and laser optics. This wealth mirrors the diversity of achievement, background, and interests in the ten- to fourteen-year-olds who learn from them. The physical features of buildings constructed specifically as middle schools and of their grounds are subtle indicators of the school's perceived mission and therefore are useful measures for a visitor or interested observer. Access points, building warmth (ambience), inside traffic control, and space priorities tend to reflect the program climate.

Architects have observed that buildings (form) are a physical expression of content. Thus, a dull, drab, unexciting building may reflect a dull, drab, unexciting educational process. On the other hand, an exciting, stimulating, dynamic structure may mirror an active, creative, total learning center.

A middle school housed in an already-existing structure, however, tells little about the current philosophy of the school. Many flexible programs are found in old buildings, and highly rigid programs are sometimes found in modern open-space designs.

Because of genuine dangers (drugs, crime) in the immediate neighborhood, many schools limit the number of access points to the school building. Others deliberately limit public access as a means of controlling the environment and the personnel. Signs of extreme control are a single entrance, a conspicuous presence of locked spaces (bathrooms, auxiliary spaces), and deliberate physical barriers to movement (long unbroken counters in school offices).

The size of spaces, scale of the environment (relationship between size of the people and objects in the environment), shape of spaces, coloration, and use of lighting all affect a school building's warmth. In the past, small classrooms with oversized furniture positioned to "fix" activity, drab coloration, and square walls were used intentionally to control environmental stimulation and to direct attention to the teacher. Such a discomforting setting presupposed that teacher behavior was of primary importance.

More recently, middle schools have used bright colors, curved walls, expansive spaces, and acoustical treatments to encourage student mobility and mental freedom. Such an environment assumes that education is highly individualized and conducted through exploration.

SUMMARY

An effective middle school must provide instructional activities, materials, and learning environments that are tailor-made for the impressionable students who use them. This chapter looked at ways in which teachers must use their own imaginations to capture the interest and (sometimes short) attention of middle graders. This means, in part, mixing core subjects with "real-world" experience. It also means using a myriad of teaching tools—from computers, cable TV, and wire services to enrichment programs and independent study.

Methods were discussed for developing programs that meet special needs—advisement; alternate programs (including mentor agreements); programs that meet *different kinds* of special needs (for the academically gifted, the academically uninspired, and those with physical, mental, and/or emotional impairment); intramurals; and so forth.

Creative ways to communicate with students, parents, and the community at large were examined, as were intelligent responses to discipline problems.

The chapter closed with a detailed look at how design and application of physical space affects students' study and learning styles. Specific topics included creating a classroom climate (using room layout, traffic flow, and furniture arrangement options); developing learning resource centers; using color and warmth to create ambience throughout the building; and including the outdoors as extensions of the classroom.

SUGGESTED LEARNING ACTIVITIES

1. With a group of colleagues, develop a catalog of creative activities found in middle schools. List each activity with a short description of how it is carried out. Also list sources for finding out more information about an activity.
2. Develop outlines for a series of workshops on building self-pacing materials, setting up learning centers, and writing interdisciplinary units.
3. Develop an outline for an interdisciplinary unit utilizing at least four disciplines, including a related arts subject.
4. Design a learning center/station for your classroom. List the materials and activities you would include and the processes by which students would move in and out of the center.
5. The school board has decided to make improvements in the building in which your middle school is housed. Develop a position paper outlining the rationale for a variety of learning areas in the school, including learning centers/stations, learning resource rooms, and flexible space for groups of students.

NOTES

1. D. W. Johnson and R. T. Johnson, *Cooperative, Competitive and Individualistic Learning* (Englewood Cliffs, NJ: Prentice-Hall 1987).
2. Jon Wiles and Joseph Bondi, "Teaching for Creative Thinking in the Intermediate Grades," *Roeper Review* 3 (October 1980) 4–8.
3. U.S. Department of HEW, National Institute for Child Health and Development, Annual Report, 1992.
4. Edward T. Hall, *The Silent Language* (Garden City, NJ: Doubleday Books, 1973), 100.

SELECTED REFERENCES

Kagan, Spencer, *Cooperative Learning Resources for Teachers* (Riverside: University of California Press, 1987).

Slavin, Robert, "Cooperative Learning and Student Achievement," *Educational Leadership,* 46 (3), October 1987.

Wiles, Jon, and Bondi, Joseph, *Motivation Techniques for Middle School Students* (Tampa: Wiles, Bondi and Associates, 1991).

_____, *Cooperative/Peer Learning in Middle Schools* (Tampa: Wiles, Bondi and Associates, 1990).

_____, *Discipline and Safety in Middle Schools* (Tampa: Wiles, Bondi and Associates, 1992).

8

Planning Considerations in Establishing a Middle School

*The establishment of a middle school is a complex activity
that requires planning as well as ambition.*

INTRODUCTION

Since its inception in the 1960s, the middle school movement has been marked by a number of milestones. In addition to firmly establishing a concept of "middle school," educators have identified the special population of learners to be targeted; the kind of teacher and professional preparation desired; elements of appropriate program design; organizational innovations that undergird the educational effort at middle schools; the instructional leadership needed to make the middle school "work"; and specific activities, materials, and environments that enhance transescent learning experiences.

These milestones coalesce into a single significant observation: The middle school is indeed a highly complex entity whose successful establishment (or conversion) calls for detailed advance planning at both school and district levels.

During the late 1980s and early 1990s, the middle school movement entered a new era of maturity, during which the past decade of practical application of concepts brought new insights to planners whose function was to establish a new middle school or convert an old facility. This chapter discusses the numerous research considerations that go into such an undertaking—type and size of community; level of community awareness; funding and personnel resources; the time required for task completion, to cite a few. The purpose here is to help readers appreciate the complexity of the planning process at all levels of operations. The chapter also provides guidelines for middle school educators so that certain problems can be avoided (or at least minimized) through careful and comprehensive preliminary planning.

BROAD PLANNING: BEGINNING AT THE PROPER LEVEL

Generally speaking, middle schools come into existence because dedicated intermediate educators are seeking a better way to serve their students. Programs and/or facilities that originate at the school level, however, sometimes are hampered in their development by lack of planning at the district level. (This chapter focuses on the district level and the school level; the latter includes classrooms and buildings.) For example, a system that constructs a building without understanding the middle school concept will handicap the program somewhere down the line.

Inherent in the planning process is *sequence* of stages, that is, the recommended order in which steps should be taken. The following subsections briefly sum up some of the broad considerations in preliminary planning.

Analysis

A middle school should arise from need. It is tempting to hope that, by proceeding through values clarification, school systems and communities will "logically" arrive at a proper middle school design. However, it is more appropriate to hope that programs will be initiated based on what is known about the students. In other words, overcrowding, integration, and building availability are poor reasons for starting a middle school. Therefore, a needs and feasibility analysis should not focus only on *problems*. It should project the kind of educational experiences desired for this special category of pupils.

Involvement

Preliminary investigation should involve all parties who have vested interests in intermediate education. Too often planning explores creation of a middle school without involving those who will be most directly affected: students, teachers, parents, and the community. Without this consideration, confrontations inevitably arise over programs and policy—for example interscholastic athletics, social events, grading policies, community-based learning.

Without considering the key players at this stage, the dedication and support needed to ensure successful implementation will not be forthcoming. In particular, community education must be undertaken so as to remedy unfamiliarity among citizens with educational "jargon" and national trends in education. If community residents understand program rationale (academic and organizational innovations for example) they are less likely to resist change and more likely to remain positively involved at later planning stages.

Commitment

Philosophical commitment to the middle school definition of education should be secured. As indicated in the preceding section, involvement leads to commitment. Emphasized throughout this book is the necessity of understanding and accepting the philosophy and concept of middle school education. Without it, no convincing rationale can be propounded legitimately, and no foundation for commitment can be expected.

Note that this commitment must exist across the board—from students, teachers, parents, and principals to the superintendent and the school board.

Funding

Appropriate monies must be earmarked to activate the plan. It has been observed time and time again that in U.S. education, finance is the fuel of progress. Few major innovations of the past twenty years have really succeeded without substantial financial support.

Dedication, involvement, and commitment aside, the middle school is a more complex form of education than traditional programs and therefore requires more money to operate. Every deviation away from standardized patterns (uniform textbooks, a classroom-confined learning, single-dimension instruction) incurs expense. Therefore, commitment on the part of school districts must translate into financial commitment to building, conversion, materials acquisition, staff development, and so forth.

Resources

Resources must be allocated that are commensurate with the task planned. A common pitfall is to assume that a middle school can operate using the same resource base used by the traditional intermediate school. Relying on teacher-made materials exclusively, overlooking a consumable materials budget, failing to allocate materials for building an instructional resource center, and making no provisions for off-campus experiences, and the like, are shortcomings any one of which spells certain doom for a program.

Personnel

Efforts should be made to staff middle schools with dedicated and enthusiastic teachers. Only a few colleges across the nation provide teacher and staff training exclusively for the middle school environment. Consequently, most teachers and support personnel will come from other more traditional educational designs. Such persons, regardless of their belief in and allegiance to middle school philosophy and concepts, will require assistance in adjusting to their new roles.

A number of middle schools open under influence of what is called the Hawthorne effect (from the Hawthorne studies, in which workers were found to be more productive—regardless of work conditions—if they are first made to feel special). Therefore, teacher enthusiasm and energy are understandably high initially. But as program development slows or resources erode with the gradual diminishment of attention, it is not unusual for old patterns of teacher-pupil interaction to recur. Thus, a "one-shot summer treatment" for middle school staff should be replaced by long-term systematic (inservice) training opportunities.

Time-Frame Considerations

The time frame for opening a middle school must allow for the magnitude of the process proposed. Preparation time required to open a middle school depends on environmental conditions in the community but ranges between three and five years. This estimate is based on certain substeps within the overall planning process:

□ Needs analysis and feasibility studies
□ Community education and commitment
□ Budgeting for development
□ Staff and site selection
□ Design and construction of detailed implementation plan
□ Intensive staff training
□ Design and development of curriculum
□ Design and construction (or conversion) of site
□ School opening

Again, time frame is influenced by the nature of the community, the school district and its central office organization, and type of support from community leaders (among many other factors). What is constant, as stated before, is the *sequence* of these activities. Skipping, or minimizing the importance of, community education, staff training, or curriculum development or proceeding with site construction without having planned a comprehensive program will all but guarantee failure.

Determining the Odds for Success

Implementation of educational change can be an unpredictable task due to the number of variables involved. One research project, sponsored by the state of Florida and directed by the authors, sought to identify the crucial variables that indicate probability for success of an educational innovation accepted at the building level. The instrument used was the probability chart (shown in Figure 8.1), which—although it in no way promises success—can serve as a pattern during the needs assessment and feasibility evaluation procedures. Not all communities are ready for a middle school, and such an instrument can help direct (or redirect) energies so as to increase the chance for a successful implementation.

Altering a curriculum at the building level is a process that is complex and difficult to control. Program changes are rarely isolated and comprise—intentionally or otherwise—a series of interrelated and interdependent events. The challenge to building planners is to develop a comprehensive monitoring device so as to observe and direct numerous ongoing changes. One such "building blueprint" is the developmental staging concept.

Developmental staging, which is basically a construct using a form of discrepancy analysis, consists of outlining anticipated change steps in program development that are interim conditions between what *is* and what *is desired.* In a sense, developmental staging attempts to close the gap between the real and the ideal while at the same time showing the comprehensive nature of the change being considered.

The utility of the "staging" concept to promote desired curricular change depends on several conditions. First, it is assumed that some philosophical consensus is present among those engaged in the change process so that goals can be described and progress toward those goals accurately assessed. It is impossible to construct a chart of progression toward desired goals in the middle school program if such ends are not clearly identified and agreed on.

Second, the staging plans leading toward desired goals must begin with an accurate portrait of present realities. A staff must use its best judgment to distinguish between educational intentions and day-to-day practices. Often the only accurate means of detecting potential discrepancies is to view the condition or practice through the eyes of a single randomly selected student: What is read? What is desired?

Finally, the use of developmental staging should always be preceded by acceptance of the fact that lasting curricular change is almost always a tedious process. A predisposition toward patience and a long view of progress will assist a staff in a thoughtful identification of stages of progress.

IDENTIFYING CONTINUUMS OF PROGRESS

In global reorientations of school programs, such as in the design of a middle school, monitoring categories of school change can provide more accurate indicators of progress toward desired ends. In one city, for instance, a planning team identified fourteen areas (see Table 8.1) in which they felt progress should be monitored.

FIGURE 8.1 Educational innovations probability chart

	High Risk ←—————————			—————————→ Low Risk	
Source of Innovation	Superimposed from outside	Outside agent brought in	Developed internally with aid	External idea modified	Locally conceived, developed, implemented
Impact of Innovation	Challenges sacrosanct beliefs	Calls for major value shifts	Requires substantial change	Modifies existing values of programs	Does not substantially alter existing values, beliefs, or programs
Official Support	Official leaders active opposition	Officials on record as opposing	Officials uncommitted	Officials voice support of change	Enthusiastically supported by the official leaders
Planning of Innovation	Completely external	Most planning external	Planning processes balanced	Most of planning done locally	All planning for change done on local site
Means of Adoption	By superiors	By local leaders	By reps	By most of the clients	By group consensus
History of Change	History of failures	No accurate records on	Some success with innovation	A history of successful innovations	Known as school where things regularly succeed
Possibility of Revision	No turning back	Final evaluation before committee	Periodic evaluations	Possibility of abandoning at conclusion	Possible to abort the effort at any time
Role of Teachers	Largely bypassed	Minor role	Regular role in implementing	Heavy role in implementation	Primary actor in the classroom effort
Teacher Expectation	Fatalistic	Feel little chance	Are willing to give a try	Confident of success	Wildly enthusiastic about chance of success
Workload Measure	Substantially increased	Heavier but rewarding	Slightly increased	Unchanged	Workload lessened by the innovation
Threat Measure	Definitely threatens some clients	Probably threatening to some	Mild threat resulting from the change	Very remote threat to some	Does not threaten security or autonomy
Community Factor	Hostile to innovations	Suspicious and uninformed	Indifferent	Ready for a change	Wholeheartedly supports the school

Shade the response in each category that most accurately reflects the condition surrounding the implementations of the middle school. If the "profile" of your school is predominately in the high-risk side of the matrix, substantial work must be done to prepare your school for change.

TABLE 8.1   Current Conditions and Desired Conditions: A Continuum

Moving From	Moving Toward
School philosophy—A written document on file in the school office, defining the school in terms of knowledge areas and administrative concerns.	An active, working philosophy known by all teachers and serving as the basis of day-to-day decision making. Defines the school in terms of expected learner growth.
School plant—Using only standard classroom spaces for instructional purposes.	Encompassing varied learning environments, using all available building spaces (school yard, corridors for instructional purposes).
Staffing patterns—Isolated teachers in self-contained classes.	Teachers grouped in cooperative arrangements, dealing with large numbers of learners collectively. Built-in planning time and home-base teaching function.
Instructional materials—Classrooms dominated by a basic grade-level text. Libraries used as study halls for large class groups.	Diversified learning materials within any given classroom setting, "something for everybody." Multiple texts, supplemental software, integrated and cross-subject materials. Heavy use of multimedia learning resource centers for independent exploration.
Organization of students—Basic pattern of one teacher and 30 students in standardized room spaces; students in the same-size groups all day.	Greater variability in the size of learning groups, from individuals to large groups (120 students). Grouped according to objective of the instruction.
Teaching strategies—Variety of approaches found, but most classes dominated by lecture, single text, question-answer format.	Greater variety of patterns of teacher-pupil interchange. Teaming when advantageous, greater use of media, possible peer teaching, counseling, more hands-on experiences.
Role of teacher—Defined in terms of subject(s) taught; teacher perceived as source of knowledge and responsible for order.	Greater concern with students. A planned teacher-counselor role. More group work (projects, issues). Teacher role an organizer, facilitator of learning experiences. Teacher monitoring "contracts" with students. Shared responsibility for order.
Role of student—Passive recipient of knowledge. Most instruction paced to group; a reactive posture.	Greater input, chance for expression, involvement in planning. Goal to become self-directed. Emphasis on self-conduct and "success." Use of contracts for student goal setting.
Role of parents—Limited access to the schools. Few parents involved at meaningful level. Involvement only in administrative concerns.	Greater parental involvement in school activities. Opportunities for more direct involvement in instructional roles in classroom and curriculum planning. Greater flow of information to parents about school objectives and program.
Role of community—Limited interface with schools. Some strong foundational ties with social services in the city.	School becoming more outwardly oriented; seeing the community as a learning environment and source of instructional resources. Systematizing the connections with social services in the community.
Rules and regulations—High degree of regimentation through rules and regulation. Little student input into process. High degree of student dependence on adults for direction.	Greater involvement of students in the design of regulatory policies and identification of the really essential rules. Aiming toward minimum acceptable level of control. Goal to foster increased student independence and self-control.
Discipline—Reactive pattern of discipline, ranging from admonishment and parent conferences to paddling and expulsion.	Designing an active program to deter disciplinary problems. Greater involvement of pupils in process. Ensured degrees of success for all students, seeking to curtail frustration and boredom.
Student progress reports—Letter grades assigned, concern with only narrowly defined academic progress.	Striving for varied student evaluation using a more descriptive medium (conferences, student folders, etc.). Focused on all dimensions of student growth. Sometimes reported as student competencies.
Staff development—Global, not closely tied to building-level needs of teachers and students.	Designed to attack building-level problems identified by teachers and students. Development of a monitoring process to measure achievement of predetermined goals.

Taking the foregoing areas of concern a step further and grouping them under specific headings (for example, learning environment, instructional organization, administrative conditions, participants' roles) will allow middle school planners to begin to see connected areas of concern.

In the model of developmental staging shown in Figure 8.2, areas within each of the fourteen categories listed in Table 8.1 are followed through five major stages of development.

DETAILED PLANNING: MANAGING CURRICULUM DEVELOPMENT

Over the past twenty-five years as chief consultants in the conversion of more than fifteen hundred middle schools in the United States and many foreign countries, the authors have found one truth to hold steady: There are no shortcuts to the process.

Early middle school models reflected a focus on innovation rather than on philosophy, and that often meant that schools were assumed to have fulfilled their obligations once they implemented teaming and an advisory program. What was lacking, we found, was a management technique for translating the philosophy into practice. To meet this need, we developed the Wiles-Bondi Curriculum Management Plan (CMP) Model, which has guided successful middle school development since the early 1980s.

The balance of this chapter provides an explication of how the CMP Model works. Examples of district action plans from successful conversions, school-based action plans, summaries of progress reports, and products of middle school transitions are presented here, with additional samples in Appendix 8. All come from actual schools and school districts in which the authors have worked.

The CMP Model: An Overview

At the very heart of implementing middle schools is curriculum development. The CMP draws from the previous work of Tyler and Taba[1,2] and from the widely used accreditation process format. Put simply, the CMP attempts to introduce regularity into the process of change. Without the logic imposed by regularity, a number of pitfalls can cripple efforts to design a middle school.[3]

The CMP Model differs from an accreditation design by superimposing a management schemata over the curriculum development framework. In recognition of the political variables of local school environments, the CMP forces values clarification and commitment at each step.

A first step in curriculum development, for instance, is to determine direction through an analysis of purpose. A prerequisite, then, is to develop a working definition of *middle school* to be endorsed by key decision makers (board, superintendent), thus setting up an administrative mandate. (*Note:* The words adopted by the board will govern behavior in the committee process and therefore should be chosen carefully. For example, if district personnel do not truly believe in the uniqueness of preadolescents, they should study the body of literature first.) Based on this attempt at arriving at a philosophy, a deductive (if-then) logic is set in motion and proceeds

FIGURE 8.2 Developmental staging—Middle schools

	Present Condition Stage 1	Awareness Stage Stage 2	Experimentation Stage Stage 3	Adoption Stage Stage 4	Desired Condition Stage 5
School Philosophy	Either lacks formal statement or has a written document on file in the school office.	School staff share beliefs, look for consensus, restate philosophy and objectives in terms of expected behavior.	Staff begins use of goals as guide to evaluating school practices. Begin to involve students and community in planning.	Philosophy and goals used to shape the program. Formal mechanism established to monitor program and decision making.	Philosophy a living document. Guides daily decisions. The program a tool for achieving desired educational ends.
Learning Environment					
School Plant	Only uniform instructional spaces. Little use of the building spaces for educational purposes.	Some deviation from traditional space utilization (classroom learning center). Possibly a complete demonstration class for bright ideas.	Limited building conversion (knock out walls). Begin to identify unused spaces. Planning for large learning spaces.	Development of a comprehensive plan for use of grounds and building. Total remodeling of spaces.	Tailor-made learning environment—all spaces used to educate. Building facilitates the learning goals.
Staffing Patterns	Building teachers isolated in self-contained classrooms. Little or no lateral communication or planning present.	Limited sharing of resources. Some division of labor and small-scale cooperation in teaching. Informal communication about student progress.	Regular cooperative planning sessions. Some curricular integration via themes. Students rotate through subject areas. Problems of cooperation identified.	Interdepartmental organization. Use of common planning time. Administrative support (such as in scheduling). Use of philosophy as curricular decision-making criteria.	Teaching staff a "team" working toward common ends. Staff patterns reflect instructional intentions. Administration in support of curricular design. Course work integrated for students.
Instructional Materials	Classrooms are dominated by a grade-level text. Library with a limited offering. Used as a study hall for large groups.	Use of multilevel texts within classroom. Materials selected after an analysis of student achievement levels. Supplemental resources made available to students.	Diverse materials developed for the students. Resource centers established. Cross-discipline selection of materials. More multimedia materials used. Some independent study.	Materials purchasing policies realigned. Common learning areas established as resource centers. More self-directed study built in.	Diversified materials. Something for each student. Integrated subject materials. Portable curriculum units (on carts). Heavy multimedia emphasis. Active learning centers.
Instructional Organization					
Organization of Students	Uniform patterns: one teacher, 30 students in 6 rows of 5 in each row in each period of each school day.	Understanding that organization of students should match curricular intentions. Some initial variation of group sizes in classroom.	Limited organization to facilitate the grouping of the students. Begin use of aides and parents to increase organizational flexibility.	Full administrative support for a reorganization of students. Building restructured where necessary. An increase in planning for effectiveness.	Group sizes vary according to the activity planned. Full support given to eliminate any problem areas.

189

FIGURE 8.2 (continued)

	Present Condition Stage 1	Awareness Stage Stage 2	Experimentation Stage Stage 3	Adoption Stage Stage 4	Desired Condition Stage 5
	Instructional Organization (continued)				
Teaching Strategies	Some variety but lecture and teacher-dominated Q-A session the norm. Homework used to promote day-to-day continuity.	Observation of other teaching models. Skill development via workshops. An identification of staff strengths and weaknesses. Some new patterns.	Building-level experiments by willing staff members. "Modeling" of ideas. On-site consultant made available for skill development.	School day divided according to the teaching strategy employed. Faculty evaluation of the effectiveness of new ways after a trial period.	Great variety of methods used in teaching, uses of media, dealing with students. The curricular plans determine strategy.
	Participants' Roles				
Role of Student	Passive recipient of knowledge. Instruction is geared to average student. Reactive communication with the teacher.	Investigation of new student roles by teacher. Limited hierarchy of trust established in the classroom. Needs and interests of student investigated.	Ground rules for increased student independence set. Student involvement in planning. Role of student connected to philosophy of the school.	Periodic staff review of student roles. Roles linked to schoolwide rules and regulations. Philosophy guides role possibilities.	Students involved in planning and conducting the program. Increased independence and responsibility. Use of "contracts" to maintain new understandings.
Role of Teacher	Defined by the subject areas taught. Perceived as the source of all knowledge. Other roles peripheral.	Perceiving roles suggested by the philosophy. Roles accepted at verbal level. Limited experimentation with new roles.	Investigation of new roles—trying on new relationship. Goal setting for individual teacher. Skills development through in-service.	Administrative reorganization for role support. Sharpened planning and action skills needed to serve the student according to the philosophy.	Teacher role is defined by student needs. Teacher the organizer of the learning activities. Teacher talents used more effectively.
Role of Principal	Solely responsible for school operation. The "boss." Enforcer of all rules. The linkage to all outside information and resources.	Awareness of role limitations. Awareness of real leadership potential. Setting of role priorities.	Limited sharing of decision making in area of curriculum. Limited joint planning with the faculty. Review of existing policy according to the philosophy.	Role perception changes to manager of resources. Emphasis on development (active) rather than on order (static). Increase in curriculum leadership functions.	An instructional leader. Administrative acts support the curriculum program. Philosophy guiding decision making. Built-in monitoring system for evaluating building-level progress.
Role of Community	Little or no access to school. Information about programs scanty. Trust low.	Some school program ties to community. Token access via PTA and media. School perceived as island in neighborhood.	Preliminary uses of community as learning environment. Identification of nearby resources. Use of building for community functions.	Regular interchange between school and community. Systematic communication. A network of services and resources established.	School programs outwardly oriented. Community seen as a teaching resource. Systematic ties with services and resources around school.

FIGURE 8.2 *(continued)*

Administrative Conditions

Rules and Regulations	High degree of regimentation. Many rules, most inherited over the years. The emphasis on the enforcement and on control.	Staff and students identify essential rules. Regulations matched against the school philosophy.	Rules and regulations streamlined. Used as a teaching device about life outside school. Increased student self-control.	Greater use of student and staff input into the regulation of the school environment. Rewards built in for desirable performance.	Moving toward minimal regulation and increased student self-control. Regulations a positive teaching device.
Discipline	Reactive pattern ranging from verbal admonishment to paddling and expulsion. Reoccurring offenders.	Staff analysis of school policies. Shift of emphasis to causes of the problems. Some brainstorming of possible solutions.	Establishment of a hierarchy of discipline activity. Begin implementing preventive strategies.	Design of curriculum programs to deter discipline problems. High-intensity program for regular offenders.	School eliminates most sources of discipline problems. The procedure for residual problems made clear to all.
Student Progress Reports	*Progress* is defined narrowly. Letter or numeric grades represent student learning in the subject areas.	Recognition of broader growth goals for students. Use of philosophy to evaluate the existing practices.	Experimentation with supplemental reporting procedures. Involvement of student and parents in the process.	Development of a diverse and comprehensive reporting procedure for student progress.	Descriptive medium used to monitor individual progress. Broadly focused evaluation. Team of teacher, student, and parents.
Staff Development	Staff development is global, rarely used to attack local needs and problems. Occurs as needed.	Staff identifies inservice needs and priorities. Philosophy assists in this process. Local staff skills and strengths are recognized.	Staff development realigned to serve needs of teachers. Opportunities for personal growth are made available.	Formal procedures for directing staff development to needs established. Staff development seen as problem-solving mechanism.	Staff development an ongoing process using available resources. An attempt to close theory-practice gaps.

SOURCE: Adapted from "Developmental Staging—In Pursuit of Comprehensive Curriculum Planning" by Jon Wiles, *Middle School Journal* 6 (September 1975): 7–10. Used by permission.

all the way to what the teacher is doing in the classroom. Thus, *if* that is what we mean by "middle school," *then* where do we stand now (enter needs assessment)? *If* that is reality (needs assessment results), *then* what is the difference between where we are and where we want to be? *If* those are the differences, *then* which of these emerging goals are most important (priorities)?

Our model is based on four key points:

1. To bring about lasting change, the people to be affected (teachers, parents, administrators, pupils) must be involved in assessing the proposed changes.
2. Change cannot happen spontaneously in a bureaucratic environment like a school district and thus must be directed from the top.
3. Decisions are best made on the basis of hard data, and such information should be open to everyone involved in planning.
4. Evaluation and accountability can "drive" change in schools.

The planning of a middle school thus goes through a standard curriculum development cycle of analysis, design, implementation, and evaluation. On top of this historic process CMP establishes a routine that pushes the process along and keeps it from becoming sidetracked. The entire effort can be conceptualized as a distance-rate-time problem: As soon as we know where we are going (*distance*), the resources needed to implement the plan (*rate*) will determine the amount of *time* needed to accomplish the desired ends. Because of the philosophical thrusts of the middle school design, some three to five years are required in most districts to make a complete conversion from the junior high school design. Figure 8.3 presents a sample statement of philosophy.

FIGURE 8.3   Sample philosophy/goal statement

The middle school curriculums are more exploratory in nature than the elementary school and less specialized than the high school. Realizing that the uniqueness of individual subject disciplines must be recognized, an emphasis on interdisciplinary curriculum development will be stressed. Curriculum programs should emphasize the natural relationship among academic disciplines that facilitate cohesive learning experiences for middle school students through integrative themes, topics, and units. Interdisciplinary goals should overlap subject-area goals and provide for interconnections such as reasoning, logical and critical thought, coping capacities, assuming self-management, promoting positive personal development, and stimulating career awareness.

The academic program of a middle school emphasizes skills development through science, social studies, reading, mathematics, and language arts courses. A well-defined skills continuum is used as the basic guide in all schools in each area including physical education, health, guidance, and other educational activities. Exploratory opportunities are provided through well-defined and structured club programs, activity programs, and special interest courses, thereby creating opportunities for students to interact socially, to experience democratic living, to explore areas not in the required curriculum, to do independent study and research, to develop and practice responsible behavior, and to experience working with varying age groups.

The CMP Team

Essentially, a management team is composed of those district administrators (assistant superintendent for instruction, director of secondary education, director of elementary education, and so forth) who make final decisions about instruction and provide resources to principals and curriculum consultants. In its role as liaison between the board (and superintendent) and various committees charged with designing and implementing middle schools, this group initiates planning, conducts a major needs assessment, and reviews committee recommendations prior to submitting them for board approval.

The CMP depends heavily on committees to clarify values and provide planning direction. Despite having a negative connotation for most teachers and administrators, committees are essential to the "valuing" process. To lessen resistance, the CMP uses ad hoc (temporary) committees where possible, which makes such committee work highly directional and product-oriented. Key committees should be formed both by nomination of management team members and solicitations from the field. The committee concept affirms the wisdom of shared decision making and the value of both public and professional input at the policy formation stage. Committee members ultimately will go out and sell the concept to those who will be affected by it. The outline for a CMP committee structure is shown in Figure 8.4.

The *coordinating committee* (fifteen to twenty members) is comprised of citizens and school personnel who will oversee the entire process during a three- to five-year period. This committee will ensure that the conversion process is smooth and will use a management plan, four primary committees, and a series of other ad hoc groups to accomplish its tasks.

FIGURE 8.4 CMP committees

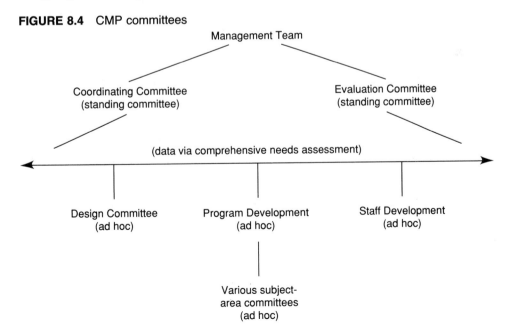

The *evaluation committee* (five to seven members including key evaluation personnel from the district) will monitor the progress of the conversion plan during the three to five years and report on that progress periodically to the board (see Figure 8.5). Major reports will include a definition of the middle school, formation of committees, results of the needs assessment, and a schedule for conversion; the middle school design and schedule of events for committees; a fully redefined curriculum complete with standards for all subjects and program areas; a staff development plan based on the projected curriculum; and a management plan for implementing the new program.

The *design committee* (about ten members) will establish general specifications for the middle school. These standards will be the product of information from a needs assessment as well as input from the public and professional literature.

The *program development committee* (about twenty members) will translate the standards of the design committee into quality indicators for all areas of the middle school curriculum. Specific ad hoc subcommittees in subject areas and special programs will be formed to assist this committee.

The *staff development committee* (about ten members) will plan and recommend inservice training for all middle school teachers charged with carrying out this plan at the classroom level. The basis of inservice planning will be the needs assessment, the program design, and local school implementation plans.

Thus, the board is sequentially asked to accept a philosophy and definition, adopt target goals and standards, accept definitions for new programs, and set aside funds for the long-term implementarion of program development and staff development activities.

Although the CMP system might appear unnecessarily cumbersome, recall that steps omitted or dealt with superficially jeopardizes the middle school concept. Teachers turn over, boards change, superintendents come and go; it is a rare district that can look ahead five years and carry out a plan to improve instruction. The bottom line is that the CMP works. The process minimizes political activity, guarantees continuity of effort across the district, manages change and resource allocation for the board, and eliminates single-issue crises for the administration. Most important for the middle school, it structures a thoughtful process whereby the philosophy of education can grow and intersect the planning process over time.

Figures 8.6 through 8.8 illustrate various components of a curriculum management plan.

FIGURE 8.5   Progress report #4: Orange County Middle School

In September 1983 the Orange County School Board committed the district to a new intermediate grade pattern (grades 6–8) based on the middle school concept. It was determined that by fall of 1987, Orange County would have the middle school organization in all of its 19 intermediate schools. Since that time, three progress reports on the transition process have been presented to the Board, with a fourth report being presented at this time.

 Progress report #1 outlined the rationale for the transition to the middle school concept, as well as a suggested approach to the conversion process. The report also listed the committees to be used throughout the process and also a review of data collected in surveys of students, parents, teachers, and administrators.

 Progress report #2 presented the proposed Orange County Middle School design, emphasizing a balanced program of subject content, personal development, and essential learning skills. Also found in this report were a suggested middle school staffing pattern, an organizational plan, and possible facilities considerations.

 Progress report #3 outlined the steps used in developing a curriculum appropriate for middle-level students. It also included a preliminary report from the staff development and public relations committees. Finally, this report presented a sample of the curriculum developed by each of the 36 ad hoc committees.

 Progress report #4 presents an overall evaluation of progress since the fall of 1983 and also projections for completion of our reorganization to the middle school concept. It should be noted that as we move closer to our target date of August 1987, the evaluation committee will have a greater role in the process. This is to guarantee that Orange County can, with confidence, say *"Coming soon, America's best middle schools."*

FIGURE 8.6 Dade County Public Schools: Action plan for middle school transition 1988–1992

The following action plan is based on the achievement of district tasks, as outlined in the attached plan, which is a part of the district's comprehensive plan to fully implement the middle school concept in all Dade County intermediate level schools. The tasks are a part of the Dade County Curriculum Management Plan (CMP) Model, a comprehensive and systematic approach to curricular and organizational change. Additional tasks may be added during the transition period as needs arise, and targeted dates accelerated when resources permit. The transition to middle school follows mandates of the state of Florida's PRIME legislation, and meets goals for educational excellence in Dade County, established by the superintendent and board.

This document is intended to serve as a guide for the board, district and school personnel, coordinating committee, and community persons in monitoring the tasks completed and pending in the middle school transition.

Task	Time Line	Person(s) Responsible
1. Develop RFP to hire consultants for development and implementation of a long-range 4-year plan. This will include training of middle school leaders, and development of the CMP for implementation of Dade County's model middle school program 1988–92.	February 1988 Due April 28 for May 11 board meeting	Management team J. L. DeChurch
2. Identify 15 pilot schools 1988–89.	March 31, 1988	Paul Bell J. L. DeChurch Management team
3. Selection of preliminary consultants to do initial training of principals and teams.	March 1988	Management team
4. Training of principal and one other building administrator for 15 pilot schools 1988–89.	April 14 and 15, 1988	Consultants (Wiles-Bondi)
5. Meeting of Management Team for middle school transition.	April 15, 1988	Management team Wiles-Bondi
6. Identification of team leaders in the 15 targeted middle schools 1988–89.	April 25, 1988	Principals of targeted schools
7. Training of team leaders for pilot schools 1988–89.	May 12–13, 1988	Wiles-Bondi
8. Preliminary needs assessment completed for selected 15 pilot schools.	March 1988	Wiles-Bondi
9. Review of present advisory program activities in middle grades.	April 1988	Wiles-Bondi Selected representatives from pilot schools (Advisory Committee)

FIGURE 8.6 *(continued)*

10. Develop materials for advisory program.	Fall 1988	Wiles-Bondi Advisory Committee
11. Piloting and evaluation of advisory program in 15 pilot schools.	1988–89 school year	Principals Advisory coordinators (pilot schools)
12. Midpoint assessment/sharing meeting of team. Implementation 15 pilot schools.	November 18, 1988	Wiles-Bondi Team leaders
13. Selection of members of coordinating committee. Board designation of all intermediate level schools as middle schools.	November 1988	Joseph Fernandez Paul Bell J. L. DeChurch Management team
14. First meeting of coordinating committee.	December 15, 1988	Paul Bell, chairman
15. Development of inservice plan for middle school transition. Inservice training to be ongoing beginning in 1988 school year.	December 16, 1988	Elvira Dopico Ken Walker Karen Dreyfuss Ed Trauschke Wiles-Bondi
16. Needs assessment conducted—all intermediate schools.	Spring 1989 completion	Wiles-Bondi
17. Training of trainers for first three training components.	Spring 1989	Wiles-Bondi
18. Identification of second group of schools for middle school transition (1989–90)	Spring 1989	Paul Bell
19. Training updating, information sessions conducted for board, district, school personnel, parents, community.	Ongoing—1988–92	Paul Bell J. L. DeChurch Management team
20. Training of administrative leadership for 1989–90 pilot schools.	May 1989	Wiles-Bondi
21. Training of team leaders for second group of middle schools 1989–90.	June 1989	Wiles-Bondi
22. Team Fair one	March 30–31	Wiles-Bondi Middle school principals Team leaders
23. Coordinating Committee meeting three.	March 31, 1989	Paul Bell

24. Progress Report #1 to board
  a. Results of needs assessment
  b. Tasks completed
	June 1989	Joseph Fernandez
		Paul Bell
		J. L. DeChurch
		Wiles-Bondi

FIGURE 8.6 *(continued)*

c. Tasks pending		
d. Evaluation or progress of year one implementation.		
25. Summer training of staff. This will lead to middle school endorsement and internal certification.	June–August 1989	Kenneth Walker Karen Dreyfuss Margaret Petersen Wiles-Bondi
26. Clinical assistance-visitation to pilot schools.	Ongoing— 1988–92	Wiles-Bondi District staff Area superintendents and staff
27. Curriculum development, refinement of middle school subject areas.	Spring 1989–ongoing	J. L. DeChurch
28. Development of middle school intramural program.	Summer 1989	District staff
29. Piloting of intramural program.	Fall 1989	District staff
30. Coordinating committee meeting four.	October 1989	Paul Bell
31. Midpoint assessment/sharing of team implementation in second group of middle schools.	November 1989	Wiles-Bondi Team leaders
32. Coordinating committee meeting five.	December 1989	Paul Bell
33. Team Fair two.	March 30, 1989	Wiles-Bondi Middle school principals
34. Identification of third group of middle schools for 1990–91 year.	March 1990	Paul Bell J. L. DeChurch Management team
35. Training of administrators in third group of middle schools (1990–91).	May 1990	Wiles-Bondi
36. Training of team leaders—third group (1990–91)	June 1990	Wiles-Bondi
37. Progress Report #2 to board—Evaluation of year two progress.	June 1990	Joseph Fernandez Paul W. Bell J. L. DeChurch Wiles-Bondi
38. Evaluation of piloted intramural program and curriculum changes in middle schools.	June 1990	J. L. DeChurch District supervisors

FIGURE 8.6 *(continued)*

39. Coordinating committee meeting six.	October 1990	Paul W. Bell
40. Midpoint assessment/sharing of team implementation in third group of converted middle schools.	November 1990	Wiles-Bondi Team leaders
41. Coordinating committee meeting seven.	March 1991	Paul W. Bell
42. Team Fair three	March 1991	Wiles-Bondi Middle school principals Team leaders
43. Identification of fourth and last group of middle schools.	March 1991	Paul W. Bell J. L. DeChurch Management team
44. Training of administrators in fourth group of middle schools (1991–92).	May 1991	Wiles-Bondi
45. Training of team leaders in fourth group of middle schools in conversion process (1991–92).	June 1991	Wiles-Bondi
46. Progress Report #3 to board—Evaluation of year three progress	June 1991	Joseph Fernandez Paul Bell J. L. DeChurch Wiles-Bondi
47. Coordinating committee meeting eight.	December 1991	Paul Bell
48. Midpoint assessment/sharing of team implementation in fourth group of converted middle schools.	November 1991	Wiles-Bondi Team leaders
49. Coordinating committee's final meeting.	March 1992	Paul Bell
50. Team Fair four	March 1992	Wiles-Bondi Middle school principals Team leaders
51. Progress Report #4 to Board—Evaluation of year four transition.	June 1992	Joseph Fernandez Paul Bell Management team
52. Final evaluation of Dade County's transition to middle schools. Publication/dissemination of report.	June 1992	Joseph Fernandez Paul Bell Management team

FIGURE 8.7 Dade County, the school-based action plan for middle school transition [Excerpts]

The following action plan is based on achievement of the standards for Dade County middle schools as outlined in the *Middle School Design Report*. The plan's purpose is to help middle school administrators focus on those standards already achieved and, more important, those standards still needing attention.

School _____

Principal _____

Standards (Sample)	Date to be Achieved	Date Achieved	Activities to Meet Standards	Person(s) Responsible
1. Middle school orientation sessions conducted for faculty to acquaint them with requirements for teaching in the middle school.			1. Provide staff with philosophical premise of middle school. 2. Share action planning concept and determine staff to work on the project. 3. Provide staff with information on components of middle schools. 4. Develop timelines for inservice. Completion of summer components A through D.	
2. Leadership training completed by all potential middle school administrators and counselors where possible. (Summer 1989)				
3. Submit time line of middle school inservice for all staff.			1. Indicate the vehicle for delivery of inservice. 2. Identify the trainers. 3. Identify the planned date of inservice. 4. Provide the TEC participant rosters to middle school office.	
4. Teams organized at the sixth, seventh, and eighth grades prior to implementation of middle school. Team members have common students, common instructional time, and common planning team.			Advanced group will have teams in all grades prior to opening of school 1989. Intermediate group will have one or more teams in place prior to 1989. Beginning group will develop staff inservice and schedule interdisciplinary teaming for 1990–91 school year.	
5. Adviser/advisee program implemented according to level of school organization.			1. Advanced group—Focus materials must be in each teacher's hands and inservice *completed.* 2. Intermediate group—must show progress or evidence of implementation by beginning of second semester. 3. Beginning group—must show evidence of inservice in time lines.	

FIGURE 8.7 *(continued)*

School _____

Principal _____

Standards (Sample)	Date to be Achieved	Date Achieved	Activities to Meet Standards	Person(s) Responsible
6. Teams organized at each grade level. Team functions monitored: Goals and objectives are directed at the needs of students and correspond with school and district goals.			Principal and assistant principals should hold weekly team leader meetings.	
21. The district's evaluation design is discussed with faculty and parents in fall of each year of middle school operation. Evaluation results provided at school and district levels in May of each year.			Pre- and post-needs assessment conducted through middle school office.	
22. Action plans for improvement of middle school program is presented by middle school principal to staff, parents, and regional office each September. Results of evaluation report from previous school year, and needs assessment data are incorporated into action plans.				

FIGURE 8.8   Products: Middle school transition, 1989–1994 (Duval County)

Middle School Design
Standards Checklist
Staff Development Plan

☐ Training Program for Teachers/Support Personnel
☐ Training Program for Development of Video Training
☐ Modules for Administration
☐ Training Program for Clinical Inservice for Administrators

Evaluation Plan
Advisory Program Developed
Intramural Program Developed
Curriculum Mapped
Articulation Plan K–5, 6–8, 9–12
Plan for Logistics—Transfer of materials for implementing new grade organization.
Plan for Building Construction—Renovations to accommodate the new K–5, 6–8, –12
Evaluation Reports
Transition Programs—Grades 4–5 and 9–10
Model Interdisciplinary Units
Cooperative Preservice Program
Alternative Program for At-Risk Students—Grades 4–10
Technology Program in Place—K–5, 6–8
County League of Middle Schools
New Grading/Reporting System
District Resource Centers
Public Relations Program

Student Goals

☐ Increase attendance
☐ Increase achievement as measured by local and state tests
☐ Decrease number of dropouts
☐ Decrease failure rate
☐ Improve student attitude toward school
☐ Reduce percentage of at-risk students

Parents

☐ Increase parent awareness of middle school
☐ Increase parent participation in middle school program

Teachers

☐ Improve teacher skills in middle school instruction
☐ Improve teacher attendance
☐ Improve teacher morale

Community

☐ Increase business/industry partnerships in middle school
☐ Increase business/industry/foundation contributions to middle school

SUMMARY

Establishing a middle school that will truly serve preadolescent youth requires extensive planning. This chapter examined middle school planning at both the district and school levels. The Wiles-Bondi Curriculum Management Plan (CMP) Model was used to illustrate the comprehensive nature of middle school planning. Actual examples from successful conversions and transitions of middle schools were presented in the chapter and are supplemented in Appendix 8 to demonstrate how theory can be put into practice.

SUGGESTED LEARNING ACTIVITIES

1. Prepare an outline of a district plan for organizing a middle school.
2. Organize a panel discussion on the topic "Why we need a middle school." What type of persons might contribute to your panel?
3. Prepare an outline of a school study designed to prepare a faculty for the middle school.

4. Develop your own goal statement for a middle school program. From this statement, extract the essential components of a middle school program and curriculum.

NOTES

1. Ralph H. Tyler, *Basic Principles of Curriculum and Instruction* (Chicago: University of Chicago Press, 1949).
2. Hilda Taba, *Curriculum Development: Theory and Practice* (New York: Harcourt Brace Jovanovich, 1962).

3. Jon Wiles and Joseph Bondi, *Making Middle Schools Work* (Alexandria, VA: Association for Supervision and Curriculum Development, 1986).

SELECTED REFERENCES

Wiles, Jon, and Bondi, Joseph, "Planning for Middle Schools—The Right Way," *Penn. Schoolmaster* (December 1981): 23–24.
———, *The Essential Middle School Resources,* 24 volumes (Tampa: Wiles, Bondi and Associates, 1992).

Wiles, Jon; Bondi, Joseph; and Stodghill, Ronald, "Miracle on Main Street: The St. Louis Story," *Educational Leadership* (November 1982): 52–53.

9

Service Delivery and Implementation

Where there is a will, there is a way.

INTRODUCTION

Chapters 6 through 8 of this book dealt primarily with design and preliminary planning of a middle school. What should be clear by now is that planning does not cease upon the opening of a new (or converted) facility, but is an ongoing process. This chapter covers implementation, which has two purposes: (1) communicating to students, parents, teachers, principals, school board members, elementary and high school staffs, support staff, and the community at large that the middle school is ready to open and (2) disseminating information about the school's goals and purposes and changes in curriculum, organization, and buildings.[1]

Concurrent with implementation and development is installation and/or development of inservice training for teachers, administrators, and support personnel. How implementation progresses is summarized in Figure 9.1.

The chapter also discusses specific guidelines and recommendations for getting program delivery under way by announcing goals and purposes; what is to be accomplished by inservice training; how physical plant facilities are to be used and adapted; and how special student needs (e.g., for exceptional students) are to be met. The programs highlighted in this chapter include advisement, intramurals, magnet schools, fine arts, vocational exploration, ESE, and ESL. Also included are guidelines for a comprehensive health program and a partnership program.

A brief description is provided on fundamental intermediate schools and on articulation. The chapter is supplemented by examples in Appendix 9.

ANNOUNCING SERVICE DELIVERY AND IMPLEMENTATION

Even though students, teachers, parents, school board members, representatives from other school levels, and community persons should have been involved in planning the establishment or conversion of a middle school, the full implications may not be realized until actual implementation is under way. Despite the best efforts to ensure community education and awareness, often critics emerge who complain about change—"It simply isn't what I'm used to!" Continuous presentation of information via handbooks, press releases, newsletters, open houses, community orientations, and the like, hopefully will overcome doubts and antagonism and will facilitate the implementation process.

Furthermore, the needs assessment and feasibility studies should have identified objectives, the agents who will carry out those objectives, a reasonable timetable for achievement, and a CMP team to oversee all stages of the overall process—design, planning, implementation, and evaluation.

The following subsections discuss a few ways to communicate the uniqueness, appropriateness, and importance of having a middle school in the community.

Handbooks for Students and Parents

A number of schools use interesting and informative handbooks to convey service-delivery information. The table of contents on page 208 was developed by a faculty undergoing inservice training for the transition of their junior high to a middle school.

FIGURE 9.1 Moving toward a model middle school program

Conventional Junior High School Program ──────────────────────────────────► Model Middle School Program

Category	Conventional Junior High School Program				Model Middle School Program
Curriculum	Single text county course guides	Interrelated scope/s sequence in at least 2 content areas	Interrelation of 4 content areas—include scope and sequence for self-awareness	Interdisciplinary instruction at maximum level—skill development	High-interest curriculum interdisciplinary program—skill, etc.
Staff	One certified teacher—300 minutes—pupil-teacher ratio	Clerical assistance to teams	Use of paraprofessionals for classroom duties	Differentiated certified personnel—task assignment	Utilization of varied personnel—task assignment
Schedule	Administrative decision is conventional	Block schedule—common instruction—common plan	Larger blocks of time—flexible time blocks	Block schedule—flexible instructional planning time	Demand schedule—flexible—individualized
Grouping	Lockstep	Proficiency interest groups	Specific diagnosis subgroups, flexible groups	Cooperative planning between students and teachers	Individual student planned program—teacher and child
Materials	State-adopted text at grade level	Multilevel texts	Supplemental texts, kits	Manipulative audiovisuals programmed texts peer production of materials	Use of community as classroom
Teaming	None	Team representing 2 disciplines	Teaming representing 4 disciplines	Include at least one exploratory	Differential use of total staff

Conventional Junior High School Program ──────────────────────────────────► Model Middle School Program

I.	Introduction	(the meaning and purpose of the middle school and when and where it will begin)
II.	Goals and Philosophy	(a summary that explains what the school will seek to accomplish)
III.	The Middle School Student	(how the system will create a more motivated student due to more individualized teaching)
IV.	Curriculum Organization	(a description of the three program phases—skills, education for social competence, and personal development; typical student schedule)
V.	Team Teaching, Interdisciplinary Instruction	(one-page summary of teaming and interdisciplinary instruction)
VI.	Enrichment	(list of activities that demonstrate how the program is designed to inspire, motivate, and enrich students)
VII.	Questions	(common questions and answers)
VIII.	Conclusion	(letter from the principal reaffirming plan's success)

Another handbook format might be "layered," with the student description on one column or page and the school description on another (see Appendix 9).

Appendix 9 also includes examples of school and team newsletters.

Advisory Groups, News Releases, Orientation Programs

Lay advisory committees keep parents and the community aware of educational changes and can be extremely valuable in promoting the benefits of the middle school. This group can select members to appear before various organizations and assist the staff in interpreting the school's programs.

As they undergo studies on the transition from junior high to middle school status, staff can submit their findings in news releases to local media (radio, TV, newspapers). The public is interested in educational changes that have local and national implications and therefore is more likely to be receptive.

Informative booklets and small group guidance sessions have been successful in preparing students for the middle school. Once convinced that the school is best for them and once they begin to enjoy individual successes, students will sell the program to parents—the best endorsement possible.

Several school districts set aside days prior to school opening during which new students can visit and "run through" a day's schedule on a shortened-time basis. This way, positive attitudes on the part of teachers and students alike help get the school off to a good start.

Figures 9.2 and 9.3 are samples of school-developed information/orientation sheets designed to acquaint parents, teachers at other levels, and the public about

FIGURE 9.2 Why change to a middle school?

Challenge:	Space-age technology demands that today's students be *challenged* to adapt to complex life-styles. Teaching methods must provide educational experiences that will help our children thrive in the environment we have created.
Habits:	Old *habits,* approaches, and structures need to give way to creative nonconformity.
Achievement:	Our children must *achieve* to their maximum potential and learn critical thinking and problem-solving techniques.
Needs:	Today's preadolescents have many *needs* (physical, social, emotional, intellectual) that must be met through a program that will foster a desire to reach the ultimate educational attainment.
Grouping:	The self-contained classroom *grouping,* with graded curriculum and static organization, must defer to flexibility and individual student needs.
Evaluation:	Continuous *evaluation* is an antidote to standard grading and unrealistic expectations of each child's progress.

Ingredients for Change

Child:	Programs must be *child*-centered to meet unique transescent needs.
Helpers:	The cooperative effort of *helpers*—professional staff, clerical personnel, aides, parents, and the community is needed for effective delivery.
Attitude:	A sincere *attitude* on the part of teachers reaffirms the Golden Rule: Teachers must respect students as they expect to be respected.
Nongrading:	A *nongraded* structure places individual student needs above standardized academic pacing.
Growth:	Each child must be permitted to *grow* at his or her own unique rate of progress.
Enthusiasm:	Teacher *enthusiasm* is the heart of the middle school system.

the new middle school. A schedule for advisory program implementation is shown in Appendix 9.

SUSTAINING INSERVICE TRAINING

As already mentioned, a major problem within the middle school movement has been the lack of sustained inservice training. Too often programs fall into decline because a faculty originally trained for the middle school environment fails to continue with follow-up staff development, or new teachers are not trained at all. Thus, a number of middle schools suffer the same fate as the junior high.

In the essential middle school, however, teacher, administrator, and support personnel training continues throughout service delivery. Effective staff development can be carried out at both the district and school levels but is more meaningful at the latter.

FIGURE 9.3 Suggested activities related to certain transescent traits

Traits	Implication for Instructional Activities
□ Physically active; short attention span; difficulty completing projects	Explanation, group discussion, demonstration, reporting, movies, workbook and practice sheets, charts and maps, drawing/painting, constructing, experimenting, decorating, role-play, quizzes and contests, field trips, textbooks and supplemental readings
□ Curious, spontaneous, enthusiastic; talents and giftedness emerge if present	Classroom is a "laboratory of life"—real life experiences form foundation for learning activities: experimentation, investigation, reporting, story telling and writing (fiction and nonfiction), poetry, art, music, building and modeling, independent projects, student officer and management projects, committees, small group work, tutoring
□ In transition from adult influences and standards to peer-group standards	Increased responsibility in management of student affairs: active student government, autonomy in classroom operating procedures and standards of achievement, distribution of responsibilities
□ Developing self-awareness, seeking identity, learning self-evaluation; attracted to clubs and cliques	Study outstanding people (historical or contemporary), analyze and determine qualities of greatness, join clubs or special-interest groups

Some districts are setting up teacher renewal centers that offer inservice training for new and seasoned teachers on a continued basis throughout the year. (One such center, the TORC Model, is discussed later in this section.) Hopefully such measures will offset the absence of special undergrad training programs in colleges and universities. Declining enrollments and a tight job market have somewhat leveled off the high rate of teacher turnover, so that experienced teachers remain for longer periods in a middle school. The renewal center concept, then, will focus on development of current staff while offering an attractive alternative to the hit-and-miss approach of quick college courses or isolated workshops.

For principals and support staff who also lack the benefit of ongoing training, a promising trend in some districts is implementation at the school level of curriculum assistants who hold administrative lines but work directly with teachers in the classroom. Many of these individuals are advancing into principalships, and good results have been observed. (Review Figure 6.1 for key characteristics of a middle school principal.)

In implementing inservice training, note that if a consultant is used, make sure he or she remains with the project for a two- or three-year period to monitor the program's evolution. Also provide adequate time for training. A number of districts not only schedule traditional summer workshops, they also provide time during the school year for inservice participation; several days a month students may be dismissed early for this purpose. Some schools undergoing transition to a middle school fall into the trap of trying to do too much too soon. A faculty should take on only what it can accomplish well the first year; this way, disillusionment is avoided if too-ambitious goals are not met. Remember, planning is an *ongoing* process.

More on Team Building

Team building was discussed at great length in Chapter 5 but a few additional points are covered here within the context of implementation. In that most middle schools rely on teaming, most training in team teaching gets under way prior to program implementation, but the process (like inservice training) is continuous throughout program development.

Teaming builds a spirit of trust and collaboration between teachers and students while at the same time setting and achieving shared goals. Thus, flexibility is a key driving force: Team members must be able to make short-notice changes without isolating themselves from the group process. Teaming also means frequent meetings, ability to compromise, and openness to innovative ideas. Because innovation is a building block of middle school philosophy, team members must be objective and examine ideas—not personalities.

Team meetings should be held in a comfortable physical environment (comfortable chairs, temperature, lighting, ventilation, and so on), with members seated in a circle so that all are visible. Once introductions are made (for a new team), a climate of openness is further established when members—of new teams as well as teams that have worked together previously—state (or restate) the team's purpose, goals, expectations, and so forth. (Review the team-building work sheet in Figure 5.3.)

Develop a clear newsprint contract between team members and individuals who have special responsibilities (such as a team leader, whose responsibilities might include grouping and scheduling students, planning team activities, planning for use of resource personnel, developing guidelines for student discipline). For example:

Step 1: Team members as a group work separately from team leader, etc. List on newsprint: How we would like (name) to function as (*person's special responsibility*) for our team. At same time team leader, working alone, lists on newsprint "How I would like to function as _____ of this team."

Step 2: Hang newsprint lists side-by-side and negotiate the differences.

Staff Development Centers: A Promising Trend

To sustain inservice training of middle school teachers, a growing number of school districts are developing teacher renewal or staff development centers. Some of the centers are classified as teacher education centers while others are extensions of the regular staff development program of the school district.

The purpose of such centers is to provide practical, hands-on types of inservice workshops for middle school teachers. The authors have participated in the development of a number of these centers and also have conducted numerous workshops at such centers. Teachers have been extremely positive about their participation in staff development centers. The follow-up help they receive in their own classroom from instructional associates and curriculum specialists attached to the centers makes the centers even more popular with middle school teachers.

An excellent example of a middle school staff development center is the TORC model, described as follows:

Teacher Orientation/Renewal Center

In recent years the emergence of middle schools has been, in many cases, in name only. The purpose of the teacher orientation/renewal center (TORC) is to provide a practical approach for teachers learning additional methods of classroom management and skills development to assist them in meeting the needs of the middle school learner. One way to involve teachers in the development and implementation of a learner-oriented classroom is to establish a center at which they can experience modeling of teacher behaviors and can explore a variety of techniques of classroom management.

TORC objectives for participants are: individualization, behavior modification, behavioral objectives, diagnosing and prescribing, classroom organization, classroom management systems, flexible scheduling, and student participation in planning, for these areas can be related to content in the various disciplines.

The rationale for TORC is based on the educational principle "learn by doing." The way to involve teachers in the development and implementation of a learner-centered classroom is to be sure teachers experience a learner-centered classroom as a learner. Teachers learn varied classroom management systems and teaching strategies by experiencing them. The trainer models the teacher's role.

Teachers may volunteer to attend a three-day training session in a center designed to model various management systems. Teachers may then sign a contract with a resource teacher and their principal to continue study of the content of TORC or to implement TORC ideas in their classrooms. They may earn component points for this work. Resource teachers provide follow-up support that includes the following:

□ Keeping the TORC center open Wednesdays from 3 to 9 P.M.
□ Helping teachers obtain instructional materials, supplies, and equipment
□ Pooling materials and ideas from various schools and making them available for sharing
□ Writing a newsletter to TORC graduates offering suggestions and encouragement
□ Working in classrooms to help teachers introduce students to new classroom procedures
□ Helping teachers make instructional materials, such as audiotapes, kits, and games
□ Helping teachers redesign their classrooms
□ Serving as a contact person with content supervisors

TORC can be used by teachers to fulfill part of the requirements for middle school certification. Participation would be on a voluntary basis and teachers interested in a learner-center classroom can receive direct help and support to put their ideas into operation. Materials would be pooled and shared among schools so that successful programs throughout the county can be shared by all district middle school students. The TTT (Teachers Teaching Teachers) Model (discussed in Chapter 3 and Appendix 3) is compatible with the TORC Model in that the TORC center is staffed by teachers on special assignment.

These proposals and alternatives offer a way to put the learner-oriented school into practice. They give the teacher concrete methods and support in implementing the middle school program. Teachers working together and sharing ideas and materials, with follow-up support from curriculum assistants and supervisors, will improve morale as well as enhance students' educational experiences. Following their attendance at the center, teachers can better determine which style, or combination of styles, of classroom management and techniques best suit them and their students.

IMPLEMENTING BUILDING FACILITIES

Chapter 7 dealt extensively with physical plant facilities and how spatial design affects the learning and teaching experience. This section recaps key points on planning, using, and implementing middle school building accommodations.

Whether the school is to open in a traditional setting or an open-space modern facility, certain points are important to keep in mind.

Planning

The entire staff should have been involved in the initial planning stages, offering specifications—either by suggesting renovations for the old plant or translating learning and teaching styles into spatial design. For example:

- First and foremost, the setting must be pleasant for students to work and play in.
- The learning resource center should be in close proximity to all other instructional areas.
- The resource center should accommodate individual and/or group independent work.
- The classroom climate should be constantly evaluated for variables that affect learning—structure, responsibility, reward, risk, warmth, and so forth.
- Access points, traffic control patterns, and the like, should be continuously monitored for conformity with the middle school philosophy.
- Color, acoustics, furnishings, and accessories should encourage mental freedom.
- The outdoors is part of the classroom setting, and easy interaction between indoor and outdoor learning areas should be maintained vigilantly.

Utilization

Students, staff, and parents should be called on to constantly look for new and better ways to utilize the middle school plant. As implementation progresses through various adaptive stages, so too must evaluation of space usage. Planners should remember that all spaces are "fair game."

- No longer is the lunchroom restricted to mealtime use and can be used during nonmeal hours as team meeting areas for more efficient utilization of space.
- School counselors must always have access to space where they can meet with students in privacy.
- Housing students in close proximity allows them to move freely from one activity to another without disturbing others.

IMPLEMENTING SPECIAL PROGRAMS

The middle school teaches not only the traditional core subjects, it hosts a variety of special programs. The remainder of this chapter offers guidelines for implementing advisory, intramural, magnet (including its spinoff, the fundamental intermediate school), fine arts, vocational exploratory, ESE, and ESL programs. Guidelines are also provided for a comprehensive health program and a partnership program.[2]

Adviser/Advisee Program

In an advisory program (or advisement), the teacher serves as adviser, school expert, and guide for each student in the group. The program focus is the social and emotional growth of the students. Difficulties arise during implementation primarily due to two reasons: (1) failure to consider the planning time and commitment required to assemble a successful program and (2) failure to provide parameters for ongoing staff development—for example:

□ Clarify purpose and objectives of the program.
□ Design adviser/advisee classes that are smaller than average class size, so that every teacher—including specialists—can lead a small student group for some scheduled part of the school day on predetermined days.
□ Try to ensure that the adviser is someone who has daily classroom contact with the advisees in the group—a factor even more significant than group size.
□ Schedule a regular class meeting time so that the class does not appear to be merely an appendage to the school day.
□ Schedule so that class time is an *uninterrupted* twenty-five minutes.
□ Try to ensure that the student/advisee remains with the same adviser throughout the middle school years.
□ Establish some broad goals so that the group's attention is focused, values-based, and goal-oriented.[3]

With input from school guidance counselors, all or most of the certificated staff maintain their involvement. The interdisciplinary planning team, expanded to include other teachers and support personnel, separates the students in the homebase unit into nonacademic advisement groups, which are an integral part of the homebase unit. Figure 9.4 shows two of several ways in which the advisement program might work. Other advisory themes are listed in Appendix 9.

Intramural Program

The organizational pattern of an intramural program is one of the most important aspects in determining its potential for success. In many instances, the administration and faculty can hold the key to success or failure. The choice of organizational pattern can be determined only after investigation of the needs, interests, student abilities, and availability of equipment and facilities. The activities program must allow for flexibility, improvements, and changes in these specific guidelines to meet the student needs of each school.

The underlying purpose of an intramural program is to provide additional experiences that will help the student achieve the broader goals of education—maximum participation in the student body; development of fundamental skills; and development of positive attitudes, social behaviors, and self-esteem.

FIGURE 9.4   Advisory program options

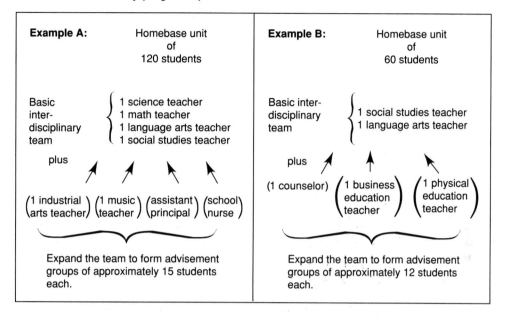

Objectives that further full participation include providing a wide variety of activities that emphasize many different skill levels and areas of interest; organizing teams such that they are balanced in terms of grade-level ability; and offering activities that are age-specific and skill level–specific.

Objectives that enhance fundamental skills include provision of skilled professional leadership through the physical education department; coordination of functions of the physical education department via continuity of skill and personal development; provision of adequate staff, facilities, and equipment for a safe environment; and solicitation of participation and cooperation of all academic teachers who are interested in and dedicated to the middle school philosophy as it applies to the intramural program.

Objectives that promote social skills are to provide opportunities for experience in human relationships (cooperation, social interaction), to build a positive learning environment through the enforcement of activity rules and etiquette, and to allow for development of leadership skills and sportsmanship.

An intramural director and intramural committee should be appointed, composed of teachers from each grade-level team and from each grade level, representatives from departments not represented on teams, and students from each grade level. The committee should establish guidelines that deal with issues such as selection and scheduling of activities, sign-up procedures, officiating, equipment and supplies, forfeits, postponements, protests, safety regulations, faculty participation, behavior on the field, evaluation, awards and recognition. The kinds of activities selected for the intramural program will help determine its success.

Each school should hold a preschool workshop to familiarize the school staff with the program.

In recognition of the diversity among schools, the following shows some scheduling alternatives:

□ Set aside one hour each day either before or after school for the intramural staff to spend with students, as part of their regular duties: The length of individual activities will be determined by the number of advisory teams or number of students in the school.
□ Designate the last period as intramurals period, three days per week: This would enable each grade level to participate one day per week and each student to participate four times a month with no loss of instructional time if the schedule is rotated on that day to have the adviser/advisee time at the end of the day. The schedule for last-period physical education classes should be restricted so as to allow for intramural scheduling.
□ Schedule during school hours utilizing adviser/advisee time: Students participate during their adviser/advisee time one day per week without rotating schedules.
□ Schedule schoolwide intramural day once per grading period: A variety of activities are provided to allow for maximum student-body participation. Points are awarded and students compete for team rather than individual recognition.

Six organizational points should be borne in mind:

1. The adviser/advisee program should be the main focus of the intramural program.
2. Students are placed on teams from within their academic team.
3. Rules and regulations are expressed during adviser/advisee time.
4. Intramural activities should be scheduled in consideration with available facilities and equipment.
5. On the designated day, students and faculty should dress down to eliminate locker-room time.
6. The intramural facilitator should be responsible for planning and organizing the entire intramural program.

Whether or not scoring, or a point system, is used, implementation depends on the individual school's philosophy.

Although intramural participation should be intrinsically rewarding, extrinsic awards may be provided on an individual or team basis.

Two recommendations are indicated:

1. Where possible, physical education classes should be scheduled by grade level and by consecutive blocked classes. This configuration will provide a more readily available time frame to facilitate intramural participation.
2. An intramural facilitator should be selected at the beginning of the school year to coordinate and organize intramural activities.

Magnet Program

Magnet programs (or schools) provide opportunities for academic excellence in the basic areas of study as well as for intensive educational experiences in areas in which students demonstrate unusual talent and/or interest. Additionally, magnet programs offer students a chance to acquire or develop skills, knowledge, and understanding necessary to pursue postsecondary aspirations in highly specialized areas of interest.

Enrollment of middle school students in magnet programs serves to further implement the middle school philosophy, which fosters the development of individual interests and encourages a high level of student performance—an outcome of which is improved self-esteem. Further, the program design of a large number of magnets calls for interdisciplinary study.

The parameters for middle school curriculum design are enhanced through the delivery of magnet experiences. For example, in terms of academic excellence, middle school classes are generally offered at the advanced and honors level. Magnet theme classes are offered in two- or three-hour blocks, providing for intensive instruction and continuous study in a specific content area. Student admission is determined by multiple criteria, which may include standardized test scores, teacher recommendation, student grades, written essays, oral interviews, and auditions. This allows for the appropriate placement of students, based on individual needs and learning styles. Finally, magnet programs are organized to maximize learning through infusion of theme-related content into the academic core, interdisciplinary study, and exposure to three types of instruction: didactic, coaching, and seminars/studios.

In terms of personal development, a student's decision to enter a magnet typically follows an exploration period. Interaction with guidance counselors and career information specialists is key to this decision-making process. The success achieved by the highly motivated student in a magnet school of his or her choosing contributes greatly to the building of self-esteem.

Along the continuous learning path, the development of magnet curricula has purposefully been established as a carefully articulated K–12 sequence. State-of-the-art equipment is installed to provide students with exposure to the technology of the 1990s. Courses are designed to provide a rigorous and challenging pace for the able middle school learner, and teachers are encouraged to utilize varied strategies to promote critical thinking and creative thinking as well as continuous learning.

Magnet programs can apply seven organizational formats:

1. *Interdisciplinary teams:* Viewed as an essential element to creating "holistic" program outcomes and limited only by the academic or elective nature of the program theme.

2. *Advisement:* Gives magnet students the opportunity to explore new avenues (e.g., interests, future careers). Extensive teacher-pupil interaction provides a vehicle for formally and informally assessing progress of each student.

3. *Block scheduling:* Facilitates in-depth instruction in magnet program content areas. Grouping students in magnet-specific content classes based on interest and knowledge of students results in homogeneous rather than heterogeneous grouping. However, potential conflict arises in the scheduling of nonacademic blocks of instructional time, which may necessarily limit scheduling flexibility, defined by the number of teams in each school.

4. *Team planning and shared decision making:* Integrating magnet students into grade-level teams to promote team continuity and appropriate course-level of-

ferings requires special consideration. The need for academic electives presents problems in team scheduling and student-teacher ratios.

5. *Exploratory and developmental experiences:* Magnet schools, with themes and/or focus related to the professions (engineering, business and finance, and teaching), provide preliminary preparation for, and specific opportunities in, career planning. Extension of the classroom into the community through frequent field trips, career shadowing, internships, and utilization of adjunct teachers facilitates career awareness. The unique curricular opportunities provided by magnets provide extended avenues for student exploration not available in the basic program.

6. *Integrated curriculum:* Required courses are infused with magnet theme and/or focus content above and beyond the magnet-specific electives. Broadly designed themes and/or focus—for example the humanities—allows for interdisciplinary curriculum development and instruction.

7. *Inservice education:* Staff development activities have been systematically delivered to address issues related to cross-cultural understanding, delivery of unique curriculum, development of interdisciplinary programs, and recent research in fields such as higher-order thinking, learning styles, and child development, as well as specific content areas. Planning and implementation of joint inservice activities between home-school staff and magnet staff is essential to creating a common knowledge base and to fostering mutual understanding. Professional development experiences, which provide opportunities for the staff to acquire state-of-the-art expertise and become acquainted with like programs throughout the nation, should be provided as a means of enhancing program quality.

The implementation strategies cited in the *Middle School Design Report* reflect those efforts necessary to deliver the unique educational programs offered by magnet schools or programs. To a large extent, the theme and/or focus of each magnet is a factor in determining strategies needed to maximize learning experiences. Additional resources are essential to the delivery of these techniques.

Seven recommendations for furthering implementation of middle school philosophy through magnet schools are:

1. Include magnet teachers in common planning period (if possible).
2. Provide extensive inservice in interdisciplinary curriculum design and implementation.
3. Conduct scheduling workshops for middle school magnet lead teachers, counselors, and administrators.
4. Review current scheduling of the school day in terms of demands for special programs (e.g., teachers as advisers).
5. Review certification issues that make it difficult for elementary teachers to add middle school certification.
6. Establish alternate transportation routes and/or times to allow magnet students the opportunity to participate in before-school and after-school activities.
7. Give special consideration to integration of magnet students into grade-level teams to promote team continuity and appropriate course-level offerings.

Fundamental Intermediate Schools

The magnet school movement led to the implementation of so-called fundamental intermediate schools which, generally speaking, are characterized by these features:

- Traditional values are rigorously maintained.
- High academic standards and a homework policy are imposed.
- Related academic subjects are taught by the same teacher, with the focus on academic skills and subject matter.
- Consistent and integrated study skills are required.
- Student and staff dress codes are conservative and ratified by agreement.
- Consistent discipline is maintained throughout the school with a signed parent-student agreement.
- Parental commitment and active participation are encouraged throughout the school program.

Many fundamental schools are misidentified as middle schools, in part because—like middle schools—they must address the developmental characteristics of emerging adolescents. Also like middle schools, fundamental programs often include advisement, teaming, intramurals, and a broad exploratory plan.

The focus on academic skills and subject matter, conservative rules on dress and discipline, and of course the name identifies the fundamental school. Yet, the delivery of instruction (teaming, interdisciplinary instruction, and an affective emphasis) is evidence of its middle school roots.

Fine Arts Program

The focus of a fine arts program should be to remove the artificial division between "academic core" and "exploratory and developmental experiences." A troublesome perception, in the authors' view, is the implied hierarchy in teaching and learning that separates the arts from the academic core. The arts should not be dismissed as "miniexperiences" because they are perceived to use less intelligence. Every individual needs to develop the multiple forms of intelligence that humans possess, and some forms of intelligence are best developed through the arts.

The arts, when taught properly, are basic to the educational process. Therefore, it is important that the program:

- Encourage creative solutions to problems in all subject matter by alternative modes of communication and expression.
- Emphasize the development of sensory skills in all disciplines by providing the opportunity to explore a variety of materials, processes, and ideas.
- Utilize a holistic approach to all teaching areas. All works of art have connecting links to specific disciplines in subject matter or in technical skills.
- Develop innovative exploratory wheels, such as the "Music Wheel," for those students not ready to elect music as an annual elective. (Wheels should not replace electives; they should promote them.)

□ Develop a middle school curriculum for dance and drama, such as now undertaken for art and music, emphasizing the goals stated in the *Middle School Design Report.*

□ Develop and seek board approval for Middle School Arts Performance Standards.

By their nature, the arts are highly compatible with middle school philosophy. For example, through the *visual arts* every child is motivated to participate and learn in a positive atmosphere in which success is based on individual interpretation and mode of expression. The scope and sequence of the curriculum offers all students an opportunity to develop individuality and to apply visual and physical concepts. The end products are creative and provide personal satisfaction, which adds to students' self-esteem. Through *dance,* students can make the connection between school experiences and their life beyond the schoolhouse doors. *Music* provides opportunity to get to know a teacher for more than one year and to participate in an organization whose population is essentially the same each year. Students engage in hands-on activities, life-related content, continual adviser/advisee relationships, and esteem-building strategies. *Drama* stimulates thinking skills, which play a vital role in script analysis and character development. For example, students must interpret a playwright's words, synthesize the information, and create a believable characterization. Drama students initially take part in a series of theater games designed to ensure a sense of group trust, which leads to a willingness to accept challenges and take risks.

Improved communication among the arts personnel, school counselors, and assistant principals can be achieved through efforts to ensure proper placement of students in arts classes—thus ensuring a sequential program. Targeting students who seek a career in the arts and apprising them of advance courses or programs while providing opportunities for them to meet professional artists should be included in the adviser/advisee program. Both these efforts promote personal development.

Objectives that enhance continuous learning skills include providing special training for arts teachers in the areas of critical thinking and creative thinking skills; including the arts, which are a basic mode of international communication, expression, and understanding, with mastery of basic communication skills; and promoting art exhibitions and performances in the middle school as a method of improving social cooperation skills and applying them to problem solving.

Seven organizational formats lend themselves to implementing a fine arts program:

1. **Interdisciplinary teams:** Include arts staff in the interdisciplinary planning of thematic units if the goal is to grasp the relationship between separate subjects, integrate each subject into a unified knowledge structure, and transfer skills and knowledge from one discipline to another. Rotate art teachers or assign them on a consultant basis, because most schools will not have enough art teachers to serve on all teams. Structure the teams by themes, grade level, or schoolwide so as to allow elective teachers to participate effectively. Schedule the electives before the teams, to ensure the proper placement of students in courses and levels.

2. **Advisement program:** Use various art methodologies, such as role-playing, during the advisement period to promote examination of peer pressure, human

relations, and self-identity. Assist students in understanding issues common to their age group through thematic exhibits and performances.

3. **Block scheduling:** Use two-period blocks rather than four-period blocks to create more flexibility in scheduling.

4. **Team planning and shared decision making:** Adjust planning periods for art teachers to give them common departmental meeting time.

5. **Exploratory and developmental experiences:** Draw exploratory experiences, such as wheels, minicourses, and special activities, from any body of knowledge or interest. (Do not have them replace electives.) Utilize artist-in-residence programs in the form of minicourses, to supplement career training in the arts.

6. **Integrated curriculum:** Make allowances for off-team elective programs as well as for off-team academic classes.

7. **Inservice education:** Provide ongoing staff development for all art teachers, emphasizing critical thinking and interdisciplinary strategies, in addition to art production and performance methodologies. Encourage music teachers to integrate more basic musicianship, listening, literature, and historical perspective into the performing classes. Provide workshops for basic education teachers to help them utilize artwork, videos, and tapes when introducing the arts into their interdisciplinary teaching. Place special emphasis on multicultural education.

Five recommendations are appropriate to fine arts instructional delivery strategies or systems:

1. Incorporate learning strategies used in the arts into the general curriculum—for example, performance and exhibits. (*cooperative learning strategies*)
2. Promote multicultural learning throughout the curriculum via the arts. (*interdisciplinary teaching*)
3. Develop creative questioning strategies in all lecture situations and provide students a chance to engage in studio or laboratory experiences in all disciplines. (*teaching and learning styles*)
4. Relate each discipline to life experiences and career implications. (*student services and career planning*)
5. Use the knowledge and expertise of parents in multicultural instruction to enhance student self-esteem and respect for the community's cultural diversity. (*home-school partnerships and communications*)

Vocational Exploratory Program

Vocational exploratory courses must afford students the opportunity to experience practical application of basic academic skills.[4] They must be designed and implemented in such a way that state program standards are maintained and offered at every middle school and at every grade level, including sixth grade. Courses should include, at minimum, programs in business, health, home economics, and technology education (formerly industrial arts). Vocational exploratory courses also must accommodate the needs of exceptional students.

Provisions must be made for students to participate in vocational student organizations (VSOs) so as to develop teamwork, competitive, and leadership skills. In that VSOs are an integral part of the curriculum, VSO activities should be incorporated into class instruction, courses should inform students of career choices, and vocational teachers should be included in the adviser/advisee program.

To assist middle school students in making informed decisions regarding career options, guidance counselors and occupational placement specialists must be kept informed of how vocational courses relate to vocational occupational clusters and specific careers. Vocational teachers should participate in the Eighth-Grade Vocation/Career Conference for exceptional students to assist in developing future career plans. An annual meeting should be scheduled with vocational teachers to inform guidance counselors and occupational placement specialists of their respective course philosophies, goals, and objectives. Students must be allowed to explore a variety of vocational exploration courses if they are expected to use the career planning system to make appropriate career choices. Vocational teachers should support home-school partnerships by providing parents with information such as vocational course descriptions and performance standards.

In terms of block scheduling and flexible scheduling within blocks, to the extent possible students should participate in vocational programs "on-team." When appropriate, vocational teachers should use flexible scheduling for various learning activities—although flexible scheduling must not jeopardize weighted funding.

In keeping with team planning and shared decision making, discussion topics should be publicized prior to the team planning meeting so that vocational teachers who are unable to attend can still provide input. Teachers must be included in team meetings that address vocational issues involving their respective courses. To enhance team planning and shared decision-making skills, vocational teachers should participate in inservice activities that address these issues. To improve the interdisciplinary approach, vocational and core teachers should share their course outlines and timelines. For all decisions that involve exceptional students participating in their respective ESE vocational courses, these teachers should be included in individual education plan (IEP) decisions.

Regardless of academic ability, gender, ethnicity, and/or disabling condition, students should be encouraged to participate in vocational exploratory courses. In the interest of safety, the appropriate pupil-teacher ratio should be maintained for hands-on activities. Where possible, vocational courses should be scheduled using the wheel approach in the sixth and seventh grades; developmental classes should be provided in the eighth grade; and a work-experience program should be available for seventh- and eighth-grade at-risk students. Flexible wheel scheduling should be made available to exceptional students, grades six through eight, who cannot benefit from a mainstream vocational exploratory situation. Courses should promote attitudes among students that will endorse nontraditional careers and provide practical experiences that demonstrate the need to work in harmony with others to achieve occupational, social, and civic responsibility.

To further mastery of continuous learning skills, vocational exploratory courses should develop an awareness among students that all careers will require commitment to lifelong learning and skills updating.

Two organizational approaches can be used to implement a vocational exploratory program:

1. Interdisciplinary teams: To ensure inclusion of vocational teachers on the interdisciplinary team and their participation during scheduled team planning time, shorten the school day so that core and elective teachers can share team planning time; increase vocational weights to defray funding lost from a shortened school day; ensure regular communication between core teachers and vocational teachers; and inform vocational teachers of scheduled parent conferences so that they can participate.

2. Advisement: Involve vocational teachers in the advisory program and make sure they receive materials to support their participation. Vocational teachers having advisory responsibilities should be informed of scheduled parent conferences and have the opportunity to participate in them. A school administrator should be assigned the responsibility for monitoring and supervising the advisement program in order to ensure its success.

Three recommendations for vocational exploratory service delivery are:

1. Include vocational teachers in all activities that involve the implementation of instructional delivery strategies/systems.
2. Encourage continued use of cooperative learning techniques among vocational educators in classroom/laboratory settings and in vocational club activities.
3. Promote incorporation of strategies such as cooperative learning, interdisciplinary teaching, and teaching methods that consider different learning styles; this way, individual differences are accommodated.

Exceptional Student Education Program

Mildly disabled students must be exposed to an interdisciplinary program with a core of basic studies—math, science, social studies, language arts. Parallel courses must be provided either in the ESE program or in the basic program to meet their needs, with interdisciplinary units incorporated into the parallel courses to the maximum extent possible. Instruction should include interdisciplinary units whenever appropriate.

A wide range of exploratory opportunities related specifically to career/vocational development and the fine arts must be an integral part of the ESE program and, when appropriate, provided through the main school program. Specially designed exploratory experiences should be created for small groups, which may be accomplished through use of supplements or assignment of a full-time teacher (where enrollment permits). Establishment of an ESE interdisciplinary team does not negate the need for some interdisciplinary units between the ESE program and the main program. An interdisciplinary team of ESE students should include a cross-grouping of special needs.

Mildly disabled students must be an integral part of the adviser/advisee program, and advisers must have a system for monitoring these students' progress. If students exhibit significant problems with attendance, behavior, grades, and such, advisers should seek the assistance of the ESE department liaison and the interdisciplinary team leader. Also, a system for facilitating parental involvement is crucial.

To the maximum extent possible, block scheduling should be used for exceptional students assigned to a regular ESE interdisciplinary team, and they should remain on-team for electives or courses taught by basic education teachers. Planning periods for teachers should be adjusted to provide for a common ESE departmental meeting time.

In schools where moderately to severely disabled students are placed on ESE teams, their teachers should be provided a common planning period.

As is the case with transescents in general, development of special interests and skills is critical to self-esteem, and prevocational and career exploration is essential to develop appropriate attitudes, skills, and interest in the world of work. Scheduling for special-needs students should be concurrent with the mainstream school population so as to guarantee equal (appropriate) access to exploratory courses. The development of realistic career goals and prevocational skills should culminate in a career plan for each eighth-grade exceptional student.

In terms of personal development, mildly disabled students should benefit from the adviser/advisee program if it is instituted with them being assigned to mainstream teams. In particular, ESE teachers should be trained in the developmental traits of middle school students and in small group dynamics, and be included in all inservices related to middle school design and implementation. Inservice for instructional staff must focus on support services available within the school and the community.

Efforts must be made to fully integrate ESE students into extracurricular activities and special-interest groups. Interdisciplinary teams must identify problem areas that are interfering with an exceptional student's success and design intervention and follow-up strategies to ensure that the adviser/advisee program makes a difference.

Agenda for team meetings must periodically address and monitor the efforts of individual team members to include continuous learning skills as a part of their curriculum. The development of good social cooperation skills must be emphasized by all teachers who work with exceptional students.

Two organizational approaches are useful:

1. Interdisciplinary teams: Include teachers of mildly disabled students in the main interdisciplinary teams (to the maximum extent possible). Assign teams without an ESE teacher one who can serve on a consultant basis. ESE interdisciplinary teams should be established only when the number of moderately to severely disabled students warrants full-time placements with limited mainstreaming. ESE center schools may need an ESE interdisciplinary team due to the range of exceptionalities and multiple needs of students.

2. Inservice education: Focus staff development initiatives on training basic education teachers in the unique needs of exceptional students and providing them with a core of strategies/skills necessary to address these needs. Help ESE teachers understand the scope and sequence of the basic education program so as to improve decisions on mainstreaming opportunities for exceptional students. Encourage joint inservices between basic education staff and ESE staff to develop trust and a common knowledge base in all disciplines. Finally, urge ESE teachers and basic education teachers to seek certification in multiple areas.

ESL Program

Increasing numbers of non-English-speaking or limited-English-speaking students are entering the middle grades. Rather than isolate them, the essential middle school seeks to assimilate those students into the mainstream program. Many of these middle graders are sensitive about their different language, dress, or cultural heritage and want to fit in.

Middle school staffs walk a delicate line when implementing an ESL program. Forcing students to remain in classes where they do not understand instruction is wrong—as is isolating them throughout the day in classes where only their dominant language is used.

In attempting to provide a workable compromise, most LEPs (limited-English programs) or NEPs (non-English programs) in the middle school have the following characteristics:

- Sheltered English teachers on each team
- LEP/NEP students clustered within each "family"
- ESL instruction
- Opportunity to enroll in regular core curriculum courses
- Sheltered English instruction used for academic core learning
- Special support services (test-taking skills, academic counseling, study skills and techniques)

Comprehensive Health Program

The term *full-service school* describes many intermediate schools. Here it refers to the fact that health care and social services are often housed in middle school buildings and are provided both for students and for their families. Health education should be a major program focus because attitudes toward self, others, and life are influenced strongly in the middle grades. Abuse or neglect of the body at this critical point of puberty can jeopardize a student's chances of becoming a productive citizen.

Appendix 9 lists some of the topics found in a typical six- through eighth-grade health education program. Figure 9.5 suggests a three-part sequence for a program that includes self-esteem, cognitive learning, and decision making.

Partnership Program

Partnerships established between middle schools and businesses and/or agencies in the community have produced excellent results. The community becomes more aware of the strengths, needs, and constraints of the education system; and educators become more aware of the needs and concerns of the community. Roles and responsibilities of schools and partners should be defined in written agreements, which need to be evaluated periodically by both parties.

For teachers and schools, benefits of such a program include:

- New curriculum/teaching resources and ideas
- Initiation of special programs

FIGURE 9.5   Comprehensive health education program

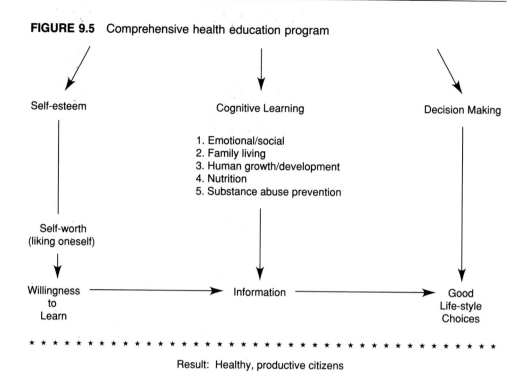

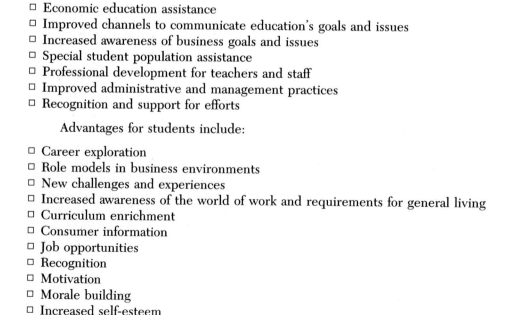

□ Economic education assistance
□ Improved channels to communicate education's goals and issues
□ Increased awareness of business goals and issues
□ Special student population assistance
□ Professional development for teachers and staff
□ Improved administrative and management practices
□ Recognition and support for efforts

Advantages for students include:

□ Career exploration
□ Role models in business environments
□ New challenges and experiences
□ Increased awareness of the world of work and requirements for general living
□ Curriculum enrichment
□ Consumer information
□ Job opportunities
□ Recognition
□ Motivation
□ Morale building
□ Increased self-esteem

Businesses benefit in the following ways:

☐ Intrinsic rewards for employees by sharing their time and talents
☐ Enhanced community image
☐ Contribution to human resource development
☐ Improved return on education tax dollars
☐ Reduction of on-the-job training time
☐ Better-prepared employees
☐ Tax deduction for charitable contributions
☐ Recognition and support for efforts

For the community there are:

☐ Recognition of education as a joint responsibility
☐ Role clarification for citizens and the role they can play in upgrading the quality of schools
☐ Parent involvement

Middle schools are particularly ripe areas for partnerships because of the need for strong role models for emerging adolescents. Whether students are "adopted" by one business or agency or work collaboratively with a number of outside partners, a number of no-cost or low-cost activities have provided meaningful experiences in both situations. Table 9.1 on pages 228 and 229 illustrates mutual benefits to schools and their partners.

ARTICULATION

In modern middle schools there has been an increased emphasis on articulation (a process by which educational goals and curricular programs are coordinated among the various levels, from preschool through high school).

Efforts should be made at all three levels to establish and implement a well-defined plan of articulation to help students make the transition from one level to the next. Such a plan might include visitation or exchange days for elementary students that will allow them to spend a day in the middle school they will enter the next year. Middle school students, in their last year, might spend a day visiting the high school they will enter. They could meet and talk with future schoolmates and teachers and get acquainted with the physical plant. Students could proceed through a simulated day in the high school. Many school districts have implemented teacher exchange days between schools in the three levels to give teachers a better understanding of the programs that precede or follow their own programs.

District committees of teachers with representatives from all three levels have developed articulated skills programs, content programs, and guidance activities. The middle school, with its emphasis on a continuous progress plan of learning, has done much to precipitate articulation activities leading to a breakdown of lockstep graded patterns of instruction. Recent reforms in the high school have seen a carrying forward of interdisciplinary teams to the ninth grade and a continued emphasis on skill building and effective activities.

TABLE 9.1 Partnership Program Activities

What Schools Can Do for Partners	What Partners Can Do for Schools
Communicate—add partner to mailing list.	Provide release time for employees to tutor students.
Provide visibility—submit partnership information (press releases, articles) for school publicity.	Recognize students who have improved in academic achievement, attendance, or behavior.
Remember to say thanks—notes from students are particularly effective.	Recognize students who enroll in honors or advanced placement classes.
Highlight partnership activities—post bulletin board announcements.	Provide incentives to identified potential dropouts to encourage their graduation.
Obtain employee birthdates—have students send cards.	Adopt an Academic Scholar Program.
Celebrate special occasions—send baked goods to partner's place of business.	Sponsor an art contest.
Provide choral or musical groups for special occasions.	Provide shadowing opportunities for students, teachers, and administrators.
Invite partner to shadow a teacher or administrator.	Provide topical seminars for students, faculty, or parents.
Initiate a student partners club or have the student council assist with planning partnership activities.	Provide curriculum support materials.
Sponsor a "Battle of Partners" contest (softball game, races, etc.).	Serve as judges for competitive events.
Provide artwork for display.	Donate used equipment or materials to schools.
Honor partner with an adoption ceremony or a reaffirmation program.	Sponsor educational field trips.
Establish *one* liaison at the school to channel all ideas and coordinate activities.	Donate tickets to cultural or other appropriate events.
Initiate a logo design contest for partnership activities.	Participate in school and community affairs, i.e., parades, ceremonies.
Invite partner to serve on advisory committees, task forces, etc.	Provide incentive awards.
Refer potential employees.	Provide display space for student work or notices of school events.
Share monthly activity calendars with partner.	Provide an award for the Teacher of the Year or Outstanding Teacher.
Provide decorations for partner functions, meetings (centerpieces, signs, etc.).	Provide opportunities for students to serve as a "Boss for a Day."
Invite partner to tour the school and explain curriculum.	Cosponsor joint beautification projects.
If applicable, have students submit designs for partner's holiday cards or publications.	Serve as (or provide) guest speakers and participate in career days.

TABLE 9.1 *(continued)*

What Schools Can Do for Partners	What Partners Can Do for Schools
Invite partner to participate in school career day.	Provide part-time, summer, or postgraduation employment.
Provide space for a partnership column in school newsletter.	Provide space in business publications to highlight partnership activities.
Invite partner to breakfast or coffee with the principal or a teacher.	Host meetings for the school.
Give an update on partnership activities at PTA/PTSA meetings.	Provide tours of your facility.
Invite partner to participate in community projects with your schools, i.e., baskets at Thanksgiving.	Purchase an ad in the school's publication(s).
Establish a referral system with partner for part-time employment.	Support substance abuse education program.
Share school and student successes with partners, particularly where the partner has been involved.	Sponsor reading incentive programs.
	Provide support for math, science, computer education, and technology.

Elementary schools have implemented additional guidance experiences and core programs in the upper elementary grades and developed special-interest classes as a result of the influence of middle schools.

Articulation among middle schools in a district or geographic area has been facilitated by the establishment of curriculum data banks that include samples of interdisciplinary units and teacher-made materials; consortiums that provide studies of grading and instructional practices; and leagues of middle schools that share ideas about successful practice in middle schools.

K–12 curriculum studies have resulted in district curriculum guides in all subject areas. Such guides have helped middle schools structure programs in the various disciplines. They have also helped all three levels to communicate better with students, parents, and the general public about the interrelationships of the various levels.

Interschool faculty meetings and shared student programs such as science and math fairs, art exhibits, and dramatic and musical performances have helped foster better relationships between school levels.

SUMMARY

Successfully implementing the middle school requires that its goals and purposes be clearly understood by students, teachers, parents, and the supporting community. This chapter included a number of practical examples of how to communicate goals and purposes.

Along with planning a middle school program and organizational structure, a plan for phasing in the middle school should be developed. An implementation schedule should include provisions for sustained inservice training of teachers, administrators, and support personnel.

Included in any implementation plan is a discussion of the types and uses of facilities available to house middle schools, most of which have had to use buildings designed for high schools, junior high schools, or elementary programs. In many cases, the buildings have had to be renovated to accommodate modern middle school programs.

Sustaining inservice training of teachers, principals, and other staff members has been a major problem in the middle school movement. Team building and interdisciplinary teaming have become major inservice areas in relation to implementation. A major stumbling block to program and organizational delivery has been that of getting middle school teachers to work together in team settings. This chapter identified a number of processes available for making the team concept work.

Successful delivery systems for carrying out inservice programs have been developed, including the teacher renewal or staff development centers. The TORC Model was presented as a good example.

Program implementation should be a part of the total grades K–12 structure of the school district. Articulation among middle schools, as well as with feeder elementary and receiving high schools, must be initiated and sustained by middle school staffs if the school is to be understood and accepted.

SUGGESTED LEARNING ACTIVITIES

1. Write a handbook for students and parents outlining the goals and purposes of the middle school.
2. Select a school facility not designed for a middle school and outline the changes you would make in the building to accommodate a middle school program.
3. Conduct a needs assessment for your faculty on types of inservice desired and delivery systems needed to carry out those activities.

4. Design a team-building workshop for a middle school interdisciplinary team.
5. You have been asked to chair an articulation committee for the middle school program with the elementary and high school programs. Outline an assignment for your committee. Assume the committee will include representatives from all three levels.

NOTES

1. Center for Research on Elementary and Middle Schools, "Implementation and Effects of Middle Grades Practice," Johns Hopkins University, 1990 (monograph).
2. The guidelines for implementing the special programs described in Chapter 9 were developed to fit the Dade County middle school design found in Appendix 4.

3. Jon Wiles and Joseph Bondi, *Making Advisory Programs Work* (Tampa: Wiles, Bondi and Associates, 1990).
4. Florida State Department of Education, "The Middle School Exploratory Wheel," State Department of Education, 1991.

SELECTED REFERENCES

Dade County School Board, "The Exceptional Education Program in the Middle Grades," Dade County School Board, 1991.

Wiles, Jon, and Bondi, Joseph, *The Middle School America Needs* (Tampa: Wiles, Bondi and Associates, 1990).

_____, *Subject Area Maps for the Middle Grades* (Tampa: Wiles, Bondi and Associates, 1990).

_____, *ESE in the Middle School* (Tampa: Wiles, Bondi and Associates, 1991).

10

Evaluating the Middle School

*There is no greater burden
than a great potential.*

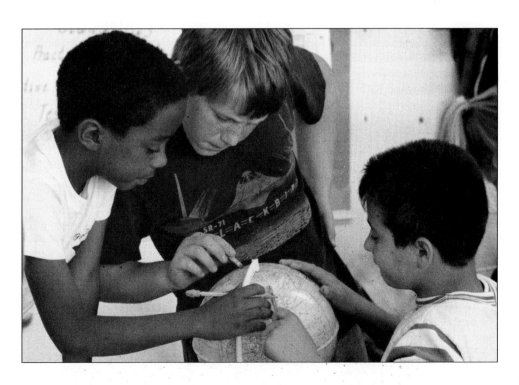

INTRODUCTION

This book has stressed the belief that, because they are *content*-centered, existing programs and organizations in most traditional intermediate schools fail to provide optimum learning conditions for students moving from late childhood into adolescence. The middle school alternative focuses on providing *student*-centered education for a population defined by its diversity and uniqueness.

This chapter raises the question of whether middle schools are meeting their purported objectives:

1. To facilitate a smoother progression between the separate components of the educational system *(articulation)*
2. To utilize staff in a way that will maximize the personal and professional development of teachers, introduce needed specialization in the upper elementary level by using team teaching and special instructional centers, and facilitate education programs for new teachers based on career opportunities in this special area *(professional preparation, staff development, specialization)*
3. To provide for more realistic and more effective guidance through use of teacher/counselors and planned guidance sessions *(advisement)*
4. To create a social and physical environment free of competitive athletics and regimented social activities that depend on adult supervision *(socialization, independence)*
5. To encourage pupils to progress at their own rate through different programs and multimedia instruction *(individualization)*

Two systems of evaluation—the feedback cycle and the validation approach—are described, as is a system for defining parameters for student evaluation. The chapter closes with a brief word about the need for more reliable middle school research.

Specific evaluation tools are included in Appendix 10.

EVALUATION CRITERIA

Like other elements in the establishment or conversion of a middle school (program design, organization, inservice training), evaluation is a continuous process that should involve students, parents, staff and administration, school district personnel, consultants, and members of the community.

Because each school operates under unique conditions and programs, each must carefully design and develop its own evaluation criteria. Failure to do so will have inevitable consequences, for in order to survive each facility must be able to identify, justify, and document its achievements as well as pinpoint areas of weakness.

Evaluation criteria might be used to test certain hypotheses about how middle school students compare with junior high students. For example, middle school learners:

□ Are more self-directed
□ Suffer fewer and less intense social and/or psychological problems

□ Demonstrate equal or greater achievement
□ Enjoy better physical fitness and health
□ Show more favorable attitudes toward school
□ Have a higher-developed self-concept
□ Have higher average daily attendance records
□ Exhibit higher measures of creativity
□ Achieve better academic records as ninth graders
□ Have a lower high school dropout rate
□ Are taught by teachers who report higher job satisfaction
□ Experience smoother program articulation K–12

In designing an instrument to measure its success, a middle school should ask questions that rely on empirical data. Figure 10.1 shows a sample basis for an evaluation questionnaire.

Feedback and Validation: Two Systems for Evaluation

Like its instructional program, a middle school's evaluation program must be comprehensive and systematic if it is to achieve its objective—*to promote better learning*. The middle school has been identified as a school designed to promote personal growth and development in preadolescent learners. That single purpose, then, defines the parameters of middle school evaluation, which serves to answer the question "Is preadolescent development being promoted?"

To answer the question posed, the evaluative focus shifts to the learning design created to achieve this end, and to the arrangements made for learning. In doing so, middle school evaluation goes beyond the areas of student growth, identified in Chapter 2, to include a much broader range of concerns: personnel, facilities, learning materials, rules and regulations, and all other program planning considerations. In effect, evaluation is defined by the purposes and activities of the middle school program.

One way of viewing evaluation is as a *feedback* or corrective mechanism, an example of which is shown in Figure 10.2. The goals of the school are translated into objectives, which in turn create a program design. Student learning, for instance, is structured into activities that have distinct foci. As evidence is gathered and analyzed, discrepancies between desired outcomes and real outcomes are discovered and adjustments in program are made. Goals are refocused and the feedback cycle is renewed.

Another system uses evaluation as a means of *validating* program goals and objectives. In this approach, data are gathered to justify specific facets of the program, and these facets (or subsystems) collectively comprise the evaluation program. Figure 10.3 shows examples of such subsystems (eight in this case), which are discussed in the next subsections.

For example, assume that a middle school is concerned with its method of teaching because students are not demonstrating growth in study skills. In such a case, each area, or subsystem, could be analyzed for probable cause (e.g., inadequate teaching materials, inadequate teacher training).

FIGURE 10.1   Evaluation questionnaire: XYZ Middle School introductory statement, instructions

	Yes	No
1. Is your school developing and testing an adequate curriculum?	_____	_____
2. Is there a policy that defines for teachers, students, and parents the purpose of the program?	_____	_____
3. Are the strategies and teaching skills acquired at inservice sessions being implemented?	_____	_____
4. Is there a change in student achievement as measured by the CAP [California Assessment Program]?	_____	_____
5. Is there a change in student achievement as measured by the CTBS [California Test of Basic Skills]? If yes, please explain.	_____	_____
6. To your knowledge, do parents hold a positive attitude toward the curriculum as implemented?	_____	_____
7. To your knowledge, is there a positive change in attitude toward XYZ Middle School on the part of teachers?	_____	_____
8. Has there been a decrease in the number of discipline referrals over the past six months?	_____	_____
9. Has there been a decrease in the number of suspensions and expulsions over the past six months?	_____	_____
10. Has teacher absenteeism diminished over the past six months?	_____	_____
11. Has there been a positive change in student mobility and attendance over the past six months?	_____	_____
12. Do students demonstrate a positive change in attitude toward school?	_____	_____
13. To your knowledge, are parents and students satisfied with the sixth grade being housed at XYZ?	_____	_____
14. Has the student failure rate declined as a result of implementation of XYZ's program?	_____	_____
15. Does XYZ's program provide for different learner levels?	_____	_____
16. To your knowledge, do students feel a sense of family and identity in the team organization?	_____	_____
17. Is there flexible grouping of students within each team?	_____	_____
18. To what degree have expanded exploratory experiences been provided?	_____	_____
19. In your opinion, have student attitudes toward self and others changed for the better as a result of the advisory program?	_____	_____
20. Are learning materials and media services adequate for the program as planned?	_____	_____
21. To your knowledge, have district personnel been provided with middle school training and kept abreast of current development and trends?	_____	_____
22. Have student profiles been developed as a result of formal and informal assessment of their skills?	_____	_____
23. Please describe the mode, frequency, and content of communication among students, parents, teachers, administration, and community as related to program implementation.	_____	_____

      Mode _____

      Frequency _____

      Content _____

FIGURE 10.2 Evaluation feedback cycle

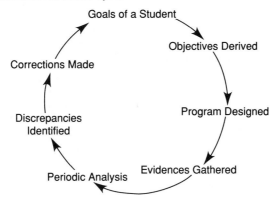

By combining these two approaches to evaluation, a school can develop a means of regularly assessing its programs and taking corrective actions where findings are unsatisfactory. Hodgkinson provides some guiding study questions in each of the areas shown in Figure 10.3.[1]

Program Design

Program design can be assessed from both an external and an internal vantage point. Viewed from the perspective of the school district in which the middle school is located, the following questions seem pertinent:

☐ Is the middle school concept as described consistent with the overall philosophy of the district and its leaders?

☐ Does the middle school articulate (fit) with the preceding elementary programs and the high school programs that follow?

☐ Are the resources allocated to the middle school (building, staff, monies, materials) commensurate with those given to other levels of schooling?

From an internal perspective, evaluating program design would focus on the structure of the curriculum and the learning opportunities for students. The following questions might guide such an analysis:

FIGURE 10.3 Evaluation subsystems

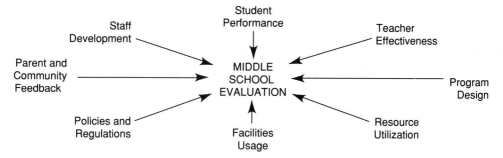

□ In what ways does the curriculum provide for the intellectual, physical, social, and emotional differences of students?

□ What materials and equipment contribute to the development of students' skills, interests, abilities, and special talents?

□ How are all learning experiences in the school integrated?

□ What provisions are made for student growth and development in health, personality, and character?

□ How are learning activities individualized to meet student needs and interests?

□ What special provisions have been made to ensure the mastery of basic learning skills?

□ What adjustments in organization have been made to promote a climate for exploration?

Facilities Usage

Regardless of its age or condition, a facility can be made to support the advancement of activities.

Some concerns are more obvious—using a building that promotes flexibility and physical movement, allows for variable grouping of students, and encourages cooperative planning and teaching—whereas others are subtle. The following questions may assist in evaluating use of facilities in the middle school:

□ Does the allocation of facility space, both in terms of location and in volume, reflect program priorities?

□ Is space utilization flexible enough to allow for individualized instructional activities?

□ Is the instructional resource center (IRC) centrally located and readily accessible to teaching spaces?

□ Are noisy spaces sufficiently separated from needed quiet areas?

□ Is the entire building stimulating in terms of its spatial and color orientation?

□ Are all available spaces, including stairwell corners and foyers, being used to educate and communicate with students?

□ Is there a sufficient number of special-use areas (like darkened projection areas, storage areas for projects, common areas, and areas for private conversations) to promote program objectives?

□ Is the administrative area accessible to students, teachers, parents, and visitors?

□ Are there provisions (tackboards and cork strips) for the display of students' work in the hallways?

Resource Utilization

The allocation and utilization of resources, both human and material, is a problem area for many middle schools. An all-too-familiar pattern is so-called territorial rights established in buildings, or available resources allocated to favored segments of a program. Middle schools must use all available resources judiciously to promote their programs. The following questions suggest some areas worth analyzing:

□ Is there a clear relationship between the allocation of funds and materials in the school, and the curricular objectives of the program?

□ Are staff members assigned to positions in the program according to function and talent, rather than by credential?

□ Are high-priority areas such as skill building given sufficient support in the form of staff and consumable materials?

□ Are immediate resources available to support innovative instructional techniques?

□ Is there an established means of assessing future resource needs and planning for their acquisition?

Policies and Regulations

Few middle schools regularly view administrative policy and regulation from a program objectives standpoint. Yet, no other single area in a middle school is so important in setting the tone or climate for learning. It is important in evaluation that the following questions be asked:

□ What policies and regulations are absolutely essential to the operation of a middle school?

□ What existing rules or policies might contradict the "spirit" of the middle school concept?

□ How might policy setting and regulation enforcement best be handled to promote the objectives of the school?

Student Performance

In that the end objectives of the educative process, in any school at any level, are concerned with student performance or behavior, evaluation in this area is generally given more attention by parents, teachers, and administrators than any other phase of schooling. In the middle school, as students are evaluated, the folly of redefining the purpose of education must be avoided while retaining the old yardsticks of measurement.

Middle schools must evaluate student performance in areas suggested by the conceptual image of the middle school design. The following questions may assist in evaluating student performance:

□ Is student evaluation perceived and conducted as a measure of personal development for each student?

□ Is student evaluation both systematic and continuous in nature?

□ Is the student fully involved in assessing and measuring his own growth and development?

□ Is the evaluation social-personal as well as academic?

□ Are progress findings related to the student's own ability and previous performance?

□ Are parents actively involved in the evaluation of their children?

□ Is the gathering of evaluative data comprehensive in nature, such as a combination of periodic testing, student self-report files, teacher-pupil conferences, observations, and such?

□ Is student progress reporting directional in nature, that is, indicating where improvement is needed?

□ Is student progress reported to parents in a positive manner, with emphasis on growth as shown in the following scheme?

C = Commendable achievement
S = Satisfactory achievement
I = Improving
N = Needing more work
NA = Not applicable

Teacher Effectiveness

Teachers in the middle school are more than simply a resource, they are in fact the medium through which the program is delivered. Without the full support of the teaching staff, the middle school will falter under the weight of ambition. Evaluation of teacher effectiveness might center around the following questions:

□ Have the talents and abilities of all staff members been fully explored and cataloged?
□ Are members of the instructional and support staffs working where they believe they can be most effective?
□ Are there organizational and administrative constraints on teaching styles?
□ Is there an active mechanism by which teachers can share ideas and activities with one another?
□ Is there an established means for program improvement input by the instructional staff?
□ Does the administration have in place a mechanism for reviewing teacher growth?

Team Effectiveness

Procedures must be developed to analyze the strengths and weaknesses of the team approach, including the role of the team leader. Evaluation of team effectiveness might center around the following concerns:

□ Is the team climate one of cooperation and teamwork?
□ Does the team use integrative, constructive methods in problem solving, rather than a competitive approach?
□ Are team goals understood by all teachers in the team?
□ Has the team put into writing the expectations of its members regarding meeting times, reviewing performance, and building agendas?
□ Does the team leader provide leadership in (1) facilitating communication within the team and with other teams, (2) coordinating curriculum planning, and (3) providing human and material resources for the team?

Staff Development

In an earlier example, staff development was seen as a corrective device for program improvement. Rather than a regularly scheduled or unfocused treatment, which characterizes many inservice programs, staff development efforts in the middle school attack real problems faced by educators. The following questions suggest a possible focus for evaluation efforts:

☐ Are sufficient monies budgeted for staff development efforts during the school year?

☐ Do staff development needs arise from analysis of other areas of evaluation such as student performance and teacher effectiveness?

☐ Can staff development efforts be conducted on short notice during the school year?

☐ Do teachers regularly have a chance to critique staff development activities and suggest areas of future need?

Parent-Community Feedback

Perhaps the most important dimension in the middle school evaluation system is that which monitors the reactions and interest of parents and the community in which the middle school is located. Without support (overt or tacit) from both of these groups, the programs cannot fully succeed.

Involvement of the community, like involvement of parents, is a matter of degree as well as frequency. These questions may assist in evaluating this part of the program:

☐ Were members of the community involved in the conception of the middle school and the drafting of formative documents?

☐ Is there in existence a school-based citizens committee whose major function is to communicate to parents and to the community about programs at the school?

☐ Is the community regularly kept informed of changes in programs or operations?

☐ Can citizens actively participate in school functions at a meaningful level of involvement?

Each of these components of the evaluation system is important in terms of program improvement and increased performance by those actively engaged in school operations. All components are interrelated and crucial to other areas.

Student Evaluation

Perhaps the greatest challenge to middle school education is developing a program of student evaluation equal to the goals of middle school education. If the goals of the middle school are comprehensive, then it is equally important that the evaluation of student performance be broad.

A useful distinction in attempting to develop a comprehensive student evaluation plan is to differentiate between evaluation and validation of performance. *Evaluation* generally refers to a judgmental process whereby decisions are made about the qualitative nature of events. *Validation*, a more recently developed process used to evaluate many federal programs, is an evidence-gathering and assessment activity. The key difference between the two is that in validation data are selected prior to activity so that the determination of progress is a result of objective analysis.

A survey of middle schools by the authors has determined a number of student outcomes regularly assessed and measured, among them work habits and academic skills; social attitudes and evidence of adjustment; physical and mental health; knowledge acquisition and goal achievement; creativity, interest expansion, aesthetic appreciation; self-concept and personal philosophy; and aspects of critical thinking.

These categories, and others, suggest that the middle school should evaluate student development in a variety of areas and that the emphasis of the evaluation program be placed on individual growth rather than on comparison to norm-referenced standards. Comparisons to norms, of course, would have no place in a program that stresses *individual* development.

Finally, it should be noted that student evaluation plays three specific roles in the instructional process. It is a *diagnostic* device, which allows the instructional staff to determine current student growth patterns. It is a *descriptive* device, which allows teachers and parents and students to communicate about the growth and development of the individual student. It is *directional,* in that evaluation of the student serves to steer future learning activity by pinpointing needs.

THE NEED FOR RELIABLE MIDDLE SCHOOL RESEARCH

As the major twentieth-century innovation in education, the middle school might be called a success story, at least in numerical terms: The number of middle schools grew from a handful in the 1960s to more than eight thousand by 1990.

Although the junior high lasted fifty years (1910–1960), its quality was subjected to criticism throughout its history. Yet, a viable alternative to that model did not emerge until the middle school gained acceptance in the early 1960s. Ironically, the goals of the original junior high model were to facilitate student progress from late childhood into adolescence and to provide an intermediate education between elementary school and high school—the very goals espoused by proponents of the middle school when it was introduced. Advocates felt that the program and grade organization of the middle school (grades six through eight versus grades seven through nine) would prove more successful than the junior high model in educating preadolescents and early adolescents.

Unfortunately, research has not yet clearly documented this premise. A review of the literature reveals that research in the field is limited, particularly with respect to studies that compare the middle school model with other models of intermediate education. Some comparative studies were conducted in the 1960s and 1970s, but the findings tend to be inconclusive and the studies generally of low quality. Since the mid-1970s, the research focus has been less comparative and more confined in scope. A number of those studies deal with components or aspects of the middle school model, but not the complete model as a unit. Studies that have dealt with the model as a unit have been primarily concerned with its current status, that is, surveying operational middle schools so as to identify practices and trends. Thus, the basic question of how the middle school model compares with other intermediate models in educating transescents still needs to be answered definitively.

The most comprehensive study on middle school effectiveness in the United States was conducted in 1989 by the Dade County School Board (Miami, Florida).[2] The Dade County project comparative study uses a multiple time series and matches pairs of students over a number of years. As a longitudinal study, it will rank in importance with the eight-year study conducted in the 1930s.

Too many middle school conferences feature speakers who intone "The research says middle schools. . . ." Scholars need to ask *whose* research? *what* design was used? *how long* did the study last? *what* were the variables and *how* were they controlled?

When speakers claim that the middle school is "better than" the junior high school or intermediate school, one needs to ask *how?* compared with what model?

To move beyond mere numerical success, the middle school must constantly evaluate both the processes and the products of its implementation (see Appendix 10 for a sample evaluation baseline and a program analysis). Only then can it gain full acceptance among U.S. educators.

SUMMARY

Although middle schools are student-focused in their orientation, there is a pressing need for specificity in the evaluation of programs. If this complex learning design is to survive, it must be able to document its achievements.

The middle school can best demonstrate its value as an educational design by using a systematic assessment of school operations as measured by a validation procedure that will provide a better justification for activities than a judgmental process.

In building an evaluation system, each school must select its own criteria for analysis.

The philosophy and objectives of middle school education will suggest the parameters of such a system.

Middle schools must pay particular attention to student evaluation because this is the area historically viewed most closely by the public. Within student evaluation, a broad spectrum of data is gathered that collectively represents a pattern of individual growth on the student's part. Such data should be used as diagnostic, descriptive, and directional tools in providing feedback about the program.

SUGGESTED LEARNING ACTIVITIES

1. Develop a list of middle school objectives that could serve as a basis for structuring a program evaluation.
2. You have been asked to chair a committee to evaluate middle school facilities in your district. What questions would you and your committee devise to study existing facilities?
3. Design a checklist for evaluating team effectiveness.

4. Develop an instrument for evaluating parent and community support of the middle school.
5. Review various reporting systems used by middle schools to report student performance. What areas of student performance would you evaluate?

NOTES

1. Jon Wiles and Joseph Bondi, "Evaluating for Effectiveness." In: *Supervision: A Guide to Practice*, 3rd ed., (New York: Merrill/Macmillan, 1991).

2. *Evaluation of the Middle School Project*, Joe Gomez, principal evaluator, Jon Wiles and Joseph Bondi, chief consultants. Dade County School Board (Miami, Florida), 1989–1990, 1991, 1992.

SELECTED REFERENCES

Archibald, Doug, and Newmann, Fred, *Beyond Standardized Testing,* (Reston, VA: National Association of Secondary Principals, 1988).

Kellogg Model Middle School Project, *Progress Reports I, II and III* (Ishpeming, MI: Ishpeming Public Schools, 1992).

National Association of Secondary School Principals, *Assessing Excellence: A Guide for Studying the Middle School Level* (Reston, VA: NAESP, 1988).

_____, *Effective Evaluation in America's Elementary and Middle Schools* (Alexandria, VA: NAESP, 1988).

Wiles, Jon, and Bondi, Joseph, *Evaluating Middle School Programs* (Tampa: Wiles, Bondi and Associates, 1991).

11

Outlook for Middle Schools

The future of tomorrow's society
can be found in today's middle school youth.

INTRODUCTION

The middle school in the United States represents a dramatic break from the past. Much progress has been made in developing and implementing new programs for preadolescents and early adolescents; yet, there is still much to be done. As with other changes in American education, the middle school has met with varying degrees of understanding and acceptance. Issues have been identified that hold continued significance for the middle school movement, and they must be addressed. This closing chapter looks at some of those issues, including the implications of change in Eastern Europe and Asia, an interdependent world community, social changes in the nation. It also raises some thoughtful philosophical questions about the demands made by progress and offers specific recommendations.

MEETING THE CHALLENGES

As the middle school becomes the dominant intermediate school in the 1990s, surpassing the junior high school, educational leaders must keep before them the purposes of the middle school. They must not let the middle school revert to the kind of school it purports to succeed. Below are some ironic comparisons of past shortcomings of the junior high school with current possible weaknesses of the middle school.

	Junior High School Movement	Middle School Movement
Reasons for Emergence	Building needs brought on by increasing or declining enrollments; integration; bandwagon effect.	Building needs brought on by increasing or declining enrollments; integration; bandwagon effect.
Teacher Preparation	Few undergraduate programs designed for middle grades preparation. Teacher preparation program usually part of elementary or secondary degree program.	Few undergraduate programs designed for middle grades preparation. Teacher preparation program usually part of elementary or secondary degree program.
Certification	Attached to existing certification program. Failed to recognize need for a difference in teacher preparation programs for middle grades teachers.	Attached to existing certification program. Failed to recognize the need for a difference in teacher preparation programs for middle grades teachers.
Teaching Methods Emulated	Lecture, recitation, static grouping, reliance on textbook.	Lecture, recitation, static grouping, reliance on textbook.

| Implementation | Usually implemented in name only with little understanding of basic underlying theory and intent. | Usually implemented in name only with little understanding of basic underlying theory and intent. |

The early years of the middle school movement were characterized by excitement, innovation, experimentation, and a sense of urgency to develop and implement a better program for emerging adolescent learners. As the middle school reaches maturity in the 1990s, its challenge is to avoid letting those qualities become lost in a sea of complacency and retrenchment.

SUSTAINING MIDDLE SCHOOLS AND PREVENTING REGRESSION TO STANDARDIZATION

In the United States, middle schools have grown in number and have resulted in positive changes in education. Over the past three decades, many middle schools came into being as the result of changing enrollment patterns, integration efforts, and the bandwagon effect. Nonetheless, many intermediate-level educators saw these "wrong reasons" for establishing a middle school as the "right opportunity" to improve school programs for an age group long ignored in our schools. At the time of this writing, declining enrollments, limited budgets, and an absence of sustained inservice training are causing some school districts to reexamine the middle school structure, encouraging those not really committed to its philosophy to take the easy way out by returning to a "cut-rate," highly structured, standardized intermediate school. Hopefully, these pressures will not overthrow the good work done to date at the intermediate level.

The middle school structure must be constantly reviewed and reaffirmed, so that the subtle but momentous change in educational objectives suggested by its design is not lost in the day-to-day tasks of operating a school. To focus an entire curriculum on the learner, rather than on content mastery, calls for a commitment to serve each learner in a personal and individual manner. Given the diversity of the preadolescent population, this can be done only through careful planning and execution of school programming.

The number of social statistics introduced in this book convey the message that many of the traditional support systems relied on during the growing-up years seem to be dissolving. At a time in our history when emerging adolescents need the kind of guidance and personal development activities that a middle school can provide, there are some who say it is time to return to the impersonal approach used in grades seven through nine of the junior high structure. Because the junior high school continued to model itself after the high school program, its curriculum development was arrested in serving adolescents rather than youth in transition.

Sustaining middle schools means reexamining existing programs. Our faculties need to restudy the nature of the age group they are serving and reestablish the philosophy of the middle school. New inservice training programs must be established to help new and seasoned teachers cope with the needs of today's middle school student.

Those committed to the middle school program must set up an effective communications network to convince the public and colleagues that the middle school is still the best alternative to the junior high school.

What Have We Learned?

As the new century approaches, educators must be aware of what does *not* work as well as knowing what does work in our schools. Certain truisms seem infallible: If we always do what we always did, we will always get what we always got. Those who ignore the mistakes of the past are destined to repeat them in the future.

Breaking the mold of tradition means we cannot continue the mistakes of the past. The euphoria brought on by the Persian Gulf victory in 1991 was followed by a deep recession, with social needs being further compromised in the United States. States in financial trouble found themselves struggling to keep up with educational needs—hardly a good time for middle school innovations, which require more funding than traditional intermediate programs. Many of the problems reported in Chapter 2—juvenile delinquency, alcoholism and drug abuse among youth, AIDS, teen promiscuity and pregnancy, jobs lost to technological advances—bear watching as we move into the new century. Will we continue to view education as just one more function of government or recognize it as being of paramount importance to the future of our society?

Will this be the last generation to use a book as a primary learning tool? Advances in information processing have provided a growing range of options for the middle school teacher. For example, as children of an electronic age, middle school students expect the same stimuli they experience in learning conditions that prevail outside the classroom; the single-text, straight-row approach simply will not work any longer.

The body of information available today will quadruple before a middle school student graduates from high school. Changes in how information is produced, transmitted, and stored are illustrated in Table 11.1.

The Future America

Studies indicate that in the future the United States will be characterized by an aging white population; a large but stable black population; rapidly increasing, diverse, and youthful Asian and Hispanic populations; a new blend of service and high-tech jobs; immigration from many nations; a declining base of middle-class people of working age; transiency and crime; environmental vulnerability; contrasts in wealth; exciting social and political innovations; and the agony of unfilled expectations.[1]

The Interdependent World

Whereas the United States may represent for some a model of democratic ideals, it is also becoming a more interdependent, cooperative member of the world community. Events in Eastern Europe and Asia, along with agreements among North Amer-

TABLE 11.1 Information Processing: Yesterday, Today, and Tomorrow

Change	Year	Mode	Speed or Density
Increasing speed of transmission—time required to send 250 words over 3,000 miles	400 BC	Runner	1.54×10^6 sec. (7 mph)
	AD 1844	Telegraph	2.56×10^2 sec.
	AD 1985	Fiber optics	1.2×10^{-5} sec.
	AD 1990	Fiber optics	9.6×10^{-11} sec.
Increasing density of information	4000 BC	Tablet	1 character/cu. in.
	2000 BC	Scroll	250 characters/cu. in.
	AD 1450	Print	500 characters/cu. in.
	AD 2000	Chip	1.25×10^{11} characters/cu. in.
Increasing rate of production	4000 BC	Tablet	½ character/sec.
	2000 BC	Scroll	2 characters/sec.
	AD 1450	Print	300 characters/sec.
	AD 1990	Printer	20,000 characters/sec.

Source: "Education Technology" (Classroom exercise, Wiles-Bondi, 1992)

ican nations and between North, Central, and South American nations, point to the need for U.S. educators and students to have a more global outlook.

It is interesting to see how the United States of the 1990s compares with the rest of the world. For example, if the world were a global village of 1,000 people, the ethnic, religious, and other demographic composition would be as follows:[2]

In the village would be:	*There would be:*	*Of all the villagers:*
564 Asians	300 Christians (183 Catholic, 84 Protestant, 33 Orthodox)	60 would control half the total income
210 Europeans	175 Moslems	500 would be hungry
86 Africans	128 Hindus	600 would live in shantytowns
80 South Americans	55 Buddhists	700 would be illiterate
60 North Americans	47 animists	
	295 agnostics or atheists	

This global scenario suggests the following changes for the middle school curriculum:

☐ Science: More time and attention; higher-skills science; technology; society; hands-on experience; moral choices arising from "progress"
☐ English: Beyond Western civilization (literature); listening, speaking, viewing skills; comprehension skills, reading rates; cultural literacy, classic works
☐ Social Studies: Global interdependence; responsible citizenship, character; geography; economics; world hunger, ecosystem, population

□ Mathematics: Application to real world problems; estimation, extrapolation, statistics; more use of calculators, computers; higher proficiency in problem solving
□ Foreign Language: Fluency in two languages; early start; balance between grammar and oral proficiency; study of Chinese, Japanese, Russian
□ Art: Required in humanities course; art history; criticism; aesthetics; studio; fuller development of creative powers
□ Vocational education: Drop wood and metals; add technology of industries; work in teams, economics of productivity

Some Recommendations

The following recommendations are suggested for the middle school:

1. Eliminate retention of students. When retained students are finally promoted to the next grade, they actually perform more poorly in the long run than would have been predicted, on average, had they not been retained.[3] Chances of a retained student graduating are about 50 percent. A student twice retained has a minus 1 percent chance of graduating. Research indicates that remedial help, tutoring before and after school, peer tutoring, individualized computer-assisted instruction, summer school, and the Individual Education Program are all more effective than retention.

2. Eliminate tracking of students. Numerous studies show there to be no benefits gained by tracking students into ability groups. Higher achievers do no better when grouped together, and lower achievers do much worse when together. Tracking clearly discriminates and perpetuates inequities among students: lower-track students tend to be black or Hispanic, poor, and from poorly educated families. Higher-track students tend to be white, wealthy, and from well-educated families.[4]

3. Eliminate corporal punishment. The United States is one of the few countries in the world where corporal punishment in schools is still practiced, although most middle schools have eliminated it. Research studies show no long-term benefits of paddling.

4. Understand that effective teaching is not a set of generic practices but a set of context-driven decisions. Nowhere is that more important than in the middle school, where teachers use a variety of classroom materials and practices to achieve certain learning objectives. Single-minded prescriptions for "effective" teacher practices in the middle school will not work. Instead, teachers need to constantly reflect about their work, observe students to make sure they are learning, and then adjust practices accordingly.

5. Revamp traditional grading policies. A's, B's, and C's do little to communicate student achievement or abilities. On the first day of school, one middle school gave each student a grade card with all A's on it. Students were allowed to keep the A's so long as they did the required work to the best of their abilities, took the tests, and observed behavior rules. Achievement, as measured by teacher-made and standardized tests, went up; the number of discipline problems were reduced; and attendance improved. Many middle schools supplement grading system information with profile folders or portfolios, but too few have broken away from the inherited junior high school grading system.

6. Understand that real-life problems and settings that allow students to display competence are more important than scores on standardized achievement tests. Successful middle schools can provide a setting, both within and outside the school, where that can happen. Cooperative learning activities, school projects, community projects, business partnerships all provide opportunities for practicing skills and displaying learning.

7. Promote the middle school as an arena for greater scholarship on the part of its leaders. Unlike well-versed writers in the junior high movement (Thomas Briggs, William Gruhn, A. A. Douglass, Harl Douglass, Maurice Ahrens, Nelson Bossing, Roscoe Cramer, Leonard Koos, for example), many modern middle school writers have spent little time in the field of curriculum writing or development.

Another concern is the lack of field service among many writers and consultants of the middle school movement. The agricultural extension agent method, whereby those persons with theoretical background on the middle school went into the field and helped school staffs develop middle school programs, has been the best way of advancing the middle school concept. Few persons have carried out major middle school transitions or conversions for which a curriculum development background provides a frame of reference to move theory into practice. Schools or school districts seeking help in this area should carefully investigate the background of prospective consultants.

8. Recognize that the quality of instruction improves with the amount of teacher time spent *away* from students during the school day. Extra planning periods, release days or half-days for inservice, and stipends for teachers to write curriculum all pay dividends. Asking middle school teachers to do more with less support courts disaster.

As pioneers of the middle school movement retire, new teachers will ascend in large numbers and must be provided with meaningful preservice. Sustaining renewal programs must also be provided for teachers already in service. The investment is indeed an investment in the future of our society.

SUMMARY

The outlook holds challenge as well as promise for middle school education. The challenge is for schools to avoid regressing into complacency and standardization, which crippled its predecessor the junior high. The promise is sparked by changing demographics within the United States, by how the nation is perceived abroad, and how it will fit into the global community by the next century.

This chapter gave some ways in which the middle school curriculum can gear up to prepare students for survival in the twenty-first century. For example, the curriculum should be stronger in the core subjects, focusing more on high-tech, hands-on learning (science); stepped-up programs in foreign language—especially Chinese, Japanese, and Russian in view of changes in Eastern Europe and Asia—and cultural literacy (language arts); higher studies in economics and geography—global interdependence and the ecosystem (social studies); and extrapolation, statistics, higher proficiency in problem solving and computer/calculator literacy (math).

The chapter closed with specific recommendations (eliminating retention, tracking, corporal punishment, and such).

SUGGESTED LEARNING ACTIVITIES

1. Develop a renewal plan for your middle school faculty to help your staff review goals and purposes.
2. Prepare a report to the community outlining the rationale for the continued existence of the middle school in your district.
3. Develop a position paper on the need for a middle school teacher preparation program

that has its own identity apart from the elementary or secondary program.
4. Organize a parents committee to study your middle school program. Outline the charge you would give that committee.
5. Prepare a report on "The Middle School of the Twenty-first Century," to be presented to a citizens group.

NOTES

1. Harold L. Hodgkinson, *The Same Client: The Demographics of Educational Service Delivery Systems* (Washington, DC: Institute for Educational Leadership, Inc., 1991).
2. *World Development Forum*, Washington, DC, 1991.
3. Irving Balow and Mahna Schwager, *Retention in Grade: A Failed Procedure* (Riverside, CA: University of California, California Educational Research Corporation, 1990) (see numerous research studies cited in this report). See also,

"Grade-Level Retention," a position paper of the Florida Department of Education, 1990 (this report supports the findings in the California report).
4. Carl Glickman, "Pretending Not to Know What We Know," *Educational Leadership*, May 1991, Alexandria, VA: Association for Supervision and Curriculum Development (Dr. Glickman presents a brilliant analysis of teaching and learning research in this publication).

SELECTED REFERENCES

Alexander, William; Williams, Emmett; Compton, Mary; Hines, Vince; and Prescott, David, *The Emergent Middle School* (New York: Holt, Rinehart, Winston, 1968).

Association for Supervision and Curriculum Development, Commission on Secondary Education, *The Junior High We Need* (Washington, DC: ASCD, 1961).

Association for Supervision and Curriculum Development, Working Group on the Emerging Adolescent, Joseph Bondi, chairman, *The Middle School We Need* (Alexandria, VA: ASCD, 1975).

Bondi, Joseph, *Developing Middle Schools: A Guidebook* (Wheeling, IL: Whitehall Publishing Company, 1972).

Bossing, Nelson L., and Cramer, Roscoe V., *The Junior High School* (Boston: Houghton-Mifflin, 1965).

Briggs, Thomas, *The Junior High School* (Boston: Houghton-Mifflin, 1920).

Carnegie Council on Adolescent Development, *Turning Points: Preparing American Youth for the 21st Century* (New York: Carnegie Corporation, 1989).

Douglass, Aubry A., "The Junior High School." In: Part Three of *Yearbook of National Society for the Study of Education*, 15th ed., (Bloomington: The Public School Publishing Company, 1916).

Eichhorn, Donald, *The Middle School* (New York: The Center for Applied Research in Education, 1966).

Grooms, Mary Ann, *Perspectives on the Middle School* (Columbus, OH: Merrill, 1967).

Gruhn, William T., and Douglass, Harl R. *The Modern Junior High School* (New York: Ronald Press, 1947).

Koos, Leonard, *The Junior High School* (Boston: Ginn and Company, 1929).

Van Til, William; Vars, Gordon; and Lounsbury, John, *Modern Education for the Junior High*

Years, 2nd ed. (Indianapolis: Bobbs-Merrill, 1967).

Wiles, Jon, *Planning Guidelines for Middle Schools* (Dubuque, IA: Kendall/Hunt Publishing Company, 1976).

Wiles, Jon, and Bondi, Joseph, *The Essential Middle School* (Columbus: Merrill, 1981).

_____, *Making Middle Schools Work* (Alexandria, VA: Association for Supervision and Curriculum Development, 1986).

Appendix 1

Obtaining Background Information About Students

School Data Sheet

Learning Behavior Checklist

Student Information Sheet

SCHOOL DATA SHEET

Enrollment (Research Department Enrollment Survey):

ADA (Research Department) 7th/8th grade:

Teacher Absence Ratio, May–June pay period (ratio = absences per teacher per month):

Number of Low Socioeconomic Recipients (Junior high school students eligible to receive free or reduced lunch):

Number of Gifted/Other Special Students (State Report Matrix):

Student Mobility (In/Out—School records indicating check-in and check-out patterns as percentage of total enrollment):

Corporal Punishment (Research Department) from _____:

Suspensions, out-of-school (Program Evaluation Department):

Expulsions, school records (Research Department):

Dropouts, 9th graders only in junior highs:

Grade Distribution (Negative if more than one-half classes show 25% failure on 40% gaining or grade of D or F in classes):

Achievement, SSAT grade 8 (CTBS—Reading/Writing/Math = total battery as compared with district average):

LEARNING BEHAVIOR CHECKLIST

Directions: For each sentence beginning, check as many responses as seem to apply to you most of the time. If none apply, fill in the blank that reads "other."

1.   When a teacher lectures in class,
_____ a.   I listen carefully and take notes which I study later.
_____ b.   I listen carefully and try to take notes, but they never help much.
_____ c.   I try to listen, but I get bored and my mind wanders.
_____ d.   I listen, and I learn a lot, but don't bother taking notes.
_____ e.   I use the time to read or do homework for another class.
_____ f.   I frequently talk, write notes, or just goof off.
_____ g.   I hope to get the notes from someone else later.
_____ h.   I daydream or sleep and hope I can get the same information from the book or from discussions. _____
_____ i.   Other_____

2.   When I read an assignment in class,
_____ a.   I always read it carefully and study it hard.
_____ b.   I change the way I read (fast or slow, skim or study), depending on what the teacher says is the purpose for reading it.
_____ c.   I read it as fast as I can just to get it over with.
_____ d.   I read it slowly but don't learn much.
_____ e.   I wait until a friend is finished and ask what it was about.
_____ f.   I just read the first few paragraphs.
_____ g.   I never finish in time.
_____ h.   I always finish early.
_____ i.   I never read, period, because I'm a poor reader.
_____ j.   I read it, but don't remember it later.
_____ k.   I take notes as I read to study later.
_____ l.   Other_____

3.   When we work in small groups in class,
_____ a.   I work harder because I can talk to other people.
_____ b.   I don't work much, but enjoy talking to my friends.
_____ c.   I try to work hard, but the others in the group don't usually listen to me.
_____ d.   I usually end up doing most of the work.
_____ e.   I don't participate much, but I pay attention and learn a lot by listening.
_____ f.   I *sit* in the group, but do the work by myself.
_____ g.   I enjoy it, but don't seem to learn as much.
_____ h.   I enjoy it and learn more than working alone or hearing lectures.
_____ i.   Other_____

LEARNING BEHAVIOR CHECKLIST *(continued)*

4. When I work by myself in class,
   _____ a.   I work harder because it is easier for me to concentrate.
   _____ b.   I talk to friends instead of working.
   _____ c.   I don't enjoy it much, but I probably learn best.
   _____ d.   I borrow answers whenever possible since I don't learn much this way, anyhow.
   _____ e.   I wait and figure out the answers during discussions.
   _____ f.   I just zip through to get done in a hurry and don't worry about it much.
   _____ g.   I do my best, but it takes me such a long time!
   _____ h.   Other_____

5. When I have assignments that aren't due for several days,
   _____ a.   I usually forget to do them.
   _____ b.   I do them right away just to get them done.
   _____ c.   I put them off until the last possible minute and then rush through them.
   _____ d.   I really worry about them even if I do put them off.
   _____ e.   I like them because I have plenty of time to do them at my own rate.
   _____ f.   I just copy them, anyway, so it doesn't matter when they're done.
   _____ g.   I wish they were due sooner because I need pressure to make me work.
   _____ h.   Other_____

STUDENT INFORMATION SHEET

Name _____ Nickname _____
          Last   First   Middle

Student Number _____

Address _____

_____ Zip _____

Phone Number _____

I live with my   mother _____   father _____   stepmother _____

stepfather _____   grandparents _____   other _____

Father's name _____ Occupation _____

Father's place of business _____ Phone _____

Mother's name _____ Occupation _____

Mother's place of business _____ Phone _____

List the names and ages of your brothers and sisters.

_____ _____ _____ _____

_____ _____ _____ _____

_____ _____ _____ _____

My birthdate is _____
                        Month   Day   Year

I was born in _____
                        City   State

Do you wear glasses to read books? _____

Do you wear glasses to read the chalkboard? _____

Do you have difficulty hearing from the back of the room? _____

How much time do you spend on homework each night? _____

My favorite subject is _____ .

The subject I like least is _____ .

My hobbies are _____ .

After school I like to _____

_____ .

When I finish high school, I would like to _____

_____ .

Appendix 2

Middle School Parent Survey (Excerpt)

MIDDLE SCHOOL PARENT SURVEY

How would you rate this school on these qualities?

	EXCELLENT	GOOD	FAIR	POOR
1. Friendly and interested teachers	1	2	3	4
2. Emphasis on basic skills	1	2	3	4
3. Strong principal leadership	1	2	3	4
4. Supportive and involved parents	1	2	3	4
5. Good student discipline	1	2	3	4
6. Quality of teaching	1	2	3	4
7. Students excited by learning	1	2	3	4
8. Opportunities for enrichment	1	2	3	4
9. Library services	1	2	3	4
10. School/community relations	1	2	3	4
11. Reporting of pupil progress	1	2	3	4
12. Communication with parents	1	2	3	4
13. Meeting needs of individual students	1	2	3	4
14. Addressing the developmental needs of students (physical, social-emotional)	1	2	3	4

. . .

Please indicate how much you agree or disagree with the following statements:

	Strongly Agree	Agree	Disagree	Strongly Disagree	Don't Know
27. The principal of this school sets high academic standards for students.	1	2	3	4	5
28. The principal of this school sets high standards for student behavior.	1	2	3	4	5
29. My child's teachers expect him/her to do well academically.	1	2	3	4	5
30. The principal communicates well with parents.	1	2	3	4	5
31. A positive feeling exists in this school.	1	2	3	4	5
32. My child's academic needs are being met.	1	2	3	4	5
33. The principal takes responsibility for the effectiveness of the instructional program.	1	2	3	4	5

MIDDLE SCHOOL PARENT SURVEY *(continued)*

	Strongly Agree	Agree	Disagree	Strongly Disagree	Don't Know
34. Decisions about what happens to students in this school are made by the principal, teachers, and parents working together.	1	2	3	4	5
35. Parents and teachers work together to monitor homework.	1	2	3	4	5
36. Parent-teacher conferences result in specific plans to improve student classroom achievement.	1	2	3	4	5
37. My child receives adequate individual attention from his/her teachers.	1	2	3	4	5
38. My child is treated fairly in class.	1	2	3	4	5
39. My child enjoys what he/she does in his/her classes.	1	2	3	4	5
40. The lunchroom at this school is orderly.	1	2	3	4	5
41. I am aware of the consequences of my child's not obeying the rules at this school.	1	2	3	4	5
42. Students at this school are generally well-behaved.	1	2	3	4	5
43. I feel my child is safe from physical harm in this school.	1	2	3	4	5
44. Students at this school generally appear respectful of their teachers.	1	2	3	4	5
45. Students at this school generally appear respectful of their principal.	1	2	3	4	5
46. In my child's classes there is a positive feeling that helps students learn.	1	2	3	4	5
47. My child's classes are generally orderly and quiet.	1	2	3	4	5
48. Goals and priorities for this school are clear.	1	2	3	4	5
49. My child's teachers let me know how my child is doing in school.	1	2	3	4	5
50. My child enjoys going to this school.	1	2	3	4	5
51. I expect my child to do well academically.	1	2	3	4	5
52. My child has friends at school with whom he/she feels comfortable.	1	2	3	4	5

MIDDLE SCHOOL PARENT SURVEY *(continued)*

	Strongly Agree	Agree	Disagree	Strongly Disagree	Don't Know
53. There is at least one staff member who has a close, supportive relationship with my child.	1	2	3	4	5
54. I have specific reasons to be concerned about my child's exposure to drugs and alcohol at this school.	1	2	3	4	5
55. The school building is neat, bright, clean, and comfortable. It is a source of school pride.	1	2	3	4	5
56. My child is respected by students from different races and backgrounds.	1	2	3	4	5
57. My child has opportunities to socialize with students from other races and cultures.	1	2	3	4	5
58. I know whom I would call to correct a situation in which I felt that my child was discriminated against.	1	2	3	4	5
59. My child's courses have included students from differing races and cultures.	1	2	3	4	5
60. My child feels welcome to participate in any school activities that he/she is interested in.	1	2	3	4	5
61. My child socializes with students from other races and cultures.	1	2	3	4	5
62. My child's courses include opportunities to learn about many races and cultures.	1	2	3	4	5

63. How would you rate the academic ability of your child compared with other students at this school?

My child's ability is much higher.   1
My child's ability is somewhat higher.   2
My child's ability is about the same.   3
My child's ability is somewhat lower.   4
My child's ability is much lower.   5

64. Do you expect your child to attend college?

Yes _____   No _____

MIDDLE SCHOOL PARENT SURVEY *(continued)*

65. Please list steps that this school could take to become more sensitive to differing races and cultures.

    a. _____

    b. _____

    c. _____

66. Please list three things you like about this school.

    a. _____

    _____

    b. _____

    _____

    c. _____

    _____

67. Please list three things you would like to see improved at this school.

    a. _____

    _____

    b. _____

    _____

    c. _____

    _____

Appendix 3

Inservice Design and Workshop Models

Inservice/Staff Development Activities (Dade County)

Inservice/Staff Development Plan (Duval County)

Teacher/Administrator Training Model (Duval County)

Preservice and Inservice: Recommendations

Training Categories

Administrator Training Model

Administrator Technical Assistance Training

Teacher Competencies Self-Appraisal

Teacher Survey of Experience and Staff Development Needs

Training: Objectives, Activities, and Evaluation

Teachers Training Teachers (TTT) Workshop in Teaming and Interdisciplinary Instruction

Sample Training Certificate

INSERVICE/STAFF DEVELOPMENT ACTIVITIES
(DADE COUNTY)

Middle School Inservice/Staff Development Committee

Chair: Ms. Elvira Dopico

Members: Dr. Kenneth Walker, Dr. Joseph DeChurch, Dr. Ed Trauschke, Ms. Karen Dreyfuss, Ms. Margaret Petersen

Consultants: Dr. Jon Wiles, Dr. Joseph Bondi

Purpose: To develop an inservice/staff development plan to train, orient and inform all persons responsible for the successful implementation of the middle school program in Dade County.

Impact Groups: School board
Senior staff
District subject area supervisors
Area administrators
Middle school principals, assistant principals, counselors
School support staffs, including clerical, security, custodial, and bus drivers
Parents
Community groups/persons

Inservice/Staff Development Activities for Middle School Transition

Group	Activity	Time Frames	Person(s) Responsible
School Board	a. Reporting to (progress report) b. Information and updating	June 1989, 1990, 1991, 1992	J. Fernandez P. Bell Management team Coordinating committee Wiles-Bondi
Senior Staff	a. Information and updating	As needed	J. Fernandez P. Bell Wiles-Bondi
District staff/area administrators	a. Orientation-training	Spring, fall 1988	Wiles-Bondi
Other school administrators (elem.–high school)	b. Information and updating	As needed	Wiles-Bondi

INSERVICE/STAFF DEVELOPMENT ACTIVITIES
(DADE COUNTY) *(continued)*

Group	Activity	Time Frames	Person(s) Responsible
Middle school principals, assistant principals, counselors	a. Leadership training in scheduling, leadership, working with teams, building parent and community involvement	Spring preceding implementation of middle school program	Wiles-Bondi
	b. Information and updating	Ongoing	J. DeChurch Wiles-Bondi
Middle school teachers	a. General training in 50-hour middle school training components	1988–1992	K. Walker K. Dreyfuss M. Petersen Subject area supervisors Training teams Wiles-Bondi University—other consultants
School support staff, clerical, custodial, security, bus drivers	Orientation and information	1988–ongoing	J. DeChurch K. Dreyfuss J. Gilyard
Parents	Orientation and information	1988–ongoing	J. DeChurch
Community groups/individuals	Information	1988–ongoing	P. Bell J. DeChurch

Training Components for Teachers

A. Three 10-hour training components developed by Wiles-Bondi for teachers:
   1. The Middle School and Middle School Student
   2. Teaming and Interdisciplinary Instruction
   3. Strategies for Adviser/Advisee Program

B. Two additional 10-hour components developed by Teacher Education Center (TEC) staff and Wiles-Bondi. This will provide a total package of 50 hours of training leading to middle school endorsement (for those eligible) and internal Dade County middle school certification. These two components will be taught by local university consultants and others. They are as follows:
   4. Teaching Strategies in Middle School (English, science, math, social studies, art, etc.)
   5. General Strategies for Teaching in Middle School.
      This component will include topics for teaching critical thinking, teaching decision-making skills, designing positive classroom management and assertive discipline programs.

INSERVICE/STAFF DEVELOPMENT ACTIVITIES
(DADE COUNTY) *(continued)*

Training Program for School Administrators

A separate 10-hour training component for school administrators developed by Wiles-Bondi will include topics such as scheduling, school leadership, working with teams, and community involvement. This component will allow principals, assistant principals, and district and area staff to update skills in middle school leadership.

Orientation and Information Components

Orientation and information components for the board, district, senior staff, supervisory staff, area staff, school site administrators, coordinating committee, and parent and community groups will be developed by the management team, middle school coordinator, and consultants. These components will begin in 1988 and be ongoing.

Delivery of Training and Orientation/Information Program

Delivery of teacher training components 1–3 will occur through the TTT (Teachers Training Teachers) Model with the consultants training the training teams to deliver each of the three components. Training in these components began in 1988 and will be ongoing. Components 4 and 5 will be regularly scheduled by the TEC beginning in 1989 and will be ongoing. The 10-hour leadership component will be regularly scheduled and taught by the consultants beginning in 1989 and will be ongoing.

Recordkeeping, Monitoring, Support, and Certification

Recordkeeping, monitoring, support, and certification will be the responsibility of the Bureau of Human Resource Development.

Overall Goal

Our goal is for Dade County to have *the* nationwide model for a middle school training program. Dade County will train 100% of our middle school teachers and administrators and set in motion a sustaining program for all new personnel. In addition, orientation and information components will be developed and delivered to orient and update all school personnel, parents, and community individuals on the middle school concept.

INSERVICE/STAFF DEVELOPMENT PLAN
(DUVAL COUNTY)

Committee Members: Linda Cugini, Barbara DeSue, Jana French, Peggy Kring, Gerlieve Oliver, Marlene Rasmussen, Franklin Smith, Dorothy Williams

Consultants: Dr. Jon Wiles, Dr. Joseph Bondi

Purpose: To develop an inservice/staff development plan to train, orient, and inform all persons responsible for the successful implementation of the middle school program in Duval County.

Inservice/Staff Development Activities

Group	Activity	Time	Person(s) Responsible
School board	Progress report	November 1989, 1990, 1991	Larry Zenke Management team Coordinating committee
District/staff area superintendents	Orientation-training	Fall 1989/ongoing	Wiles-Bondi
Other administrators (Elem.–high school)	Information and updating	Spring 1990/ongoing	Wiles-Bondi
Middle school principals, assistant principals, counselors	a. Leadership training in scheduling, leadership, working with teams	January–February 1990/ongoing	Wiles-Bondi
Middle school principals (24)/vice principals/counselors/ assistant principals	a. Leadership Training II b. Information	April–June 1990 Ongoing	Wiles-Bondi Management team Wiles-Bondi
Middle school training team	a. Trainer inservice	Fall 1989/ongoing	Wiles-Bondi Staff development coordinator Teacher Education Center
Middle school teachers/staff	a. General training in June; 40-hour middle school training component	November— 1989— 1990/Ongoing	Training team Teacher Education Center Staff development coordinator
School support, staff, clerical, custodial, bus drivers	Orientation and information	1989/ongoing	Barbara DeSue Staff development coordinator

INSERVICE/STAFF DEVELOPMENT PLAN
(DUVAL COUNTY) *(continued)*

Group	Activity	Time	Person(s) Responsible
Parents	Orientation and in-formation	1989/ongoing	Barbara DeSue Staff development coordinator
Community groups/individuals	Information	1989/ongoing	Barbara DeSue Staff development coordinator Committee members

The Staff Development Coordinator will release two newsletters, one in the winter of 1990 and one in the spring of 1991.

TEACHER/ADMINISTRATOR TRAINING MODEL
(DUVAL COUNTY)

Training Components for Teachers-Administrators

A. Four 10-hour training components for teachers/administrators:
  1. Characteristics of the Middle Grade Student and Middle School Program
  2. Organization of Instruction (Teaming) in the Middle Grades
  3. Counseling the Middle Grade Student
  4. Middle Grade Curriculum: Planning and Evaluation

   Delivery of Teacher Training components 1–4 will occur through the TTT (Teachers Training Teachers) Model with the consultants training the training teams to deliver each of the four components. These components will be scheduled through the TEC and will begin in 1989 and will be ongoing. Components 5 and 6 will be regularly scheduled by the TEC office and middle grades staff development coordinator beginning in 1990 and will be ongoing. Training in components 7, 8, and 9 will be regularly scheduled through the TEC and the middle grades staff development coordinator.

B. Five additional 10-hour components are:
  5. Teaching Strategies in Middle School (math, English, art, social studies, science, etc.)
  6. General Strategies for Teaching in Middle School (will include topics for teaching critical thinking skills and designing positive classroom management techniques)
  7. Team Leader Training
  8. Utilizing Interdisciplinary Units
  9. Trainer Component (Teachers will be trained to deliver the 40-hour inservice.)

C. Training program for school administrators will include:
  10. Leadership in Middle Schools I: A 10-hour general training component for school administrators, developed by Wiles-Bondi, will include general topics such as scheduling, school leadership, working with teams, and community involvement. This component will allow principals, assistants, and district and area staff to update skills in middle school leadership.
  11. Leadership in Middle Schools II: A 10-hour training component for middle school administrators (principal, vice-principal, assistant principal) developed by Wiles-Bondi will focus on identified needs of administrators. This component will permit work on a real schedule, building organization, curriculum, team organization, and leadership strategies.

   Recordkeeping, monitoring, support, and certification will be the responsibility of the staff development coordinator.

PRESERVICE AND INSERVICE: RECOMMENDATIONS

Teacher Education Experiences

A. Underlying Principles: In addition to guidelines for the three phases of teacher education—general education, individual specialization, and professional preparation, the following underlying principles are suggested:

1. Middle school teacher education should promote continuity of educational experience. All aspects of the teacher education program should be closely interrelated to provide a meaningful professional experience for the prospective middle school teacher.
2. Middle school teacher education should ensure the development of personal qualities as well as professional abilities.
3. Middle school teacher education should be highly personalized. It is important that the individualization of instruction sought for the middle school also be a goal of middle school teacher education.
4. Middle school teacher education should be a simultaneous blending of didactic instruction and practical experience. Practical experiences should be coordinated with didactic course work to provide meaningful professional education experiences for prospective middle school teachers.
5. Middle school teacher education should use those principles, techniques, and materials appropriate to middle school teaching insofar as they are consistent with the level of understanding and maturity of prospective middle school teachers.

B. General Education: Middle school teacher preparation should include sufficient experiences of a general or liberal education nature to qualify the teacher as a literate, self-directed learner, able to understand and interpret current developments in a changing society.

C. Individual Specialization:

1. As early as possible in the teacher education program, teacher candidates should have opportunity to study the operation of schools at different levels, so that the individual's choice of middle school specialization is based on special interest in work at this level.
2. Each middle school staff member should have both breadth and depth in preparation. The depth of preparation should be in a curriculum or service in which the person could function as a specialist in team teaching or other instructional organization appropriate to middle school–age children.
3. Specialization should be planned for each middle school teacher in terms of his interests, competencies, and pattern of college courses to ensure an adequate preparation in the field of specialization.
4. Some experiences in the field of specialization should parallel the school laboratory experiences described below, so as to provide adequate opportunity for relating general professional preparation and individual specialization. Periodic reviews of each teacher competencies should be used in determining further training needs.

D. Professional Preparation:

1. Basic to the entire program of teacher education for the middle school is study of the characteristics of middle school–age children. In that continuous and prolonged experience in working with these children is desirable in the program, a combination of laboratory observation, case study, and systematic instruction seems indicated.

PRESERVICE AND INSERVICE:
RECOMMENDATIONS *(continued)*

2. The middle school teacher should participate in a middle school laboratory experience program for at least one year. These experiences would include observation of teaching and learning situations; involvement in parent conferences and school-community activities; participation in team planning, team teaching, and evaluation, and other differentiated staff arrangements: direct instruction of individuals, small groups, and variable-size classes, and participation in schoolwide and special-interest activities. The program should include both extensive and intensive phases to provide experience with a wide variety of instructional situations.

3. The school laboratory experience should be paralleled by, or include, experiences of a curricular and instructional laboratory type. These experiences would include preparation of curriculum objectives, plans and units, and instructional materials; practice in use of a variety of instructional media and resources; development of tests and test analyses; and the use of systematic observation, simulation, and other techniques for developing teacher skills.

4. Paralleling the laboratory experiences should be a professional seminar devoted to developing professional understandings, skills, and attitudes for working in the middle schools. Seminar participants (in addition to teacher candidates and college professors) might include supervising teachers in the laboratory situations and resource personnel as needed and as available. Experiences in the laboratory settings would be analyzed with attention to alternative procedures, relationships between schools and units within particular schools, and in general the application of theory and research to practice. The seminar would include opportunities for grouping participants both by curriculum area and across roles.

Program Admission

A. Preservice:

1. The institution has a procedure for identifying and selecting candidates for admission to the program for middle school teachers. Sections II and III of these guidelines are used in developing the procedure for admission.

2. Procedures for admission include criteria relating to selection, placement, and retention.

3. Procedures provide for individual assessment utilizing Section II of these guidelines as criteria. They also provide for a design of an individual program for the applicant that is based on his needs as revealed by this assessment.

4. The assessment should include the capacity of the candidate to complete the program; familiarity with the objectives of the program; an understanding of the competencies, attitudes, and skills needed in the middle school teacher; and an initial commitment to teaching the middle school child.

5. Procedures provide for candidates to enter the program after completion of an undergraduate program in another area of concentration.

B. Inservice: The inservice teacher, for all practical purposes, is admitted to the inservice program of a school district when that school district employs the teacher to teach in a middle school. However, admission to certain parts of the inservice program for middle school teachers should follow an organized procedure:

1. The local education agency or school has a cooperatively developed procedure for assessing the inservice needs of middle school teachers.

PRESERVICE AND INSERVICE:
RECOMMENDATIONS *(continued)*

2. Procedures provide for individual assessment based on Section II of these guidelines and the system's ability to improve the needs revealed. Assessment only includes the competencies in Section II of which the local system is capable of improving through inservice education.
3. Procedures provide for the cooperative development and use of the assessment procedures by teachers, supervisors, and administrators.
4. Procedures provide for candidates to use both the local education agency's inservice education program, and institution-based programs.

Follow-Up of Program Participants

A. Preservice:
1. There is a planned program for assessing changes in attitudes and behavior of students as they move through the program.
2. The program utilizes the results of the assessment procedures to revise individual student programs.
3. Personnel in cooperating schools participate in the education process.
4. Evaluation of the effectiveness of the program is accomplished through evidence obtained from former students, the schools in which they work, and the Department of Education. This evidence is based on the stated objective of the program.
5. The follow-up program includes early leavers as well as those who complete the program.
6. A record of revisions in the program includes the follow-up data on which the revisions were based.
7. Data appropriate for preservice/inservice program articulation are shared with the cooperating school system.

B. Inservice:
1. There is a planned program of evaluation of the effectiveness of each inservice education component.
2. The assessment of competencies developed in the program includes not only changes in teacher behavior, but an assessment of the resultant changes in student behavior.
3. A record of revisions of inservice education components includes the evaluation data on which revisions were based.
4. Personnel from teacher education institutions participate in the evaluation of the program.
5. Supervisors, principals, and teachers participate in the evaluation of the program's effectiveness.

TRAINING CATEGORIES

In an effort to provide top-quality administrative training, we will divide our training into three specific categories (Beginning, Intermediate, and Advanced). This will allow us to focus our efforts to meet the specific needs of individual schools. The following is a description of the three categories with an explanation of the type of district support attached to each.

Advanced

This category of schools will open their doors in September with a master schedule that reflects *true* interdisciplinary teaming in *all* grade levels within the school.

District Support

1. Salary supplements for team leaders and advisory leader (contingent on state funding)
2. Salary supplement for an advisory leader—if schoolwide advisory program exists (contingent on state funding)
3. Summer training for administrative staff (generic and technical assistance)
4. Training of teacher training cadre
5. District support services
6. $6,000 for interdisciplinary team development

Intermediate

This category of schools will open their doors in September with a master schedule that reflects *true* interdisciplinary teaming in *one* or *more* grade levels. **Or,** this group comprises those schools that will revise their master schedules during the first semester so that *true* interdisciplinary teaming will be in place in *one* or *more* grade levels during the second semester.

District Support

1. Salary supplements for team leaders (contingent on state funding)
2. Salary supplement for an advisory leader—if a schoolwide advisory program exists (contingent on state funding)
3. Summer training for administrative staff (generic and technical assistance)
4. Training of the teacher training cadre
5. District support services
6. Some portion of the $6,000 for interdisciplinary team development (exact amount determined by the school principal and the middle school office)

Beginning

Those schools will use the 1989–1990 school year as a planning and training year. They will train staff and use the 1989–1990 school year to develop a master schedule, which will allow for full-scale interdisciplinary teaming during the 1990–1991 school year.

District Support

1. Summer training of administrative staff (generic and technical assistance)
2. Training of the teacher training cadre
3. District support services

TRAINING CATEGORIES *(continued)*

Categories

Advanced	Intermediate	Beginning
Arvida	Allapattah	Brownsville
Campbell Drive	B. T. Washington	Carver, G. W.
Carol City	Centennial	Hammocks
Citrus Grove	Hialeah	Highland Oaks
Cutler Ridge	Miami Lakes	Kennedy, J. F.
Drew	Richmond Heights	Lee, J. R. E.
Edison	Thomas Jefferson	Mann, Jan
Filer	Westview	Marti, Jose
Glades	W. R. Thomas	McMillian, H. D.
Homestead		North Dade
Horace Mann		Palmetto
Kinloch Park		Riviera
Lake Stevens		Rockway
Madison		Southwood
Mays		South Miami
Miami Springs		West Miami
Nautilus		
Norland		
North Miami		
Palm Springs		
Parkway		
Ponce de Leon		
Redland		
Ruben Dario		
Shenandoah		

ADMINISTRATOR TRAINING MODEL

Premise: Principals should receive *useful,* hands-on training. Training configuration must be taken in order:

1. Middle School Development (Component "A")
   A. Role of intermediate education
      How is it different and why should it be different?
   B. Middle school curriculum: establishing a philosophy; establishing a climate; focusing the learning design; establishing major curriculum developmental tasks
2. Effective Administration of a Middle School (Component "B")
   A. Development of an action plan based on a needs assessment
   B. Determination of progress points and observable criteria
   C. Elements of the basic middle school components
   D. Building the administrative team
   E. Special problems of the new middle school administration
3. Leadership and Change in a Middle School (Component "B")
   A. How to create change
   B. Meeting with resistance and overcoming challenges
   C. Leadership theory in practice
   D. Inservice training needs and the development of a yearlong implementation plan
4. Retooling the School and Staff (Component "C")
   A. Prepare ways to orient teachers to middle school
   B. Develop orientation presentation
   C. A new look at the middle school classroom
   D. How to humanize instruction (total development versus subject priority)
   E. Learning styles/instructional strategies
   F. Organizing the classroom for instruction
   G. Teams and team leaders—what are they and what do they do?
   H. Obstacles/challenges/helpful hints
5. Developing a Middle School Curriculum (Component "D")
   A. Scheduling process
   B. Issues and concerns
   C. Hands-on training
   D. Adviser/advisee

Training with a different edge (for assistant principals) includes:

1. Middle School Model/Philosophy (Component "A")
   A. Role of intermediate education
   B. Focusing of the learning design
   C. Major curriculum developmental tasks
2. Supervision of the Middle School (Component "B")
   A. Teams/team leaders/department heads
   B. Team leader council
   C. Interdisciplinary planning/implementation setting
   D. Setting expectations, adviser/advisee, etc.
3. Retooling [Same as principals, plus supervision of team leaders] (Component "C")
4. Scheduling (Component "D")

ADMINISTRATOR TECHNICAL ASSISTANCE TRAINING

Teams of two to three training principals will be assigned to work with schools on an individual basis. Each school will set its own schedule for technical assistance with its assigned principal training team. Technical assistance will be offered throughout the summer and will include these areas:

A. Scheduling
B. Teaming
C. Adviser/advisee
D. Interdisciplinary instruction
E. Curriculum
F. Exploration

G. Intramurals
H. Needs assessment
I. Action plan
J. Follow-up
K. Inservice

TEACHER COMPETENCIES SELF-APPRAISAL

Name _____   School _____

Date _____   Grade _____

Directions: Below are a list of competencies deemed important for effective teaching in the middle school. Please examine each competency and appraise your own abilities in this area. Indicate whether the competency is an area of strength, adequacy, or weakness for you. Do so by using the following code to mark the boxes to the right of the competency: S = Strength, A = Adequacy, W = Weakness.

At the end of the list, you are asked to select several competencies for further professional development. The competencies that you select may be strengths that you wish to capitalize on, or weaknesses you wish to erase.

Part One: Middle School Teacher Competencies   **Appraisal**

A.   Competency Area: Interpersonal Relationships
1. The teacher manages the classroom with a minimum of negative or aversive controls.   _____
2. The teacher creates a climate in the classroom which rests somewhere comfortably apart from an authoritarian tenseness or a laissez-faire chaos.   _____
3. The teacher uses himself (herself) as a tool in promoting the personal growth of students and colleagues.   _____
4. The teacher's relationships with colleagues, administrators, and supervisors are harmonious and productive.   _____
5. The teacher is aware of the needs, forces, and perceptions which determine his (her) personal behavior.   _____
6. The teacher accepts behavior, and values individuals and groups which depart from his own.   _____

TEACHER COMPETENCIES SELF-APPRAISAL *(continued)*

Part One: Middle School Teacher Competencies   **Appraisal**

B. Competency Area: Basic Instructional Skills
    1. The teacher exhibits variety as a basic facet of instruction both during the hour and from class to class.   _____
    2. The teacher uses a multimedia approach.   _____
    3. The teacher maintains a balance between teacher-directed learning and student-directed learning.   _____
    4. The teacher individualizes instruction in the classroom.   _____
    5. The teacher promotes student self-direction, initiative, and responsibility.   _____
    6. The teacher selects learning activities and executes them in a way that promotes student interest and involvement.   _____
    7. The teacher's efforts in curriculum and instruction proceed from a problem-solving framework, involving the students in relevant inquiry. _____
    8. The teacher plans lessons thoroughly and in advance, using specific objectives and smooth transitions from one lesson to another.   _____
    9. The teacher utilizes a variety of group sizes and devices in instruction. _____
    10. The teacher possesses skill in asking questions which encourage student thinking beyond the level of "recall."   _____
    11. The teacher avoids common pitfalls of expository teaching, such as in faulty speech patterns, pacing the room, use of chalkboard, physical appearance of the classroom, etc.   _____
    12. The teacher knows about and applies modern learning theories in the classroom.   _____

C. Competency Area: Curriculum
    1. The teacher knows what is relevant to the lives of students and finds ways to include it in the curriculum.   _____
    2. The teacher chooses curriculum materials that are appropriate for the learning abilities and styles of the students.   _____
    3. The teacher, individually or with a team of teachers, involves students in interdisciplinary studies.   _____

D. Competency Area: Relationships with the Community
    1. The teacher establishes positive relationships with the parents and families of students.   _____
    2. The teacher works at understanding, accepting, and being accepted by members of the subcultures in the school and in the community.   _____
    3. The teacher is interested in and participates in affairs of the community and school.   _____

E. Competency Area: Understanding the Student
    1. The teacher understands the intellectual nature of middle school youth. _____
    2. The teacher understands the physical nature of middle school youth.   _____
    3. The teacher understands the socio-emotional nature of middle school youth.   _____

TEACHER COMPETENCIES SELF-APPRAISAL *(continued)*

Part One: Middle School Teacher Competencies   **Appraisal**

F. Competency Area: Commitment to Middle School Teaching
    1. The teacher is enthusiastic and vigorous in the daily activities of teaching middle school youth.   _____
    2. The teacher understands the middle school concept and attempts to apply it in the classroom, and in the school as a whole.   _____

Part Two: Areas for Development
Please list below the numbers of the competencies which you have selected for further development. They may be either strengths or weaknesses, and you may select more than five or fewer than five.

1.
2.
3.
4.
5.

TEACHER SURVEY OF EXPERIENCE AND STAFF DEVELOPMENT NEEDS

Instrument: Teacher Survey Form (administered to 6–8 teachers, counselors, and administrators)

Findings: This questionnaire was designed to gather data from the above-mentioned sources regarding experience and training. The findings include:

Degrees:	22% hold a B.A. degree
	28% hold a B.S. degree
	39% hold a Master's degree
	8% hold a higher degree
Years of service:	22% over five years
	42% over ten years
	22% over twenty years
Years in middle school:	33% over five years
	44% over ten years

Skills identified as most useful in implementing the middle school concept include:

1. Dealing with motivation and discipline problems in the classroom
2. Effective teaching strategies
3. Understanding characteristics of middle school students
4. Strategies for dealing with low achievers
5. Techniques for guiding and advising students

Implications:

1. Middle school teachers represent a veteran, highly trained staff. Almost half of the teachers surveyed have ten or more years in middle school; however, one-fourth of these teachers do not have middle school certification.
2. Teachers are anxious to improve skills relating to discipline, motivation, and advising students. In order to do this, they need a clearer understanding of middle school students and strategies for working with them at all levels.
3. Inservice and staff development should continue to provide teachers with retooling skills needed to carry out an effective middle school program and provide means to gain proper certification.

TRAINING: OBJECTIVES, ACTIVITIES, AND EVALUATION

Number: 5–01–49–2–13

Inservice Points: 60

General Objective: To identify the characteristics of the middle school; to identify the needs of and develop a curriculum for the middle school students

Specific Objectives: At the conclusion of training, each participant will be able to:

1. State the rationale for the middle school
2. Examine the history of the development of the middle school
3. Develop a program description for the middle school
4. Describe the physical, social, emotional, and intellectual development of students between the ages of ten and fourteen
5. Suggest specific program needs suggested by growth and development characteristics of emerging adolescent learners
6. Develop a block schedule, given the number of teachers and students in their middle school
7. List the advantages and disadvantages of a nongraded structure
8. Plan a lesson for a block of time in their classrooms
9. Learn to use the thirteen-category Flanders System of Interaction Analysis and Gallagher-Aschner System for Analyzing Classroom Questions
10. Develop a system for dealing with classroom discipline
11. Identify the ten most important teacher competencies for the middle school
12. List the advantages and disadvantages of team teaching
13. Develop a team agenda
14. Practice teaming skills
15. Learn the steps necessary in developing an interdisciplinary unit of instruction
16. Outline the steps of a needs assessment
17. Learn to state Level I, II, and III goals and learning objectives
18. Identify the major skills, concepts, and content in their subject for grades 6 through 8
19. Learn to diagnose needs of creative and talented students
20. Master the sequential skills in the Wiles-Bondi skill clusters for creative thinking
21. Develop and teach one or more skill-learning activities in the Wiles-Bondi Creative Thinking Skills System
22. Develop and implement a series of guidance exercises for their students that will enhance their self-understanding and respect for others
23. Practice learning skills and other skills necessary for serving in an advisory role to middle school students
24. Learn what persons and agencies are available to assist the classroom teacher in working with students having special school and home problems
25. Develop and teach a creative learning lesson
26. Plan and implement several new classroom activities for that unit
27. Present a plan to restructure the seating arrangement of the classroom and utilize other school spaces for their students in teaching the learning unit
28. Develop a plan for a learning center in their classrooms
29. Develop strategies for working with students with special needs

TRAINING: OBJECTIVES, ACTIVITIES, AND EVALUATION *(continued)*

30. Develop a plan to enhance the learning environment for middle-level students
31. Identify and sequence the steps necessary in planning a middle school
32. Develop an instrument to judge the effectiveness of a middle school. The instrument will examine both curricular and instructional practices

Description/Activities:

Objectives 1 through 3:　Participants will view the film "Profile of a Middle School," write a philosophical statement defending the middle school design, and develop a parent information brochure outlining the essential elements of a middle school.

Objectives 4 and 5:　Participants will develop procedures for studying students in their middle school and develop one instrument to carry information about student needs and interests in their school.

Objectives 6 through 8:　Given enrollment and the staffing pattern of a middle school, participants will develop an actual middle school schedule. In groups of four or five, participants will organize a week's activities for a block of instructional time.

Objectives 9 through 11:　Participants will practice using certain instruments utilized in assessing classroom instruction and develop an actual set of discipline procedures they will use in the classroom. Case studies will be provided to examine in detail teaching-learning situations found in middle schools.

Objectives 12 through 15:　Participants will role-play in team meetings and work together in interdisciplinary teams to develop an outline for an interdisciplinary unit.

Objectives 16 through 18:　Participants will work individually and in teams to analyze the curriculum of the middle school, focusing on the subject areas they are teaching. A skill continuum or checklist will be developed for each subject area represented by the participants.

Objectives 19 through 21:　Participants will develop a series of learning activities utilizing the Wiles-Bondi Creative Thinking Skills System and organize several learning activities that will enhance the creative thinking skills of their students.

Objectives 22 through 24:　Participants will structure a series of guidance activities. Role-playing techniques will be used to acquaint teachers with actual student-teacher roles and expectations.

Objectives 25 through 30:　Participants will utilize existing classroom materials and teacher-made materials to develop a learning unit. The unit will require the development of innovative classroom activities and a restructuring of the physical arrangement of the classroom in which the unit is being taught.

Objectives 31 and 32:　Participants will work in small and large groups to develop a planning checklist for those organizing a middle school and also develop an evaluation instrument for judging the effectiveness of a middle school.

TRAINING: OBJECTIVES, ACTIVITIES,
AND EVALUATION *(continued)*

Evaluation:

Objectives 1 through 3:   Participants will
—list the essential elements of a successful middle school.
—explain the rationale for the middle school.
—design a program description for their own middle school.

Objectives 4 and 5:   Participants will
—discuss characteristics of adolescent learners and implications for effective school level programs.
—describe the physical, social, emotional, and intellectual development of students between the
  ages of 10 through 14.
—list and develop appropriate instructional strategies for middle-level learners.

Objectives 6 through 8:   Participants will
—list advantages of interdisciplinary teams with regard to the instruction of middle-level learners.
—develop an appropriate block schedule and flexible time schedule for middle school students.
—list the advantages and disadvantages of a nongraded structure.
—plan a lesson for a block of time in their classrooms.

Objectives 9 through 11:   Participants will
—list kinds of teaching strategies appropriate for preadolescents.
—discuss appropriate classroom questioning techniques.
—discuss necessary competencies for the middle school teacher.

Objectives 12 through 15:   Participants will
—list advantages and disadvantages of team teaching.
—develop an agenda for a team meeting.
—list, discuss, and practice effective teaming skills.
—list the steps used in developing an interdisciplinary unit of instruction.

Objectives 16 through 18:   Participants will
—analyze curriculum and discuss its impact on middle-level learners.
—develop appropriate goals/objectives for middle-level instruction.
—identify skills, concepts, and activities to achieve specific learning levels.

Objectives 19 through 21:   Participants will
—list activities/strategies that develop thinking and creativity in middle-level students.
—discuss the sequential skills used in developing higher thinking.
—develop and teach an activity which addresses higher/creative thinking in middle-level students.

Objectives 22 through 24:   Participants will
—list support personnel with expertise in counseling middle-level students.
—list and practice skills necessary for serving in an advisory capacity.
—develop, assemble, and practice a series of activities designed to enhance the self-concept of
  middle school students.

TRAINING: OBJECTIVES, ACTIVITIES,
AND EVALUATION *(continued)*

Objectives 25 through 30:   Participants will
—implement a plan designed to enhance the learning environment for middle-level students.
—design and implement a creative learning unit.
—plan classroom activities for the unit mentioned above.
—design a plan to fully utilize classroom space in a variety of ways.
—develop a learning center for use in their subject area classrooms.
—plan activities for students with special needs.

Objectives 31 and 32:   Participants will
—develop a list of criteria with which to evaluate their team/school effectiveness.
—identify a sequence of steps for use in planning a middle school and critique their own school.

Participants and consultants will assess the degree to which specific objectives have been addressed by the component activities.

Pretests and posttests designed by the instructor(s) will be administered to each participant. Mastery of the component will be demonstrated by a minimum score of 80 on the posttest.

A workshop evaluation form will be administered to all participants to assess their perceptions of the training received.

Coordinator: District staff development director/middle school supervisor

TEACHERS TRAINING TEACHERS (TTT) WORKSHOP IN TEAMING AND INTERDISCIPLINARY INSTRUCTION

Agenda

    I. What Is Teaming? Advantages and Disadvantages of Teaming

   II. How Teams Make Decisions
1. Autocracy
2. Voting
3. Consensus

  III. Team Building
1. Expectations of team members
2. Expectations of team leader
3. Expectations of principal, assistant, counselors
4. Working with special-area teachers
5. Goals for your team

  IV. Goals for Your Team Students
1. Achievement
2. Team spirit
3. Attendance

   V. Developing a Discipline Plan for Your Team

  VI. Evaluating Team Effectiveness

 VII. Working Tasks
1. Profile folders
2. Recordkeeping
3. Scheduling students
4. Who's who in our school
5. Team agenda—minutes
6. Day one, week one, month one tasks

VIII. Developing an Interdisciplinary Unit

  IX. Materials Needed
1. *Teaming in the Middle School* (Wiles-Bondi)
2. *Designing Interdisciplinary Units* (Wiles-Bondi)
3. Tear-off sheets, marking pens, masking tape

Working Tasks

1. Profile folders
2. Schedules for students; grouping, regrouping
3. Traffic patterns: lunch, changing classes
4. Place and schedule of team meeting: physical resources
5. Scheduling of administrators, counselors, media, and other support persons in school and outside school
6. Rules for use of staff support persons—secretary, custodians
7. Communication with special-area teachers—exceptionalities teachers
8. Plans for adviser/advisee
9. Recordkeeping—files
10. Team rules for students
11. Roles of team members

TEACHERS TRAINING TEACHERS (TTT) WORKSHOP IN TEAMING AND INTERDISCIPLINARY INSTRUCTION *(continued)*

12. Roles of team leader
13. Team agenda
14. Plans for reaching goals
15. Rules for communicating with parents
16. Orientation of students—communications to parents
17. Day one
    Week one
    Month one
18. Curriculum maps
19. Determination of ID topics
20. Plans for first ID unit
21. Evaluation
22. Inservice follow-up

SAMPLE TRAINING CERTIFICATE

NASSAU COUNTY PUBLIC SCHOOLS

MIDDLE SCHOOL TRAINING CERTIFICATE

awarded to

_____

FOR SUCCESSFULLY COMPLETING THE PRESCRIBED COURSE OF STUDY FOR

MIDDLE LEVEL EDUCATION

Given this _____ day of _____,19___

Craig Marsh	Eugene W. Grant	Dr. Joseph Bondi
Superintendent	Director of Middle Education	Middle School Consultant

Appendix 4

Middle School Design Parameters
(Excerpts), Dade County

DESIGN PARAMETERS FOR THE MIDDLE SCHOOL IN DADE COUNTY PUBLIC SCHOOLS

Prepared by the Middle School Design Committee

John Moore, Co-chairperson
Principal, Cutler Ridge Middle School

Murray Sissleman, Co-chairperson
President, United Teachers of Dade (UTD)

Thelma Davis, Principal
Madison Middle School

John Gilbert, Principal
Norland Middle School

Michael Jones, UTD

Al Maniaci, UTD

Dorothy Mazine, Teacher
Miami Springs Middle School

Kim Rubin, Teacher
Nautilus Middle School

Pat Tellis, Asst. Principal
Drew Middle School

Dan Tosado, Principal
Centennial Middle School

Developed under the direction of the Middle School Office—J. L. DeChurch, Executive Director. Consultant services provided by Jon Wiles and Joseph Bondi.

Foreword

The Middle School Design Report was developed through a collaborative effort between staff of the Dade County Public Schools and members of the United Teachers of Dade (UTD). This collaboration represents the continued effort of the district and union to work together for the betterment of education in Dade County's public schools.

The *Design Report* is to be considered a working blueprint that allows individual school communities maximum flexibility in developing programs and implementing the philosophies of the middle school.

The document is the result of the work of an ad hoc committee formed to provide a model for education to all middle schools in the district. The model recommends a shared philosophy and identifies programs and components, objectives, standards, and evaluative criteria for all middle schools.

The Dade County School Board has adopted a four-year plan to convert all its intermediate-level schools to fully functioning middle schools by 1991–92. This four-year conversion process utilizes a Curriculum Management Plan (CMP) as a guide. The CMP focuses on using needs assessment, developing a clear set of goals, tying school needs to program needs, involving teachers, administrators, union, parents, and community, and providing an analysis of progress to the general public.

It is the hope of Dade County Public Schools that this type of long-range planning and collaborative working arrangement will allow us to accomplish our goal of "National Excellence in Middle Grades Education."

Joseph A. Fernandez
Superintendent of Schools

DESIGN PARAMETERS FOR THE MIDDLE SCHOOL IN
DADE COUNTY PUBLIC SCHOOLS *(continued)*

Executive Summary

Design of the DCPS Middle School

The design parameters for middle school education in the Dade County Public School (DCPS) System are described in the accompanying document.

The document sets forth the essential parameters of an appropriate middle-grades education program in Dade County. Information is presented in three ways:

1. Critical Elements: narrative text explaining critical aspects of our middle school program
2. Design Checks: specific questions or criteria, which school-site practitioners may use to monitor progress during the transition
3. Perspectives: charts and diagrams showing the relationships between significant elements of the middle school program

The Critical Elements Summarized

The middle-grades education program has important functions different from the elementary and high school programs.

Middle school students (transescents) have special needs that identify them as a unique group in the K–12 learning continuum. Specific philosophical approaches, educational strategies, and school organizations are effective during this period. Twelve critical elements are needed in the DCPS middle school:

1. The philosophical core of the middle school education program is based on the following beliefs:
    □ Every child can learn.
    □ Middle school is a key experience whereby students learn that the various disciplines and subjects are all related to people's search for understanding (i.e., "big picture" or holistic knowledge structure).
    □ Learners must feel physically and psychologically safe for our educational goals to be achievable.
    □ Thinking skills instruction is a middle school responsibility.
    □ Respect for every child's individual differences must be maintained.

2. To accomplish its mission, the middle school curriculum has three interwoven and connected threads:
    □ The pursuit of academic excellence as a way to achieve social competence in a complex, technological society
    □ The pursuit of self-understanding and personal development
    □ The pursuit of continuous learning skills

3. The traditional academic core must be taught in a way that ensures the following:
    □ Students recognize the relationships between such disciplines as math, language arts, science, and social studies and can transfer learning from one discipline to another.
    □ Students recognize that their exploratory and developmental experiences are related to the academic core and are a way to broaden each individual's insights and potential for personal growth.

DESIGN PARAMETERS FOR THE MIDDLE SCHOOL IN DADE COUNTY PUBLIC SCHOOLS *(continued)*

4. The middle school curriculum contains a variety of exploratory experiences (into disciplines beyond the academic core), which will enable students to:
   □ Recognize, through exploratory experiences, that there are a multitude of routes to take to understanding and successful independence
   □ Sample fields they may wish to pursue in greater depth in high school or beyond
   □ Develop a realistic overview of talents, aptitudes, and interests
   □ Begin to develop talents and special interests in a manner that provides balance and perspective

5. Thinking skills expand in scope and nature during the middle grade years. Although problem-solving strategies need to be part of the K–12 learning continuum, formal instruction in critical and creative thinking skills is essential in the middle grades program.

6. Middle school students need someone to whom they can relate as an adviser and guide during transescence. Middle schools provide such advisers and ensure that advisers and advisees have time to work on the developmental issues of early adolescence.

7. Middle schools integrate academic knowledge and skills through use of interdisciplinary teaching teams. The structure of such teams may vary widely from school to school, but the essential elements are common planning time and teaching the same group of students.

8. Teachers of the academic core and of the exploratory/developmental programs work together to foster transfer of learning from one discipline to another, enhance application of basic skills, and help students develop a "big picture" on the scope and nature of people's efforts to understand themselves and the environment.

9. The exploratory program is provided in a variety of ways in addition to formal classes. These may include minicourses, clubs, special activities, and interest-group meetings built into the school day at regular intervals.

10. Inservice education and methods for teachers to share insights and information are an important part of the middle school conversion.

11. Instructional delivery strategies used at the middle grades allow for the developmental traits of the students. Cooperative learning strategies, accommodating different learning styles, recognition of attention span limitations, and understanding the transescent's preoccupation with personal development issues are all needed in the middle-grades program.

12. The middle school must develop a closer relationship with the parents and community and serve as a guide to each student's departure from childhood and embarkation on the route to adulthood and citizenship.

The middle school transition and the professionalization of teaching are complementary efforts to improve the educational programs we provide our young people. Within the parameters, which set the goals of middle-grades education, school sites should have as much flexibility as possible in structuring programs and experiences to meet the needs of students in their feeder pattern.

Appendix 5

Sample Proposal for Organizing a Middle School

Proposed Organization: Guidelines

Developing a Team Philosophy

Curriculum Mapping Guidelines

Sample Interdisciplinary (Thematic) Unit

Suggested Interdisciplinary Unit Format

Interdisciplinary Topics: Suggestions

Flexible Block Schedule: A Sample

Sample Letter to Parents

Teaming Processes: A Critique

Techniques for Effective Team Teaching

PROPOSED ORGANIZATION: GUIDELINES

All middle schools consist of students, teachers, time, space, and media/curriculum. This outline proposes general organizational standards for a middle school that address teacher grouping, student grouping, time, staffing, and facilities (space).

General Organizational Standards

Organization within the middle school is such that a smooth transition may be made from the self-contained classroom of the elementary school to the departmentalized high school. Provision is made to meet the unique social, academic, and personal needs of children as they emerge from childhood into adolescence. Flexibility in time utilization, and in the grouping of students and teachers, is provided to allow for balanced instruction.

1. Teacher Grouping
   - Teachers are organized into interdisciplinary teams to provide instruction in the core subjects of reading, language arts, science, mathematics, and social studies.
   - The interdisciplinary team serves a common group of students.
   - The interdisciplinary team controls a block of time.
   - Interdisciplinary team members are assigned classrooms that are in close proximity to one another.
   - Interdisciplinary team members have a common planning period.
   - A member of the interdisciplinary team shall be designated as team leader.

2. Student Grouping
   - Students are organized by grade levels.
   - Each grade level is divided into teams of approximately 90 to 135 students as is compatible with the interdisciplinary instructional team.
   - Provision is made for instruction at differing ability levels, at differing skill levels, and in different interest areas.

3. Time
   - Provision is made for a flexible daily time schedule.
   - A block of time equivalent to five 45-minute time segments (225 minutes) is assigned to the interdisciplinary team for academic instruction.
   - A 90-minute block of time is provided for exploration and physical education activities.

Sample Middle School Student Schedule

The day schedule contains seven 45-minute periods, one 25-minute A/A period, one 25-minute lunch period, and accumulative passing times (total of 25 minutes). The total student day is 6 hours 30 minutes (as blocked below):

25 min A/A	225 min Academic Block	25 min Lunch	45 min Enrich.	45 min P.E.	25 min Passing

Staffing Standards

An effective middle school is dependent on professional and nonprofessional staff who possess special understanding, skills, and a positive attitude in working with middle school students, parents, and community members. An effective middle school staff supports, understands the need for, and implements the middle school concept. These personnel see the middle school as neither elemen-

PROPOSED ORGANIZATION: GUIDELINES *(continued)*

tary nor secondary, but as an institution designed to meet the special needs of emerging adolescents. The schoolwide philosophy should be student-centered, not subject-centered. Each staff member's role is to help all students develop emotionally, socially, and academically. Recommended administrative staffing pattern (school of 1,200 students):

1. Administrative Staff
   - One principal
   - Two assistant principals

2. Support Staff
   - Three grade coordinators (10-month contract with provisions for contract extension)
   - Guidance counselors; recommended counselor/student ratio is 1 to 350
     (*Note:* Special consideration given for additional staffing for exceptional education centers housed at some schools.)
   - Media
   - Alternative education
   - Nurses
   - Aides
   - Psychologist
   - Social worker
   - Police liaison
   - Additions (school volunteers)

3. Teachers
   - Team teachers
   - Exploratory education teachers
   - Exceptional education teachers

Facilities Standards

The instructional program and the organizational pattern of the middle school dictate the facility requirements. Facilities should allow for varied instructional experiences, support the middle school concept, and meet the needs of personnel and support staff.

1. Essential Considerations
   - Increased attractiveness by use of color schemes and graphics
   - Adequate instructional space and equipment for each curricular program
   - Clustered interdisciplinary team instruction rooms
   - Team planning/work/conference area
   - Flexible classroom space
   - Computer instruction area
   - Alternative education area
   - Clinic area
   - Closable stalls in boys restroom and girls restroom
   - Adequate area for physical education and recreational activities
   - Private shower and changing facilities for boys and for girls
   - Exceptional education/student services

2. Desirable Considerations
   - Inhouse television capability
   - Adequate acoustical treatment (ceiling tile, floor covering, etc.)

DEVELOPING A TEAM PHILOSOPHY

Dear Principal:

During our team leader workshop, we developed a list of fifteen questions that will help define teaming in our pilot middle schools. We have asked that our participants meet with you to discuss these items. Thank you for your input into this planning process.

1. What is teaming at our school?

2. What is the composition of teams?

3. What is the role of team members?

4. What is the role of the team leader?

5. How will we make decisions?

6. How will we solve "big" problems?

7. What things should teams *not* do?

8. What are the most important tasks of our teams?

9. How will we form teams?

10. How often should teams be formed? Re-formed?

11. What steps lead to team success?

12. What is our time frame for team development?

13. How can we evaluate team progress?

14. What do we expect for this effort?

15. How will we motivate team members?

CURRICULUM MAPPING GUIDELINES

1. Introduce concept to coordinators.
2. Pull together vertical mapping—coordinators.
3. Introduce and validate the mapped curriculum—coordinators and lead teachers.
4. Look for logical connectors (horizontal). Identify by six weeks. (Lead discipline each six weeks.)
5. Select a six-week link and develop interdisciplinary unit.
6. Introduce concept of mapping to interdisciplinary teams in all schools—coordinators and lead teachers.
7. Each team selects a six-week link and develops an interdisciplinary unit.
8. Build bank of interdisciplinary units.
9. Network units/instructional strategies (printed media, electronic media).
10. Establish review group to monitor, update, and revise existing mapped curriculum.
11. Train administrators at school level in monitoring mapped curriculum.
12. Include all other disciplines in interdisciplinary approach.
13. Evaluate total process.

SAMPLE INTERDISCIPLINARY (THEMATIC) UNIT

Grade: Six
Grading Period: First nine weeks
Title of Interdisciplinary Unit: Contributions of ancient civilizations
Content: To acquaint students with the contributions of ancient civilizations on modern culture.

Math	**Language Arts**	**Science**	**Social Studies**	**Health**
Numeration	Reading	Plants	Rise of Civiliza-	Interpersonal Re-
Integers	Writing	Animals	tion	lationships
Measurement	Thinking		Ancient Civiliza-	Personal Health
Decimals/metric	Speaking		tions	Practices
Geometry	Listening			Substance Abuse
Graphing				Prevention
				Human Growth
				and Development
				Disease/AIDS
				Education
				Safety/First
				Aid/CPR

Generalization/Concepts

Math	Language Arts	Science	Social Studies	Health
Renumeration is the foundation of any mathematical system.	Sharing common human experiences assists in defining one's own humanity and in developing a positive self-concept.	The environment depends on plants to maintain the balance of life.	People alter their environment to meet their needs.	Relationships within the family and among peers affect potential well-being.
Positive and negative numbers can be used to describe the world.	Literature is a reflection of its historical era.	The study of plants includes the structures, the reproductive systems, and the process of photosynthesis.	People whose basic needs are met begin to develop a more complex culture.	Knowledge of personal health practices is basic for potential development.
Measurement involves primary and intermediate students in measuring metric units of time, money, capacity, weight, and temperature. In addition, intermediate students are involved in working with perimeters, areas, volumes, and measuring angles.	Personal values are enhanced through exploring the values of others.	All animals are classified as vertebrate or invertebrate.	Development of shared language, religion, and government unifies a culture.	
	Functional literature provides the skills necessary and/or relevant to business and personal management.	Knowledge of the structure and function of human systems increases the awareness of health problems associated with these body systems.		

SUGGESTED INTERDISCIPLINARY UNIT FORMAT

A. Theme/Cover Sheet
   □ Title
   □ Names of unit developers
   □ School

B. Introduction Sheet
   □ Information for the teacher
   □ Background information for the student
   □ Acknowledgments

C. Goal Statement/Broad Objectives

D. Specific Objectives for Each Subject Area

E. Activities and Materials
   □ Glossary
   □ Classroom activities
   □ Student record sheet
   □ Homework and enrichment materials
   □ Resources
   □ Evaluation procedures
   □ TAP (advisory program) activities
   □ Culminating events/activities
   □ Bibliography

F. Calendar/Schedule

G. Modifications/suggestions sheet/student evaluation/teacher evaluation
   □ Involvement of other subject areas:

INTERDISCIPLINARY TOPICS: SUGGESTIONS

Imagination and Discovery

Bicentennial

Sports and You

Careers in Transportation

The Concrete Jungle

People Accept the Challenge of City Living

The Law and You

International Trade

Rural Life

Communications

Temporary Living: Camps and Camping

Greece

You Are What You Eat

Let's Get Personal

Foreseeing the Unforeseeable

Be It Ever So Humble

Cities: What You Always Wanted to Know

Shock: A Serious and Dangerous Condition

Elections

MAN: Minorities Are the Nation

Of Mice and Men: An Interdisciplinary Unit

Sports and Your Identity

Changing Sex Roles in the Twentieth Century

The Wheel in Human Social Development

Animal and Human Interdependence and the
Necessity for Cooperation

Feeding the Population

Evolution: Process of Change

America: The First Two Hundred Years

How Environmental Factors Affect Shelter

The Civil War and Reconstruction

Anchors Aweigh to a New World

The World Series

Sports in America

The Pollution Problem

People as Consumers

Then and Now

The Westward Movement

Westward Expansion

Take Me Out to the Ballgame

FLEXIBLE BLOCK SCHEDULE: A SAMPLE

Adviser/Advisee, Study Skills, and Silent, Sustained Reading Block

Academic Block

- □ Language arts
- □ Social studies
- □ Math
- □ Science

———— Lunch ————

Activity and Special-interest Block

Physical Education Block

Exploratory Block

SAMPLE LETTER TO PARENTS

Dear Parents:

We welcome you and your child to Team II. Teaming is an instructional program in which four teachers share their resources and expertise. It provides better instruction and classroom experiences. Teaming also gives students and teachers the feeling of belonging to a small group that has common goals and whose members are supportive of each other. It provides the opportunity for you as parents to join with students and teachers in sharing ideas, plans, information, and activities.

Successful team teaching is based on common and consistent rules for behavior. Our team rules for this school year are as follows:

1. Respectfully enter and leave the classroom.
2. Be on time to class—be seated.
3. Be prepared for work.
4. Listen carefully, answer respectfully.
5. Allow others a turn to speak—be patient.
6. Be considerate of others—no interruptions.
7. Stay seated in your own space.
8. Complete your work.

Your team teachers will be Ms. Brown, Mr. Green, Ms. Smith, Mr. Jones.

We all look forward to having you work with us in making this a productive year.

_____

Please indicate you have read, and discussed with your child, our common team goals by signing below and returning this section tomorrow.

Date _____   Parent's Signature _____

                                  Student's Signature _____

TEAMING PROCESSES: A CRITIQUE

	Always	Sometimes	Never
Agenda used			
Remained on task			
Good listeners			
Ideas and decisions clarified			
Decisions summarized			
Meeting critiqued			
Opportunity for everyone to speak			
Evidence of domination			
Ideas accepted			
Mutual respect			
Trust			
Decisions reached by consensus			
Freedom to express ideas			

Topics Discussed

_____ Content planning   _____ Student concerns

_____ Content evaluation   _____ TLC Minutes

_____ Teaching strategies   _____ Organizational concerns

_____ Grouping or placement of students   _____ Parent involvement

Other:_____

_____

_____

TECHNIQUES FOR EFFECTIVE TEAM MEETINGS

1. Plan meetings cooperatively.
2. Acknowledge the schedules of others.
3. Provide ample lead time.
4. Keep a portion of the agenda open.
5. Stay on task.
6. Keep presentations/discussions short and to the point.
7. Make space ready and presentable for the meeting.
8. Eliminate distractions.
9. Schedule time to socialize if possible.
10. Feed the troops.
11. Value humor.
12. Learn to read silence.
13. Manage hostility.
14. Respect differences.
15. Protect confidentiality.
16. Stretch for closure.
17. Invite participant feedback.
18. Retire useless practices.

Appendix 6

Middle School Instructional Checklist

MIDDLE SCHOOL INSTRUCTIONAL CHECKLIST

Directions: This instrument is to be used during a ten- to fifteen-minute classroom observation. The observer is to place a check in the space beside those items that *are observed or present.* Items not observed or present are to be left blank.

School _____   Subject Area _____

Teaching Is Personal

_____ 1. Student work is displayed prominently in the classroom.
_____ 2. Teacher/student-made bulletin boards rather than purchased displays are in use; ideally, bulletin boards are activity-oriented.
_____ 3. There is a seating pattern other than straight rows.
_____ 4. Living objects (plants, animals) are found in classroom.
_____ 5. Teacher moves about room freely while instructing.
_____ 6. Teacher calls students by first name without difficulty.
_____ 7. Constructive student-to-student communication is allowed during class.
_____ 8. Teacher uses specific praise and encourages comments frequently.

Teaching Is Individualized

_____ 9. Multilevel texts or materials are in use for instruction.
_____ 10. Some students are doing independent research or study in classroom.
_____ 11. Learning centers are present in the room.
_____ 12. Students are working on assignments together in small groups.
_____ 13. Supplemental learning materials are available in the classroom for student use.
_____ 14. Student work folders are used by teacher for work management.
_____ 15. Skill continuum cards are kept on individual students.
_____ 16. Instructional activity allows for creative or multiple outcomes over which the student has some choice.

Teaching Skills Are Utilized

_____ 17. One-to-one conferences with student in the classroom.
_____ 18. Diversifies instructional approach or method during observation.
_____ 19. Utilizes small groups to increase learning.
_____ 20. Groups and re-groups students for instructional purposes.
_____ 21. Teaches at varying level of difficulty around an idea or concept.
_____ 22. Stylized learning materials for the group.
_____ 23. Uses real-life illustrations or examples during instruction.
_____ 24. References student interests or needs during instruction.
_____ 25. Maintains student discipline through nonpunitive behavior.
_____ 26. Uses student-teacher contracts for learning.
_____ 27. Works with other teachers across subject-matter lines.
_____ 28. Teaches general study skills while instructing.
_____ 29. Uses teacher-made interdisciplinary units during instruction.
_____ 30. Uses questioning techniques that encourage participation.

Appendix 7

Instructional Activities and Materials

Broad-Unit Topic: A Mathematics Continuum

Research, Enrichment, and Development (RED) Program

Sample Recognition Certificates

Disciplinary Notice to Parents

Student Recognition Referral

Community Involvement Techniques

BROAD-UNIT TOPIC: A MATHEMATICS CONTINUUM

I. Origin of Various Numeration Systems (Words, Symbols, and Their Meanings)

II. Whole Numbers
   A. Recognition of Whole Numbers (Each student should be able to read or write any number to 1 billion)
   B. Prime, Composite, and Relatively Prime Numbers
   C. Computation and Related Problems of Application in Equalities and Inequalities
      1. Addition
      2. Subtraction
      3. Multiplication
      4. Division

III. Fractions
   A. Basic Understanding of the Fraction Concept
   B. Computation and Related Problems of Application in Equalities and Inequalities
      1. Addition
      2. Subtraction
      3. Multiplication
      4. Division
      5. Ratio and proportion

IV. Decimal Fractions
   A. Basic Understanding of the Decimal Fraction Concept
   B. Computation and Related Problems of Application in Equalities and Inequalities
      1. Addition
      2. Subtraction
      3. Multiplication
      4. Division

V. Percent, Interest, etc.
   A. Meaning of Percent (%)
   B. Computation
   C. Application

VI. Statistical Graphs—Bar, Circle, Picture, Broken Line, and Smooth Line
   A. Reading and Interpreting Graphs
   B. Construction of Graphs from Given Data

VII. Metric System
   A. Length—Meter
   B. Capacity—Liter
   C. Weight—Gram

VIII. Geometry
   A. Nonmetric Geometry
      1. Basic terminology (ray, curve, polygon, parallel lines, etc.)
      2. Elementary constructions

BROAD-UNIT TOPIC: A MATHEMATICS
CONTINUUM *(continued)*

B. Metric Geometry
   1. Perimeter
   2. Area
   3. Volume

IX. Directed Numbers
   A. Basic Understanding of Directed Number System
   B. Computation and Related Problems of Application in Equalities and Inequalities
      1. Addition
      2. Subtraction
      3. Multiplication
      4. Division

X. Eighth-Grade Algebra
   A. Four Basic Operations of Whole Numbers and Rational Numbers
   B. Solution Sets for Equations and Inequalities (All Types)
   C. Word Problems—Reading, Interpretation, and Translation of Data to Variable Expressions
   D. Polynomials—Basic Operations of Monomials and Polynomials, Powers
   E. Factoring
   F. Quadratic Equations
   G. Algebraic Fractions—Simple and Complex
   H. Graphs and Analytic Geometry
   I. Systems of Linear Equations
   J. The Real Number System
      1. Meaning of square roots
      2. Computation and simplification of square roots
      3. Equations with irrational solutions

RESEARCH, ENRICHMENT, AND DEVELOPMENT
(RED) PROGRAM

Management of time and class schedules in a middle school provides the time which can be used in a program of interest activities, developmental or remedial activities, and research activities. Such a program is often called ER & R, or Special Interest, or Enrichment Class. Since our school colors are red and white, and since Research-Enrichment-Development produced the acronym RED, our program became known as the RED classes.

By shortening each of seven periods by a few minutes, we developed an "R Day" schedule for use on the days that these classes met.

Surveys of students and faculty members produced the list of activities attached. The A-B-C lists apportion participation among the activities and ensures a variety of experiences for the students.

Registration for RED classes was effected through the three academic centers by reserving one-third of the membership of each class for each center. Every care was taken that all students took part in RED classes, and their satisfactory participation was recognized with a certificate.

RED Period Courses

Below are described the various special-interest courses being offered in the RED period. Read them over carefully, discuss them with your council teacher and with your parents, and make a list of the numbers of the ten courses you are most interested in. Bring your list of numbers and this description sheet back to Council Group.

Activity Number

1. *Applied Mathematics:* A study of the applications of mathematics to social studies, science, athletics, art, home economics, and mechanics. Activities in mapping, use of the slide rule, and independent study and research.
2. *Baby Sitting:* Those who successfully complete this course will receive a Red Cross certificate identifying them as a certified baby sitter.
3. *Basketball—Basic Fundamentals:* Learn and improve your basic skills in basketball through skill drills and game playing.
4. *Beginning Backgammon:* Learn an exciting new game. Develop strategy and compete with other students.
5. *Beginning Typing:* This course is designed to present an introduction to the keyboard and development of correct typing techniques. These skills might be a good way to improve your papers and grades. Students in 8th grade Business Careers *should not* sign up.
6. *Cheerleading:* This course is designed for all cheerleaders. They work on improving their cheers and help others learn cheers. (Cheerleaders will work with 40 additional students every 6 weeks.)
7. *Cheerleading Clinic:* Open to all students who would like to learn cheers and to improve their cheerleading ability.
8. *Chess—Advanced:* This course is for students who already know the moves and rules of the game. Emphasis will be on strategy and improving skills.
9. *Chess—Beginning:* Learn the basic moves and explore the fascinating game of chess.
10. *Creative Stitchery:* An exploration of various kinds of sewing with emphasis on handwork. Crewel, embroidery, needlepoint, and patchwork will also be included.

RESEARCH, ENRICHMENT, AND DEVELOPMENT
(RED) PROGRAM *(continued)*

11. *Creative Communication—Art and Speech:* Participants will do speech and/or art activities such as children's storytelling, puppet theatre, and choral reading. Culmination of activities should be visits to other schools and local organizations to present programs.

12. *Creative Writing:* Do you want to write creatively and with purpose? In this course you will create short stories, personal journals, poetry, and biographies. Some may even compose a novel. Depending on this group's work, we may publish a literary magazine containing your best work.

13. *Current American Issues:* To research current American issues for presentation to the rest of the group. Students will be divided into approximately four committees for work on various current problems. Examples of topics are overpopulation, pollution, and the state of the economy. Each group will give a presentation to the class.

14. *Debate:* Students learn to organize their ideas and arguments in a formal manner with the correct debate procedure. Important issues of the day such as politics, environment, and sports will be used in this activity.

15. *Developmental Math:* Acquire a better understanding of the world of math, increase basic skills, and improve your grades. Teacher recommendations required.

16. *Developmental Spanish:* Improve your skills in this subject and improve your understanding of Spain and the Spanish language. Teacher recommendation required.

17. *Dissection—Internal Affairs:* Learn techniques of dissecting by starting with the lower forms such as mollusks and insects. Then progress to more advanced life such as fish and frogs.

18. *Emergency Treatments:* Students learn how to care for someone who has had a heart attack or other emergency. This course could save your life.

19. *Environment—Get Involved:* This course deals with environmental concerns. The activities will be set up to prepare the student to become involved in the functions of his city.

20. *Everything You've Always Wanted to Know About and Not Had Time to Investigate:* This course will offer the opportunity to work on a subject of interest to you from comic strips to archeology. Goals will be determined by contract between students and teacher.

21. *Experiments Can Be Fun:* Interested in science? Want to do some fun experiments? Here's something that offers a little instruction and a lot of doing. Make things like an electric quiz board, a fire extinguisher, a 002 boat, and more.

22. *Foreign Language Newspaper:* Improve that language! Help design and publish a foreign language newspaper. Make cartoons, puzzles, and illustrations.

SAMPLE RECOGNITION CERTIFICATES

NORCO TEAM PRIDE

HAPPY BIRTHDAY

BONANZA

TO BE USED FOR EXEMPTION FROM ONE DAY'S
CLASSWORK OR HOMEWORK ON THE DAY OF
BEARER'S BIRTHDAY OR A SUBSTITUTE DAY.
MANY HAPPY RETURNS.

BIRTHDAY _____   SIGNATURE _____

NORCO TEAM PRIDE

HOORAY

NO HOMEWORK

THE BEARER OF THIS CERTIFICATE IS HEREBY ENTITLED TO USE IT IN
EXCHANGE FOR ONE DAY'S HOMEWORK WITHOUT FEAR OF
CHASTISEMENT, DEFAMATION OF CHARACTER, OR BODILY HARM.

TEACHER SIGNATURE _____

DATE USED _____   SIGNATURE _____

DISCIPLINARY NOTICE TO PARENTS

_____ has engaged in the following unacceptable behavior:

I have taken the following steps to correct this behavior:

_____ A thorough discussion of the team discipline plan with the entire class

_____ A verbal warning

_____ A conference with the individual student

_____ Time out

_____ Parent contact (phone conference or letter to the parent)

_____ Detention

_____ Parent conference with the team, perhaps including a dean or administrator

In spite of all my efforts, the student continues to exhibit unacceptable behavior. Therefore, I have requested administrative intervention in the matter.

Sincerely,

Date _____   _____
                                                            (Signature)

STUDENT RECOGNITION REFERRAL

Date _____ Time _____

Student's Name: _____ Grade _____ Period _____

Referred by: _____

1. Reason for Referral (check as appropriate):

_____ Respect for others
_____ Classroom participation and completion
        of assignments
_____ Possession of classroom materials
_____ Any act which promotes the orderly con-
        duct of a class, a bus, the school, or
        school function.

_____ Always on time to school/class
_____ Exhibits good manners

_____ Shows concern for other students/others
_____ Other

2. Each reason checked is to be supported by factual comments. (Use reverse side if needed.)

3. Action by Teacher/Faculty Member

    _____ Acknowledged with student

    _____ Phone call to parents

    _____ Written communication to parents

    _____ Acknowledgment submitted for school bulletin

    _____ Other

4. Action by Administrator

    _____ Acknowledged in conference with student

    _____ Phone call to parents

    _____ Written communication to student

    _____ Formal letter of recognition to parents

    _____ Other

_____
                    Signature

COMMUNITY INVOLVEMENT TECHNIQUES

1. *School Board Meetings:* School board meetings should be a central place for the members of the community, educators, and board members to exchange ideas about their schools. Meetings must be scheduled for the convenience of all members.
2. *Citizen Advisory Councils:* Advisory councils provide excellent opportunities for members of the community to meet with school officials and educators and discuss new issues and situations. Advisory councils can also be developed for special-interest areas such as sports, music programs, current issues, transportation, and many more.
3. *Volunteers and Aides:* The community has many people who would like to assist the schools. Often they are retired and have a wealth of knowledge and available time. Volunteers have an opportunity to see what is taking place in the schools while students have an opportunity to work with the not so young.
4. *Adult and Continuing Education Programs:* Less than one-third of the U.S. adult population have children in school today. These people are also taxpayers and want to see a return on their money. Evening and adult classes can be offered for academics as well as for recreational reasons.
5. *Community Coordinator:* Many school districts are now employing a professional advertising/promotion coordinator. Frequently, this responsibility is placed with the superintendent or another high-level administrator, who often is too busy or inadequately skilled at promoting programs.
6. *Schools as Community Centers:* This is not a new concept, and many more schools now work hand-in-hand with the local government to utilize the schools to the fullest. Both parties share expenses and facilities, and both realize greater financial savings while improving the community's contact with the school and its activities.
7. *Adopt-a-School Programs:* Although there is some disagreement concerning the name, the idea remains the same. Specific schools will be supported by partner businesses.
8. *Administrators and Principals:* Administrators may be in the best position to obtain community support for a district or a school. Administrators should become involved in community activities, organizations, and clubs. If an administrator strongly believes in good community-school relations, these bonds usually exist. The opposite holds true as well.
9. *Teachers:* Although the most important individual in the educational system, the teacher is usually overlooked as a resource speaker to represent the school to the community. Teachers and their discussions concerning their schools do have great impact on how a community perceives the school.
10. *Open House and Parent Visitations:* Most educators will agree that a school enjoying a great deal of parental involvement usually provides a better climate for learning. These schools are also perceived to be doing better, as well.
11. *Newsletters and Releases:* Schools and individual teachers should prepare newsletters for parents and the community. They should be distributed in grocery stores, doctors' offices, and other high-visibility locations.

Appendix 8

Planning Considerations

Curriculum Management Plan (CMP) Model: Highlights

Comprehensive Plan for Middle School Development (Excerpts)

School-Based Standards (Sample)

CURRICULUM MANAGEMENT PLAN (CMP)
MODEL: HIGHLIGHTS

1. Needs Assessment
   - Of the school and the community

2. Philosophy and Goals
   - Determined by students, administrators, teachers, parents, community, board
   - Based on needs of students and community

3. Curriculum
   - Based on needs and philosophy
   - Includes defined sequence of content, concepts, skills
   - Provides for all levels of learners
   - Includes skills continuums, checklists for progress
   - Provides balance between personal development and skill and content acquisition
   - Provides for uniform, articulated curriculum for K–12

4. Instructional Program
   - Management system to assure implementation
   - Grading and reporting system follows curriculum
   - Articulated guidance program smooths transition
   - Materials are current and appropriate

5. Organization
   - Self-contained classes, teaming, departmentalization used when appropriate
   - Flexible rather than static grouping of students
   - Maximum time-on-task for teachers and students

6. Staff
   - Only qualified teachers employed
   - Responsibilities for all are clearly identified
   - Systematic inservicing for teachers and administrators
   - Systematic evaluation of teachers and administrators

7. Facilities
   - Flexible spaces to meet a variety of instructional programs and organizational structures
   - Lab and computer areas provided for high-tech training

8. Evaluation and Reporting
   - Checkpoints for monitoring student progress (K–12)
   - Norm-based and criterion-based testing for progress
   - Reporting system that shows clearly extent of student progress in each grading period
   - Grading system that matches curriculum

9. Budget
   - Resources allocated based on alignment with plan

COMPREHENSIVE PLAN FOR MIDDLE SCHOOL DEVELOPMENT (EXCERPTS)

Duval County Public Schools, 1990–1995

CMP Committees

The organization of the middle school conversion will feature four primary committees under the direction of a general oversight committee known as the Coordinating Committee. Other ad hoc committees will be employed as needed to design programs and coordinate changes.

The *Coordinating Committee,* a select committee of about 30 members (key citizens and school personnel), will oversee the entire four-year conversion process. The role of the Coordinating Committee will be to ensure that smooth progress is maintained in moving from a junior high structure to the middle school structure. Tools used by the Coordinating Committee include a Management Plan (based on needs assessment data), four primary committees, and a series of ad hoc committees. The primary committees will include: The Design Committee, the Program Development Committee, the Staff Development Committee, and an Evaluation Committee.

The *Design Committee,* consisting of about 10 members, will establish general standards or specifications for all 50 middle schools in the district. These standards will be arrived through a study of needs assessment data and input from both the professional literature and the public.

The *Program Development Committee,* a committee of about 20 members, will translate the standards of the Design Committee into quality indicators for all aspects of middle school programming. Specific ad hoc committees will be formed to define subject areas and special programs such as mathematics, computer literacy, or physical education.

The *Staff Development Committee,* consisting of about 10 members, will recommend and plan inservice for teachers, administrators, and parents connected with the 50 middle schools. Inservice planning will be based on needs assessment data, the program design, and local school plans for conversion.

The *Evaluation Committee,* consisting of five members and assigned staff members from the Program Evaluation Section, will monitor the progress of the conversion process throughout the four-year period. Periodic reports from the Evaluation Committee to the Coordinating Committee will assess the accomplishment of tasks.

The governance structure calls for the four primary committees to report findings and recommendations to the Coordinating Committee. The Coordinating Committee in turn will make recommendations for conversion through periodic reports to the Board. The Board will then set policy to be implemented by the Superintendent and the staff.

The role of the Management Team in the conversion process will be unique. The Management Team will serve as a liaison between the Coordinating Committee and the Board for purposes of planning, policy formation, research allocation, and policy implementation. The Deputy Superintendent will coordinate this mediating role between the professional staff and the various committees of the conversion process. The Consultants will provide general advice and input through the Management Team and will serve as a resource to the committees and the Board.

COMPREHENSIVE PLAN FOR MIDDLE SCHOOL
DEVELOPMENT (EXCERPTS) *(continued)*

CMP Tasks Timetable (Sample)

Program	Activity	Time Frame	Person(s) Responsible	Costs
Middle School Program Design 8.0	Training of team leaders for 1990–1991	July 30–July 31, 1990	Wiles–Bondi	Stipends for team leaders (2 days × 6 hrs. × number of participants) Materials— $2,000 (provided by Wiles–Bondi as part of contract)
Middle School Program Design 12.0	Study/development of K–5 pilot technology program— selected sites	1990–1991	Charles Cline Michael Walker Betty White Wiles–Bondi Selected participants from district/ community	None
Middle School Program Design 3.0	Five-year plan (1990–1995) for renovation, construction of schools to house grades K–5, 6–8, 9–12 by 1995—to board	Summer, 1990–1991	Board Dr. Zenke Charles Cline Management team	To be determined by board, superintendent, management team

SCHOOL-BASED STANDARDS (SAMPLE)

Standards	Date Achieved	Person(s) Responsible

XIII. Flexible block scheduling—The goal of scheduling is to provide teachers with a flexible instructional block of time to satisfy students' academic needs.

    A. Provision is made for a flexible daily time schedule.

    B. A block of time is assigned to the interdisciplinary team for academic instruction.

    C. A block of time is provided for exploration and physical education.

    D. An established time is set aside each day for adviser/advisee (between 25 and 30 minutes per day).

    E. Provision is made for varying the daily schedule to allow for club and intramural activities to occur during the regular school day for all students.

    F. Provision is made for interdisciplinary team planning each day.

              * * *

    G. The interdisciplinary team is responsible for the coordination of curriculum and for the delivery of instruction to the students on its team.

    H. Members of the team plan cooperatively.

    I. Common pools of information about students are shared among team members.

    J. Teams meet with parents to discuss individual student's academic and developmental progress.

    K. Team members participate in a team meeting at least once a week.

SCHOOL-BASED STANDARDS (SAMPLE) *(continued)*

Standards	Date Achieved	Person(s) Responsible
L. Team members provide support for each other.		
M. Activities are planned to foster a sense of team identity and pride among teachers and students.		
N. The school's adviser/advisee program is implemented.		
O. Interdisciplinary units of instruction are developed and implemented.		
P. Action plans are developed for individual students who are experiencing difficulties academically or socially.		
Q. The team operates on a consensus basis, so that when a decision must be made and agreement has not been reached, the team leader will make the decision based on available input.		

Appendix 9

Implementation Communications

Booklet for Parents (Sample "Layered" Format)

Health Education Program, Lesson Topics

Team Newsletter

School Newsletter

Advisement Themes: Monthly Schedule

BOOKLET FOR PARENTS (SAMPLE "LAYERED" FORMAT)

The Middle School Student . . .	The XYZ Middle School . . .
☐ Is enthusiastic	☐ Has a team of specialists ready to challenge your child, to capitalize on and support his or her enthusiasm
☐ Must be motivated to learn	☐ Encourages students to progress at their own rate, motivated by repeated success in an individualized program—*nothing succeeds like success!*
☐ Has short-term objectives and attention span	☐ Provides flexible scheduling, arranged around students' ability to maintain interest and complete tasks
☐ Differs widely in physical attributes and maturity. He or she is growing rapidly and is subject to overexertion.	☐ Offers a wide range of activities designed for the developmental variations that mark this age group. Some activities will be instituted at student request.
☐ Is activity-minded	☐ Provides carefully planned physical education classes tailored for this age group. Intramural sports give an outlet for competitive feelings *without* serious injury to rapidly growing bodies.
☐ Desires freedom, but fears loss of security	☐ Allows students autonomy to create their own schedules and select areas of interest with counselor and teacher support and encouragement.
☐ Needs communication with peers and adults outside the home	☐ Affords opportunities for students to meet peers in small groups to foster social interaction with peers and adults

HEALTH EDUCATION PROGRAM, LESSON TOPICS

6th Grade
Knowing about Health
Making Decisions
Self-Examination
Plan for Good Mental
   Health
Belonging to a Family
The Importance of Rela-
   tionships
Abuse Prevention
*Endocrine System
*Puberty, Male and Fe-
   male
*Fetal Growth and Devel-
   opment
*Immune System
*AIDS
Facts about Drugs
Types of Drugs
Drugs in Your Life Now
   and in the Future
Alcohol and Health
Alcohol and Behavior
Tobacco and Health
Smoking and Behavior
The Chew Story
Weight and Energy
Eating Disorders
Physical Hygiene
Dental Care
Health Products
Health Services
Chronic Diseases
Nervous System Disorders
Common First Aid Proce-
   dure
Safety around You
Safety from Disaster

7th Grade
Adolescence and Values
Life Management Skills
Self-Concept
Emotional and Social
   Changes during Adoles-
   cence
Responsibilities and
   Earned Privileges
Families and Characteris-
   tics
Dating, Purposes and Re-
   sponsibilities
Dating Risks
Abuse Prevention
*Endocrine System
*Puberty, Male and Fe-
   male
*Fetal Growth and Devel-
   opment
*STDs, Communicable
   Diseases
*AIDS
Drugs Affect People Differ-
   ently
Controlled Drugs
Drugs That Promote Good
   Health
Preventing Drug Misuse
   and Abuse
Illegal Drug Prevention
The Effects of Alcohol
Dynamics of a Chemically
   Dependent Family
Smokeless Tobacco
Diet Alert
Consumer Decisions
Teeth and Disease
Cancer
Cardiovascular Disease
Health Care Providers
Careers in Health

8th Grade
Introduction to Health, Val-
   ues, and Decision Mak-
   ing
*Adolescence: Physical,
   Mental, and Social
   Changes
Self-Concept
Communication/Media
Parent Relationships and
   Characteristics
Dating Purposes
Dating Responsibilities
Causes and Conse-
   quences of Inappropri-
   ate Sexual Activities
Teen Pregnancy Statistics
Abstinence and Return to
   Abstinence
Abuse Prevention
*Body Talk, Male and Fe-
   male
*Fetal Growth and Devel-
   opment
*STDs
*AIDS
Illegal Drugs
The Innocent Victims
Facts about Alcohol
Alcoholism: A Chronic Dis-
   ease
Treatment and Prevention
Understanding Chemical
   Dependency
Tobacco and Your Health
Issues Related to Smok-
   ing
Weight Watching
Diet Choices
Good Dental Health
Effects of Physical Fitness
Consumer Protection
Choices about Time and
   Money
Health Careers

*Will be taught by a trained nurse in separate classes for boys and girls.

TEAM NEWSLETTER

Dear Team F parents,

Team F is a four-subject interdisciplinary team involving Language Arts, Social Studies, Math, and Science. In order to keep you informed as to what your child is doing in these areas, we will begin sending a newsletter home with your child at the end of each report period.

Following is a description of what has taken place these past six weeks.

1. *Social Studies* this past grading period was assigned the concept of exploration and discovery. We grouped the students in sections so that poor readers and those with above-average reading ability could move at their own speed.

    Using skill kits designed to help both groups, the average students were given task sheets to work from, designed as to teach inquiry and concepts. We tried to have task sheets made up so that the student would use outside resources and the media center.

2. *Science* classes have been involved in a study of physiology. We have studied various body processes and also briefly reviewed various systems of the human body.

    Some students have been reading from a selected text, which covers various scientific topics from geology to biology. There are selected groups who are working in packets made from the Steck-Vaughn series, which includes various biological topics. Students have been allowed to proceed in their work on an individualized basis within a time framework. Extra-credit reports were submitted by those who desired to upgrade their work. Students are allowed to complete or submit extra-credit work on any scientific topic throughout the six-week period.

    Various students were assigned book reports on science-related books.

    The entire team was moved from a class-type situation to the lab. We will begin the new semester with various laboratory experiences.

3. In *Mathematics* students have been grouped according to their ability. The different topics being studied at this time include whole numbers, fractions, integers, rational numbers, and algebra. The groups are exposed to a variety of teaching techniques including skills kits, cassette tapes, worksheets, workbooks, textbooks, and lectures.

4. In *Language Arts* the students have been working on two skills kits and a six-week literature and creative writing unit. The skills kits covered usage, vocabulary, punctuation, and spelling. Each student worked at his own rate.

    The literature unit centered around a book called *Imagination, the World of Inner Space.* At the beginning of the unit students contracted for their grade, different amounts of work being required for each grade. The book contained short stories, poems, and plays. After reading the material students did creative writing assignments from a logbook. Students were also assigned a group project for completion of the contract. At the end of the six weeks the *Imagination* notebook and group project were handed in. I enjoyed reading them! Many students did good work.

SCHOOL NEWSLETTER

One of the highlights of the _____ Middle School program is the Humanities exposure. The students are encouraged to have encounters in art, music, and foreign language. Such experiences could be playing a musical instrument, singing songs, dancing, designing a leather disc, making a clay object, and learning to speak either Spanish or French. The general goal of the humanities program is to provide myriad opportunities for the student to gainfully use his or her leisure time. This knowledge could become invaluable later on when these people become involved in the world of work.

ATTENTION PARENTS—You must see to believe. Our agriculture program headed by Mr. _____ has developed faster than expected. His students are growing about anything you can name and have a hothouse second to none in the county. There are now 72 boys and girls learning to plant and grow things and appreciate the effort put forth by the farmers of America in growing what we eat. These kids are doing an outstanding job and enjoying what they are doing.

The academics are also being introduced to the vocational world. Many fine people from the local business and industrial community have come to the school to lecture and to show through slides how their particular business operates. We have recently had Mr. _____ from the _____ _Times_ who had a slide presentation on "How to Make a Newspaper." This was a field trip which was brought to the school to give the students an insight into something most people take for granted, that is, our daily paper. Ms. _____ , a writer for the _Times,_ also talked to many students about writing and the importance of getting as much as possible out of English.

Midshipman _____ also visited us. He is a second classman at the U.S. Naval Academy at Annapolis, Maryland. He is a math major, aspiring to be either a jet pilot or be stationed aboard nuclear subs. He told many of our students the importance of attaining as much proficiency in this area as possible and to be continually thinking about making a career choice. He emphasized that our students should explore a few career choices now and then make a final choice of one or two.

Including the people now attending, we have 18 boys and girls involved at the Work Evaluation Center in _____ . Here they are observed by several evaluators who assist them and test them in performance tasks. An example is taking a telephone apart and putting it back together by following directions. They are graded on time and quality of work. All tasks require a certain amount of reading and math to be able to perform. This nine-day series of work-related tests tells the students in which area they are proficient and a lot of times motivates them to stay in school and study harder. Several of our _____ students have also been given either the Ohio Vocational Interest Survey test or the Kudex Interest test. These tests are given on a voluntary basis and many times are a motivating factor in that they show the student where his or her interests lie.

_We would at this time like to extend an open invitation to all parents to visit us at _____ Middle School and observe our students in action._

ADVISEMENT THEMES: MONTHLY SCHEDULE

Corona-Norco Unified School District

Grade Seven

1. Orientation/Rationale/Rules	
Group Building/Get Acquainted/Goal	September
2. Study Skills/Time Management	October
3. Self-Esteem	November
4. Stress Management/Conflict Resolution	December
5. Interpersonal Relations (Peers/Adults/Family)	January
6. Accepting Responsibility/Decision Making	February
7. Communications (Peers/Adults/Family)	March
8. Community Involvement	April
9. Goal Setting, Career	May
10. Evaluation	June

Grade Eight

1. Orientation/Rationale/Rules	
Group Building/Goals	September
2. Study Skills/Time Management	October
3. Self-Esteem	November
4. Self-Awareness/Attitudes	December
5. Inter-/Intra-Personal (Peers/Adults/Family)	January
6. Accepting Responsibility	February
7. Career Plannings/Future Communication (Peers/Adults/Family)	March
8. Problem Solving/Decision Making	April
9. Job Skills/Attitudes	May
10. High School Attitudes/Where Are You Going?	June

Appendix 10

Evaluation Instruments
Evaluation Baseline

Middle School Program Analysis

EVALUATION BASELINE

1. *Discipline:* Number referrals by school and grade—corporal punishment
2. *Achievement:* Stanford and SSAT Reading/Math Listening Range by school—Percentage of skill passage by school
3. *Grading:* Percentage of grade awarded by subject, grade, and school
4. *Attendance:* Quarterly ADA averages—baseline
5. *Student Mobility:* By school—internal and external
                            Transportation report
6. *Low/High SES:* Lunch programs
                    Migrant programs
                    Chapter 1 eligibles
7. *Vandalism:* By school
8. *Age of Students:* By school, sex, race
9. *Teacher Experience:* Form
10. *Student-Teacher Attitudes:* Form
11. *10th Grade Follow-Up:* Form
12. *Instructional Practices:* School visits
13. *Facilities:* School visits
14. *Instructional Resources:* Supervisors

MIDDLE SCHOOL PROGRAM ANALYSIS

Directions:

Please check those items that are descriptive of the middle school program at your school.

Philosophy and Goals

_____ 1. A formal middle school–oriented philosophy exists and is accepted by principal and teachers.

_____ 2. The goals of the middle school program reflect a three-part thrust: personal development, skills for continued learning, and education for social competence.

_____ 3. Philosophy and goals are developed at my middle school based on an assessment of the needs of students attending the school.

Organization/Organization

_____ 4. The middle school day is flexibly scheduled using large blocks of time and "modular" time arrangements.

_____ 5. Teachers are organized into interdisciplinary planning/teaching teams that share a common group of students and planning period.

_____ 6. Teaching teams are located in physical proximity to one another.

_____ 7. Parent involvement/community involvement is built in to the school curriculum.

Curriculum/Organized Learning

8. The formal program of organized learning includes the following components:

_____ Core academic learning consisting of language arts, mathematics, social studies, and science

_____ Remedial and enrichment opportunities such as gifted programs

_____ Exploring electives to expose new fields of knowledge and expand aesthetic and creative horizons

_____ Career education components for all students

_____ Physical development and health education for all students

_____ Student-initiated elective choices in art, music, and other related areas

_____ A required course in the area of computer literacy

9. General skill development is planned and included in major subject areas including:

_____ Reading

_____ Spelling

_____ Writing

_____ Library use skills

_____ Problem solving

_____ Finding and organizing information

_____ Critical and creative thinking

10. A continuous progress approach to learning is present and does the following:

_____ Assesses each student at entry level on a continuum of course objectives

_____ Has ongoing monitoring to determine each student's readiness to progress in curriculum

_____ Allows student to attain proficiency in skills and performance objectives at rate/level that matches the student's instructional needs

_____ Assesses student performance based on progress through a skill-and-objective continuum

MIDDLE SCHOOL PROGRAM ANALYSIS *(continued)*

11. Schoolwide advisement programs are present and do the following:
    _____ Include a separate, planned nonacademic program
    _____ Include direction by guidance counselors
    _____ Have a regularly scheduled group activity
    _____ Involve all certificated personnel, staff, and support personnel
    _____ Provide ongoing personal interaction between staff (adviser) and students (advisee)
    _____ Maintain a teacher/pupil ratio of less than 1:20
    _____ Provide individual guidance opportunities when needed

12. A physical development/health program is present and is characterized by the following:
    _____ Experienced by all students
    _____ Students grouped on basis of development rather than grade level
    _____ Intramural program available to all students and organized around skill development
    _____ Formal health program to assist students in understanding and accepting physical and intellectual changes in themselves and others
    _____ Health screening and monitoring for all students
    _____ Graduated physical education program according to student development

Instructional Patterns

_____ 13. Students are grouped by intellectual, social, and/or physical characteristics in classes.
_____ 14. A variety of instructional methods are used in classes at any given time.
_____ 15. Instructional strategies other than lecture are used in most classrooms.
_____ 16. Varied instructional materials are regularly used in most classrooms.

17. There are interdisciplinary team planning/teaching approaches that provide for the following:
    _____ Teachers of different subjects meet during scheduled time to coordinate instruction for common groups of students.
    _____ Teachers of different subjects meet during scheduled time to monitor progress of common groups of students.
    _____ Teachers of different subjects teach common group of students within a block of time and group/re-group students to meet varied instructional objectives.
    _____ Teachers of different subjects participate in delivery of interdisciplinary units on periodic basis.
    _____ Teachers of different subjects meet together with parents of individual students to discuss the student's program.

Glossary

adviser/advisee program Daily or weekly period during which students interact with peers and teachers about personal and school-related concerns. Also called *advisement* or *advisory* program.

articulation Process by which the educational goals and curricular programs of a school system are coordinated among the various levels from preschool through high school. For example, a relationship with the elementary school is designed to make transition into the middle school easier; a relationship with the high school is designed to make transition there more comfortable and effective. Within a middle school, articulation is expected to facilitate movement between grade levels and learning levels and between continuous progress programs.

balanced comprehensive/curriculum Incorporates all three areas—essential learning skills, subject content, and personal development.

block schedule Organization of the school day into units of time that may be utilized in various ways by the school staff. A block of time allows a teacher or a team of teachers to teach a class in two or more subject areas, with the teacher or team determining the relative amount of time to be devoted to each subject, according to a daily estimate of needs. *See also* modular scheduling.

cognition Process of logical thinking.

cognitive learning Academic learning of subject matter.

common planning time Regularly scheduled time during the school day during which a given team of teachers is able to meet for joint planning, parent conferencing, or lesson preparation.

core (fused) curriculum Integration of two or more subjects; for example, English and social studies. Problem and theme orientations often serve as the integrating design. *See also* interdisciplinary program.

cooperative learning Two or more students working together on a learning task.

crisis intervention center A special center within or outside of the school designed to assist students with severe emotional problems. The center is staffed with psychologists, social workers, etc.

deductive learning Learning process that moves from larger generalizations and principles to illustrative examples and concepts.

departmentalization Students move from one classroom to another, with different teachers for each subject.

developmental physical education Instruction based on the physical development of the individual preadolescent learner, as opposed to a team sport approach.

developmental tasks Social, physical, maturational tasks regularly encountered by all individuals in our society as they progress from childhood to adolescence.

discovery learning A type of inquiry, emphasized especially in individualized instruction, in which a student moves through his or her own activities toward new learnings, usually expressed in generalizations and principles; typically involves inductive approaches. *See also* inductive learning.

early adolescence Stage of human development generally between age ten and fourteen when individuals begin to reach puberty.

essential learning skills Basic skills, such as reading, listening, and speaking, introduced in the elementary schools that must be reinforced and expanded within the middle school curriculum.

exploration Regularly scheduled curriculum experiences designed to help students discover and/or examine learnings related to their changing needs, aptitudes, and interests. Often referred to as the *wheel* or *miniclasses*. *See also* minicourses.

feedback   Evidence from student responses and reactions that indicates the degree of success being encountered in lesson objectives. Teachers seek feedback by way of discussion, student questions, written exercises, and test returns.

formal operations   Higher-level thinking skills; moving from concrete to abstract.

fundamental intermediate school   Middle-grades school that emphasizes basic skills, dress codes, strict adherence to discipline, and parental involvement.

heterogeneous grouping   Student grouping that does not divide learners on the basis of ability or academic achievement.

homogeneous grouping   Student grouping that divides learners on the basis of specific levels of ability, achievement, or interest. Sometimes referred to as *tracking*.

house leader   Educator who will act as a liaison between and among teams and other houses (units). This person reports directly to the principal.

house plan   Type of organization in which the school is divided into units ("houses"), with each having an identity and containing the various grades and, in large part, its own faculty. The purpose of a house plan is to achieve decentralization (closer student-faculty relationships) and easier and more flexible team-teaching arrangements.

independent study   Work performed by students without the direct supervision of the teacher so as to develop self-study skills and to expand and deepen interests.

inductive learning   Learning that results when individual concepts in examples and illustrations lead to larger generalizations and principles.

innovations   New instructional strategies, organizational designs, building rearrangements, equipment utilizations, or materials from which improved learning results are anticipated.

integrated curriculum   Translation of the concepts of core subject areas into meaningful relationships for students.

interdisciplinary program   Instruction that integrates and combines subject matter ordinarily taught separately into a single organizational structure.

interdisciplinary team   Combination of teachers from different subject areas who plan and conduct coordinated lessons in those areas for particular groups of pupils. Common planning time, flexible scheduling, and cooperation and communication among team teachers is essential to interdisciplinary teaming.

interscholastic program   Athletic activities or events whose primary purpose is to foster competition between school and school districts. Participation usually is limited to students with exceptional athletic ability.

intramural (intrascholastic) program   Athletic activities or events held during the school day, or shortly thereafter, whose primary purpose is to encourage all students to participate regardless of athletic ability.

learning center   Usually a large multimedia area designed to influence learning and teaching styles and to foster independent study. Also called a *learning station*.

magnet program   A specialized school program usually designed to draw minority students to schools that historically have been racially segregated.

metacognition   Process by which individuals examine their own thinking processes.

middle school   A school in between elementary and high school, housed separately and, ideally, in a building designed for its purpose, and covering usually three of the middle school years, beginning with grade five or six.

minicourses   Special-interest (enrichment) activities of short duration that provide learning opportunities based on student interest, faculty expertise, and community involvement. Also called *exploratory courses*, *short-interest–centered courses*, or *electives*.

modular scheduling   The division of the school day into modules, typically fifteen or twenty minutes long, with the number of modules used for various activities and experiences flexibly arranged.

nongraded organization   System in which grade levels are abandoned and students move upward in continuous progress, associating in every subject field with other students who are at approximately the same point of development.

performance objectives   Purposes pursued by the teacher expressed in terms of pupil behaviors, which in themselves act as evidences that the purposes have been achieved.

personal development   Designed to foster intellectual, social, emotional, and moral growth of students through such programs as adviser/advisee, developmental physical education, and minicourses.

process-pattern learning   Learning design that focuses on each student's experience rather than on a predetermined body of information.

programmed learning   Materials built on a rational step-by-step development basis, usually presented in the form of a workbook or for use in a teaching machine, designed for independent study and learning. Emphasis is on subject-matter development.

scope   The parameters of learning; for example, a subject-matter discipline sets its own scope, often by grade level.

self-contained classroom   Students are housed in one classroom, with one teacher. Variations may occur in such subjects as music, art, shops, and physical education.

sequence   The organization of an area of study. Frequently the organization is chronological, moving from simple to complex. Some sequences are spiraled, using structure, themes, or concept development as guidelines. A few schools use persistent life situations to shape sequence.

special learning center   Instructional center that provides programs for special-needs students.

staff development   Body of activities designed to improve the proficiencies of the educator-practitioner.

subject content   A type of curriculum that stresses the mastery of subject matter, with all other outcomes considered subsidiary. The school may employ tracks, units within subjects, and ability grouping. Despite recent shifts from encyclopedic learning to structural recognition (e.g., from facts to understanding), the central focus at many traditional schools remains subject-matter mastery. Also called *subject-matter curriculum*. See also homogeneous grouping.

support personnel   Ancillary personnel such as guidance, media, custodial, clerical, social services persons who help facilitate the instructional program.

systematic observation   A method of observing teaching practices in a classroom using an observation instrument such as the Flanders System of Interaction Analysis.

team house   Designated self-contained section or area of the school that contains a team of teachers and their assigned students to maximize feeling of team identity and minimize unproductive movement of students from class to class.

team-oriented course   Emphasis is placed on the principles that hold the subject together. The micropedagogy of textbook teaching is changed to the macropedagogy of underlying principles.

team teaching   Method of teaching that utilizes teacher strengths and allows teachers to work flexibly with individuals and with small or large groups. Also referred to as *teaming*.

time-out room   Designated area in which disruptive students can receive specialized instruction under the guidance of a single teacher. Students sent to a time-out room are a step away from out-of-school suspension.

transescence   The period in human development that begins in late childhood prior to the onset of puberty and extends through the early stages of adolescence.

TTT (Teachers Training Teachers)   Inservice process by which teachers receive instruction from peers, usually at the school level.

unified arts   Usually a grouping of subjects including art, music, industrial arts, drama, homemaking, and so forth, for which a time is scheduled with a team of teachers organizing the pupils into groups.

unified studies   An approach to curriculum design in which a unifying theme is used to tie together many subjects; for example, the theme "conservation" could attract contributions from many fields. Often, team teaching is used for this type of organization. Also called *broad themes* or *broad-unit topics*.

unstructured time   Time used for independent study, individual projects, and open laboratory activities. The student assumes responsibility for his or her own learning.

wing plan   A number of classes at the same grade, housed in closed proximity to each other, usually facilitating a horizontal interdisciplinary team-teaching arrangement. A wing plan can be part of a house plan.

work study   Program that allows students to work outside the school during a portion of the school day.

Name Index

Subject Index

About the Authors

Jon Wiles and **Joseph Bondi** are considered the foremost authorities on middle school education in the United States. For more than 25 years they have served as active leaders in the development of middle schools and as consultants to more than 500 school districts in the United States and in a number of foreign countries. They have been chief consultants for conversions in major U.S. school districts, including districts in Denver, Dallas, and St. Louis; and, in Florida alone, in Orlando, Long Beach, Tampa, Jacksonville, and Miami. The Miami (Dade County) conversion of 52 junior high schools was the largest curriculum conversion in the history of U.S. education.

They are authors of a number of textbooks, articles, booklets, and training programs. Among the latter is *Making Middle Schools Work*, published by the American Society of Curriculum Development. Other publications include *The New Training Program for Middle School Teachers*, *The Middle School We Need*, and *Profile of a Middle School*. The authors contributed to the Carnegie report on young adolescents (entitled *Turning Points*) and a number of state middle school guides, including California's *Caught in the Middle* and Florida's *The Forgotten Years* and *Development of Middle Schools*.

Drs. Wiles and Bondi are also authors of leading texts in the fields of curriculum development, supervision, instruction, and administration. Among these are *Curriculum Development: A Guide to Practice* and *Supervision: A Guide to Practice*, both published by Macmillan. Having served as teachers, administrators, and curriculum directors in the middle grades (as well as for other levels of education), the authors currently are professors of education at the University of South Florida in Tampa. They are also partners in the consulting and publishing firm of Wiles, Bondi and Associates, Inc., in Tampa. Both Dr. Wiles and Dr. Bondi received their doctorates from the University of Florida.